The Heroism of Queen Victoria

The Heroism of Queen Victoria

And How The Monarchy Was Saved by Princess Alice

Gerard Noel

First Published 2012

Published by Baptist Publications
Westington Mill
Chipping Campden
Gloucestershire
GL55 6EB

Designed by Loose Chippings
The Paddocks
Chipping Campden
Gloucestershire
GL55 6AU
www.loosechippings.org

Printed and bound in England by The Dorset Press, Dorchester

ISBN 978-0-9573798-0-0

Other books by Gerard Noel

The Renaissance Popes:
Statesmen, Warriors and the Great Borgia Myth

The 100 Most Notable Popes
The Most Remarkable Papal Saints, Sinners, Martyrs, Heretics, Warriors, Rulers and Patrons from St Peter to the Present

Pius XII: The Hound of Hitler

Princess Alice: Queen Victoria's Forgotten Daughter

The Journey of the English-speaking Union

Ena, Spain's English Queen

Sir Gerard Noel M.P.: And the Noels of Chipping Campden and Exton

Miles: A Portrait of Miles 17th Duke of Norfolk

The Great Lock-Out of 1926

Cardinal Basil Hume

The Montini Story. A portrait of Paul VI

The Anatomy of the Catholic Church:
Roman Catholicism in an Age of Revolution

A Portrait of the Inner Temple

Harold Wilson and the "New Britain."

Harold Wilson: A Biographical Study

Goldwater. A pictorial sketch. With portraits

Front cover illustration: *The Queen and Prince Albert's Polka*
by John Brandard. Chromolithograph, 1840s.

Contents

Introduction

This story begins logically, if not chronologically, with Queen Victoria's eldest daughter, the Princess Royal, known at home as 'Vicky'. For she it was who was first discovered, comparatively recently, to have displayed symptoms of porphyria, the deadly gene associated with the madness of King George III. She passed the gene on to her daughter and granddaughter. Even more significantly, there has now been discovered the hitherto unsuspected fact that she must have inherited the gene from her mother.

It has now been established that, almost certainly, the Queen was a carrier of this gene. This throws valuable new light on to her life and accounts for many facts and features of her reign not previously fully understood.

Vicky was her favourite grandchild despite the invaluable services and love she received from her second daughter Alice, who plays a major role in the story told in this volume. History repeats itself and the sterling qualities of Princess Victoria continue to be among the stoutest bulwarks of the monarchy. This book is published close to the 150th anniversary of her marriage to the future Emperor of Germany. She it was, moreover, who endowed with enduring lustre the title of Princess Royal.

Evidence of the presence of the deadly porphyria gene is one of two crucial factors in the reign of Queen Victoria which have recently emerged; the other is the extent to which the monarchy owed its survival to the Queen's second daughter, Alice. These two aspects of Queen Victoria's reign reveal, when considered together, a formerly unsuspected dimension in the life of the world's most written about monarch.

The supposition, amounting to virtual certainty, that Queen Victoria carried the porphyria gene, largely accounts for her frequent bouts of ill health, often associated with severe and alarming nervous disorders. The latter provided the principal contributing factor to her nervous breakdown, following the death of her beloved husband, the Prince Consort. During this horrendous period, fears were expressed that the Queen's mental state would completely break down and that she would succumb to insanity. The fact that she did not do so was due to her gifted and sensitive second daughter, Alice, to an extent that received scant attention until the publication of my book on that neglected Princess.[(1)] I also explain the sub-title to the book as to the relative but very real nature of the description 'Forgotten Daughter'.

The symptoms suffered by the Queen during this period (1861-2) recurred for the rest of her life, though not always in so traumatic and violent a form. Though brought back at that critical juncture from the brink of insanity (by Princess Alice) the longer term effect of this struggle occasioned the retirement by Queen Victoria from public life for a potentially disastrous ten year period. During that time, there was a progressive and disturbing rise of republican feeling throughout the country. This might well have resulted in the collapse of the monarchy. This feeling receded due to the recovery from a near-mortal illness by the heir to the throne, 'Bertie', Prince of Wales. His recovery was due in great measure to none other than that self-same Princess Alice, his favourite sister.

Because of her intervention on these two crucial occasions, it can be persuasively argued that Alice was truly the saviour of the monarchy. The circumstances in which this came about were described – for the first time in any detail – in my book about that remarkable Princess. The salient facts of this process are reprised in this volume. The combined effects of this with the discovery of the Queen's association with the destructive porphyria gene have made possible an entirely new assessment of what might have come to be known as the 'madness of Queen Victoria'.

The crucial factors in how this came about were first revealed in the breakthrough researches of three authors, John C.G. Röhl, Martin Warren and David Hunt. They are embodied in their work published as *Purple Secret*, with the sub-title of 'Genes, 'Madness' and the Royal Houses of Europe', Bantam Press, 1998.

The reasons why the theory that the porphyria gene was carried by Queen Victoria had not previously been examined are given by these same authors. They are ascribed to the assertion by Cecil Woodham-Smith, in her unfinished biography of Queen Victoria (George III's granddaughter) that the illness did not affect the Royal Family after 1837. Dame Cecil categorically states that 'there is no evidence to suggest that Queen Victoria suffered from porphyria or passed it on to any of her children.'(2)

Röhl, Warren and Hunt point out that this belief led historians to abandon their search for signs of the disease in subsequent generations. They go on, moreover, to demonstrate that an overwhelming amount of evidence existed to indicate that Queen Victoria's eldest child Vicky had the porphyria gene and passed it on to subsequent members of the royal family. This led them to the inescapable conclusion that the Queen must herself have carried the gene, although previous historians had failed to deduce this from any of her known symptoms; hence their efforts to review her own medical history in a fresh light.(3)

The same authors go on to describe the numerous symptoms displayed by Queen Victoria to substantiate their theory. They give scarce attention, however, to the crucial part played by Alice in saving the Queen from total and possibly permanent nervous collapse.

The combination of these two scenarios provides the main theme of the present volume, summarising as it does the findings in *Purple Secret* as to the Queen's 'peculiarities'.

Thus unfolds the full story, for so long undisclosed, of how and why the monarchy under Queen Victoria hovered, at a tantalisingly prolonged juncture, in deadly peril from which it would surely have perished but for her daughter Alice.

I owe a special debt of gratitude to my old and valued friend Helen Broughton for first drawing my attention to the book *Purple Secret* which has played such an important part in the background research to the present work.

I am extremely grateful to Michael Ward without whose work as an expert research assistant this book could not have been completed.

Chapter One
The Questionable Madness of George III

It is terrifying to consider that a king might be mad. Certainly we do not expect monarchs to be perfect; often their frailties allow us a welcome sense of shared humanity. But, although we do not expect omniscience and would be fearful of omnipotence, we imagine monarchs to have an eagle's eye view of their subjects and their countries. In English history, that expectation has often been met.

A contemporary film, *The Madness of King George*, brought Alan Bennett's play *The Madness of George III* to a mass audience. Viewers were invited to consider the dilemma of whether George III (1738-1820) was suffering from temporary delirium or insanity. If irrevocably insane, should George be deposed by parliament in favour of his eldest son? Although the dilemma was resolved by George's semi-recovery, as the respective titles of the film and book suggest, audiences were left with the notion that George was, in some way or another, mad. The problem with madness, however, is that it is a nebulous concept which requires further definition. A Victorian study came to the conclusion that King George had suffered from 'mania', i.e. violent mood changes leading to impaired judgement, rapid speech and possible delusions. Although the diagnosis of mania was consistent with the mental symptoms exhibited by King George, it left both his physical symptoms and their periodic nature unexplained.

In time, the mania theory was extended to one of manic-depressive psychosis, a condition characterised by savage mood swings between depression and manic 'high'. All of us have good and bad days; for the sufferer of manic-depression, however, the good days will be impossibly perfect, while the bad days will be stolen by Doctor Johnson's 'Black Dog' of despair. While such a theory might accommodate King George's mood swings, it failed to explain their causation. Manic-depressive mood changes are triggered by specific events to which the sufferer responds with an intensity denied to the rest of us. But there was no evidence of any such triggers predating George's periodic breakdowns.

George III came to the throne in 1760 and ruled for sixty years until 1820. For almost 150 years after his death, his 'madness' was awarded the status of accepted fact. Given a widespread fear of mental illness and an almost primeval terror of the mental instability of kings, there was an inevitable slur not only to the reputation of King George in particular but to the British monarchy in general.

Entirely unknown to most people, this slur has been challenged, with a marked degree of success. In 1966 a fascinating paper about King George was published in the British Medical Journal. It was written by a mother and son team, named Ida Macalpine and Richard Hunter. Macalpine and Hunter were both psychiatrists, with a keen interest in the history of psychiatry. Despite their British names, both had been born in Germany and were relative outsiders to the prevailing intellectual establishment. They considered the supposed madness of King George with reference to both of the relevant disciplines – psychiatry and history. And they brought to bear not only considerable research diligence but also the freshness of outlook sometimes shown by outsiders. What they found was startling. King George's 'madness' was not a normal condition; instead it was periodic. In fact, in a lifetime which spanned eighty two years, there were only five major attacks – in 1765, 1789, 1801, 1804 and 1810. On closer examination, the 1765 attack was found to be physical and not psychiatric; thus it may be ruled out. The 1810 attack, when the King was seventy two, appeared to mark the onset of senility, rather than 'madness' per se. So the 1966 researchers were left with only three unequivocal attacks within a fifteen year segment of an eighty two year life. Furthermore the King had lived for fifty one years before the onset of the first such attack.

Try as they might, Macalpine and Hunter could not locate King George's 'madness' within any psychiatric taxonomy. The breakthrough came when they discovered that each of his attacks had been preceded by a series of physical symptoms. These included severe pain in the chest and abdomen, hypersensitivity to sound and light and rapid, often incoherent speech. They also found several references to the King's urine being discoloured. In 1812 it was described as having a blue tinge, while in 1819 it was described as bloody. Macalpine and Hunter concluded that the attacks were preceded by an 'almost specific combination of seemingly unconnected symptoms' which allowed only one satisfactory explanation. Accordingly, their ground-breaking 1966 medical paper was entitled *The Insanity of King George III: A Classic Case of Porphyria.*(1)

* * *

What is porphyria and how is it caused? To answer these questions, we need to turn to yet another discipline: biology. In 1962 the Nobel Prize in Physiology and Medicine was awarded to Watson, Crick and Wilkins for their classic work on the structure of DNA. Each chromosome, i.e. a single molecule of DNA, is akin to a piece of computer code, with sub-codes of biological information (genes) which determine key reactions in the body. As with computers, this information can become corrupted. Such corruption will have two results: key reactions in the body will be affected, to a greater or lesser degree and, as corruption can be passed from linked computer to computer in the form of a virus, so may genetic mutations be passed from parent to offspring and to their offspring. The Biblical comment about the sins of the fathers being visited onto other generations is frighteningly apt.

A particular component of one chromosome, the PPOX gene, contains biological information to create an enzyme which is involved in the final stage of production of a molecule called haem. Haem is present in haemoglobin, which carries oxygen throughout the blood. Corruption (known in biology as mutation) of the PPOX gene results in a deficiency of this enzyme, creating impaired production of haem.

This condition is known as variegate porphyria. Because of the impaired haem production, transportation of oxygen in the blood is diminished; consequently harmful products accumulate in the body. When such accumulations reach critical mass, the afflicted person may suffer symptoms such as acute abdominal pains, skin photosensitivity, muscle weakness, seizure, fever, loss of sensation, and mental changes, such as anxiety and hallucinations. These harmful products can be detected in the blood, urine and faeces of affected individuals. One product is purple and causes urine to be discoloured to what has been termed 'the colour of port wine'.

Undoubtedly Macalpine and Hunter had performed some extremely worthwhile scientific detection. As outsiders, they had approached the tragedy of King George in a fresh and revealing light. But, if they had gone some way towards dispelling the madness of this particular King, they had also opened a different, and scarcely less alarming, Pandora's Box. In 1968, two years after their first scientific paper, they published another scientific paper in collaboration with the eminent chemical pathologist Professor Claude Rimington. The nature of the particular Pandora's Box which they opened is revealed in the title of this paper: *Porphyria in the Royal houses of Stuart, Hanover and Prussia.*(2)

As MacAlpine, Hunter and Rimington well knew, once a gene is mutated, it will almost invariably remain mutated. Such mutations may be passed from parent, to offspring, to their offspring. While it appeared that King George's affliction was medical and not psychiatric, it also appeared that his descendents might be subject to the same afflictions. Specifically, in the case of King George, every one of his fifteen children had a 50% chance of inheriting 'the porphyria gene'. Statistically there was a significant probability of the royal families of England – even to the present day – being afflicted by porphyria in exactly the same way that George III had been.

The politics of science is a fascinating subject. Proposers of scientific breakthroughs would do well to tread carefully. Macalpine and Hunter did not tread carefully. Incomplete 160 year old medical records, however well researched, scarcely constitute normal scientific evidence. Acting as though a tentative theory was scientific fact was practically guaranteed to rouse academic umbrage. Variegate porphyria had been well researched in South Africa, where it was common among the Afrikaner population. It was asserted that some of King George's symptoms, far from being specific indicators of porphyria, were 'so non-specific [as] would fit many other diseases'.(3) For instance, discoloured urine may have many causes. It was further contended that not only was 'the evidence insufficient to support a diagnosis of variegate porphyria but in many cases it contradicts it.'(4) The British Medical Journal received letters pointing out that the porphyria theory was 'not proven' and indeed, 'highly unlikely'.(5) Perhaps Macalpine and Hunter had been carried away by their enthusiasm? Dr Geoffrey Dean, the discoverer of variegate porphyria, memorably promised 'to eat my hat if the authors [Macalpine and Hunter] can produce convincing evidence that they are right.'(6)

While scientists remained unconvinced, the porphyria theory received more sympathy from historians. Professor Hugh Trevor-Roper noted that he found 'the medical argument both fascinating and convincing. No one can now continue to maintain that George III was a neurotic… who took refuge from his responsibilities in madness.'(7) Prince Charles, a keen amateur historian, wrote thus of his direct ancestor: 'I think there can be little doubt that George III suffered from periodic attacks of a metabolic illness.'(8) The British Medical Association entitled their review of the debate *Porphyria – A Royal Malady*.

If porphyria was genetically transmitted (perhaps from King George III to members of the present royal family), then the question arose: had a gene mutation occurred in King George or had he, in turn, inherited it? In their research, Macalpine and Hunter came across extensive case notes relating to the medical treatment of King James I of England (King James VI of Scotland). He too was subject to a wide variety of conditions, including stomach pain, difficulty in breathing, mood changes, delirium, melancholy, and sensitivity to sunlight (a symptom of some types of porphyria). In addition, he too had discoloured urine, which he described as being the dark red colour of Alicante wine. Macalpine and Hunter contested that King James had been an earlier sufferer of porphyria. Certainly his character 'stammering, slobbering, shedding unmanly tears, trembling at a drawn sword and talking in the style alternately of a buffoon and a pedagogue' was uneasily reminiscent of that of King George.[9] Finally Macalpine and Hunter located the person whom they regarded as the most likely source of the porphyria gene in the royal family of England – the mother of King James; Mary Queen of Scots.

Mary Queen of Scots is one of the most charismatic and tragic figures in history. She has also been described as 'one of the great invalids of history'.[10] She suffered from a wide variety of symptoms, some of which certainly seem indicative of porphyria. In 1566 and in 1570, when she was twenty four and twenty eight respectively, she suffered fits where, after terrible abdominal pain and protracted vomiting, she became delirious. She then lost her powers of sight and speech and, eventually, her consciousness, to the extent that she was thought to be dead. One theory advanced was that she suffered from a gastric ulcer. However her biographer, Lady Antonia Fraser has concluded that: 'It certainly seems far easier to relate these symptoms [of porphyria] rather than those of gastric ulcer.'[11] She further noted that 'the mysterious hysterical manner of the death of James V' may also have been due to porphyria. Mary may, in turn, have inherited the gene from her father. There is something horrible in the sinister thought of this rogue porphyria gene being transmitted through succeeding generations of the interconnected royal families of Britain and Europe. Were the sufferers dimly aware of 'something wrong' in the family, something for which they had no name, a curse emanating perhaps from the doomed Mary Queen of Scots?

With their theory of porphyria, albeit unproven, Macalpine and Hunter had uncovered a controversy which raged through the medical and academic establishments of the day. In 1974, eight years after the publication of their original paper, Ida Macalpine died of cancer. Seven years later, in 1981, her son, Richard Hunter, succumbed to the same disease. With their deaths, investigation ceased. Worse, myth was substituted for rumour, with some authorities treating the porphyria theory as established fact and others giving it no credence whatsoever. Any fair-minded person would have to admit that Macalpine and Hunter had uncovered a singularly intriguing line of enquiry; but it was not one which the medical establishment seemed inclined to pursue. The deaths of Macalpine and Hunter were followed by the death of rigour in consideration of their work.

It took the emergence of the popular film, *The Madness of King George*, a decade later, to renew attention on the controversy. The bane of the original theory was the lack of empirical evidence. If the porphyria gene was transmitted throughout the royal families of Britain and Europe, there must have been many victims. In the years between the deaths of Macalpine and Hunter and the screening of *The Madness of King George*, one discipline had advanced almost beyond recognition – DNA profiling. It had become possible to take DNA samples from human remains. Scientific detection could extend across the centuries. If the porphyria gene was present in the descendents of George III (and Mary Queen of Scots), it might be found in their remains.

* * *

This line of enquiry led to a fascinating interdisciplinary collaboration between an historian, John C.G. Röhl, and two biological specialists, Martin Warren and David Hunt. They began by going back to Ida Macalpine's previously ignored files, by then dusty relics tucked away in the archives of Cambridge University Library. Macalpine had identified (but not named) the so-called patients A and B, four and five generations respectively descended from George III. Patient B, an elderly lady in Germany in the 1960s, was reputed to have urine stained the colour of port wine. However when it was tested by Rimington, the collaborator of Macalpine and Hunter, the results were deemed inconclusive. It was thought that patient B had died with no issue; thus no more evidence could be gleaned from that quarter.

Patient A was identified as Princess Adelaide of Prussia. In World War II she had been treated by doctor Alfred Vannotti, an authority on porphyria. Typical of porphyria sufferers, she suffered abdominal pains and had discoloured urine. When Vannotti analysed her urine, he concluded that 'it was not doubtful that the patient suffered from an abdominal form of porphyria.'[(12)] Unfortunately Vannotti had only treated Princess Adelaide for a single month, many decades before, and the results of the analyses were long lost. Back in the Macalpine and Hunter era, their collaborator, Rimington, had asked his colleague, Vannotti, to request permission for more samples to be taken. Permission was refused by Princess Adelaide; an attempt to obtain samples from her daughter also met with failure. Thus, the Patient A lead, seemingly so strong, also remained inconclusive. However, when the later research team of Röhl, Warren and Hunt asked the noted authority Sir Abraham Goldberg whether he would place reliance upon Vannotti's diagnosis, Goldberg's reply was unequivocal, 'Quite definitely, yes.'[(13)]

The original assertion was that King George III had suffered from porphyria; thus each of his children had a 50% chance of inheriting 'the porphyria gene'. With fifteen children, thirteen of whom had survived into adulthood, there was ample history, medical and otherwise, to investigate. Röhl, Warren and Hunt expected to find either a lack of symptoms (indicating that George III's malady was other than porphyria) or symptoms in approximately half of the offspring. What they actually discovered astounded them. Nearly all of George III's thirteen adult children exhibited symptoms of porphyria, ranging from mental disturbance, acute headaches, pain in the side, chest and back, lack of breath, constipation, and vomiting. For instance, King George's sixth son, Prince Augustus, Duke of Sussex (1773 – 1843), was 'so delicate... that the air of England was found too severe for his system.'[(14)] At the age of fifteen, he suffered 'fearful paroxysms',[(15)] so violent in their intensity that his doctors feared he would suffocate. His urine went from a normal pale to deep amber and reddish when the attacks occurred.

Lacking specific analysis, all of this evidence is necessarily circumstantial. But its weight is compelling. We do not have signed, witnessed photographic evidence of the great battles of antiquity. Nevertheless we believe that they took place because we place our trust in chroniclers who seem reliable. And we cross-reference when we can. The four doctors attending the unfortunate Duke of Sussex were brave enough to declare their ignorance of his malady to the King; and they were brave enough to voice their great fear. The Duke, they concurred, had 'a peculiar disposition to paroxysms of a violent kind, but in what this disposition consists we are unable to determine... It has come to our knowledge that several members of the royal family and in particular His Royal Highness the Duke of York and Price Edward [the Duke of Kent] are subject to the same paroxysms and this arouses our suspicions of a hereditary predisposition.'[(16)] The Duke of Sussex felt that there was a 'peculiarity in my conformation'.[(17)] Queen Victoria's father Edward, Duke of Kent (1767-1820), believed that there was a common disorder among his brothers and sisters; furthermore he believed that it was the same disorder as was suffered by their father, King George III.

Macalpine, Hunter and Rimington's Patient A had provided strong circumstantial evidence of porphyria. In their medical analysis of thirteen children of King George III, Röhl, Warren and Hunt, uncovered a plethora of evidence, albeit also circumstantial. They continued their quest down the family tree, from Mary Queen of Scots and King George. When they came to investigate Victoria, (Vicky, the Princess Royal, 1840 – 1901, daughter of Queen Victoria and great-granddaughter of George III), they found that, as with the Duke of Sussex before her, she too was a frail child. In 1858 she suffered severe headaches and nausea which may, or may not have been due to pregnancy. In 1861 she had 'violent lumbago', followed by terrible pain in 'the nerves of the head'.[18] [19] In 1862 she had 'violent pains in the left side and back'.[20] The following years saw headaches, vomiting and severe abdominal pains. She was 'feverish from nervous mood swings', as had been her great-grandfather before her.[21]

An 1868 account of an attack of 'most severe neuralgic headache!' is pitiful to read.[22] 'I have been in the most excruciating pain all day long… I could only cry and moan while it lasted… I cannot go on like this any longer.'[23] Upon taking quinine for relief, her face went 'fire-red' with swelling so severe that 'my eyes are almost completely shut, making it impossible to look up or down. My ears are so swollen that I can hardly hear… The tautness of my skin, the burning heat and the itching are almost intolerable.'[24] [25]

Sensitivity to heat is a symptom of porphyria which Vicky shared with fellow descendants of King George. Her attacks seem to have been brought on by what we would now term stress, either from confrontations with her domestic staff or from meetings with her mother-in-law, Queen Augusta. She admitted that meeting the latter caused her to be, 'quite ill after – my knees shaking and my pulse galloping. [sic]'[26] And this leads us to yet another important point. The mutated PPOX gene ('the porphyria gene') is termed 'low penetrance'. This means that individuals with the faulty gene may still excrete the chemicals (porphyrins) yet not show symptoms of affliction unless they are triggered. Environmental factors such as certain prescription drugs, a low-calorie diet and progesterone in the contraceptive pill can trigger attacks. So too can 'lifestyle factors' such as sunbathing, excessive drinking… and stress.

In the 1870s, Vicky, heiress both to the Prussian crown and the imperial title, received a surfeit of stress as Europe was riven by bloody war. Her life became scarcely worth living, with 'agonising rheumatic pains', 'severe nervous headaches' and 'horrible neuralgia'.[27] Her legs and back were terribly affected and her condition became almost unendurable. 'I cannot describe what I have suffered,' she wrote, 'I have been nearly mad.'[(28)] Horrifyingly she admits, 'I took arsenic without any effect.'[(29)] Many of the supposed medicines of the time, such as arsenic, belladonna and aconite, were downright poisonous.

In 1898 Vicky was diagnosed with cancer; she died three years later in 1901. For thirty years she had suffered sporadic attacks of pain in nearly every part of her body. Typically these attacks occurred several times a year. They could last for a few days; or they could last for up to two months. They seemed to be triggered by such factors as changes in environment, such as heating and lighting, and stress. The sons of George III had suspected the existence of a hereditary condition; Vicky also seemed to suspect it. In 1891 her brother, Bertie, the Prince of Wales, later King Edward VII (1841 – 1910), became seriously ill with a raging fever and terrible pain in his back. Vicky noted in a letter to her mother, 'These are the sorts of attacks I used to have at Berlin, & take weeks to recover from.'[(30)]

Voluminous correspondence existed for Röhl, Warren and Hunt to accumulate more evidence of porphyria in Vicky, the great granddaughter of 'mad' King George III. In fact virtually the only symptom of porphyria which they were not able to locate in the surviving records was discoloured urine. However when they came to study the records of Vicky's eldest daughter, this last piece of evidence clicked into place.

* * *

Charlotte, Princess of Prussia (1860 – 1919) was the daughter of Princess Vicky and the sister of Kaiser Wilhelm II. A sickly childhood was the prelude to an adulthood plagued by ill health. Her maladies included the familiar symptoms of acute pain in the abdomen, side and back, terrible headaches, neuralgia, fever, fainting and 'fits of violent excitement'.[(31)] Abscesses made her gums 'lumps of crimson, or strings of white flesh' which were so 'disgusting' that, in company, she had to keep her mouth covered with a thick veil.[(32)] As with her mother, she could be afflicted for weeks and months at a time, then well again… then afflicted once more. However, as she entered middle age, her life became a struggle with constipation, abdominal pain, swellings, abscesses, boils, headaches and fainting fits.

Besides seeking the best medical help available, Charlotte devoured medical journals in a search for information relating to her condition. A visit to Cannes in 1905 promised 'blue sea & sky' which, she felt, would 'soon pick me up again'.[(33)] Tragically she did not realise that the Mediterranean sun would trigger her condition. Her dream of respite quickly turned into an agony of despair as one of her worst attacks occurred. Her urine was 'dark red'.[(34)] Four years later, in 1909, she noted, 'Urine is bloody again.'[(35)] Charlotte had shown the same periodic symptoms of porphyria as her mother, Princess Vicky. And she had displayed the final piece of the medical jigsaw – discoloured urine.

* * *

Röhl, Warren and Hunt went on to examine the life of Charlotte's daughter, Princess Feodora of Reuss, whose tragic end in 1945 has echoes of that of her remote ancestor, Mary Queen of Scots. Throughout her sad existence, Feodora exhibited the same dreadful symptoms as had her mother, Charlotte and her grandmother, Vicky. In 1996 Röhl, Warren and Hunt went to Poland to obtain bone samples from Feodora's remains. Their hope was that DNA profiling might reveal existence of the mutated porphyria gene. However, although the researchers returned to England with bone samples, there was some doubt as to whether they actually belonged to Feodora. Earlier they had run into the same problem when they had taken DNA samples from a bloodstained burial sheet and clothing supposedly worn by Charles I (1600 – 1649), the grandson of Mary Queen of Scots, at his beheading. In neither case was it possible to determine the provenance of the samples, both of which could also have been contaminated from other sources. In the case of Charles, there was, of course, almost 350 years for such contamination to have occurred.

Hoping for a third DNA sample, the research team succeeded in having the grave of Princess Charlotte exhumed in 1997, nearly eighty years after her death. Pitifully Charlotte's funeral dress was intact; stems of a flower posy were clasped in the skeletal remains of her hands. Bone fragments were taken. Of the three DNA samples, only that of Charlotte was regarded as being of proven authenticity.

DNA provided by Prince Philip, Duke of Edinburgh, (1921 -), a related family member, was used to authenticate biologically the supposed remains of Feodora and Charlotte. The former failed to match; thus it was impossible that the remains were those of Feodora and accordingly they were discarded from the study. However, when it came to the remains taken from Charlotte's grave, there was an identical match. The researchers now knew, beyond any reasonable doubt, that they had samples of Charlotte's DNA.

Frustratingly, the results proved inconclusive. While a mutation of the PPOX gene was found in Charlotte's DNA, it is uncertain as to whether it would cause variegate porphyria. With the DNA profiling trail fast petering out, the researchers tested their last sample – DNA supposedly taken from the bloody shroud of Charles I. No evidence of mutation was found. If this DNA is authentic, the implication is that, if porphyria did indeed exist in King James I of England, it was not passed on by his son King Charles I to his two sons, King Charles II (1630 – 1685) and King James II (1633 – 1701). With a 50% chance of porphyria being passed on to children, it is entirely possible that Charles I did not have the ailment and his sister, Princess Elizabeth (1595 – 1662), the ancestor of George III, did. She could have passed the gene on to George III and to his descendents, such as Vicky, Charlotte and Feodora.

If porphyria was present in the descendents of George III, was there a chance that it was present in members of the present British royal family? James Brough, a biographer of Princess Margaret, recounted a 1970s rumour that she had been treated for porphyria at that time. Some facts relating to the Princess seemed to fit this rumour. Although she often had difficulty sleeping, she refrained from taking sleeping tablets; barbiturates, a component of many sleeping tablets, would very likely trigger an acute attack in a porphyria sufferer. A 1967 stay in hospital was said to have been caused partially by over-enthusiastic dieting. Again fasting will cause attacks in porphyria sufferers, who are typically advised to adopt a high carbohydrate diet; such a diet might have been responsible for her weight gains in later years. Lastly, despite her love of the tropical paradise of Mustique, she was assiduous in using sunscreen long before such use was widespread. As we have seen, many sufferers of porphyria display extreme sensitivity to sunlight.

It must be emphasised that all of this is no more than speculation. But it raises a valuable point. Porphyria is a disease which may be managed, to a considerable extent, by taking care with environmental and lifestyle factors. Present day sufferers have valuable information which was not available to unfortunates such as Vicky, Charlotte and Feodora.

* * *

Trawling through the mass of correspondence from Ida Macalpine, the later research team found a reference to Professor Ian Magnus, an expert on porphyria. Claude Rimington, their collaborator, believed that Magnus had relevant information about a member of the royal family of Hesse, in Germany, related to our own royal family. Assiduous as ever in their research, Röhl, Warren and Hunt contacted the by now retired Professor Magnus, who gave them the disappointing news that Rimington was mistaken. However he mentioned a story which he had heard about an RAF physician who was believed to have seen several members of the British Royal Family in connection with porphyria. Professor Magnus warned that this physician was much older than himself and might no longer still be alive.

Röhl, Warren and Hunt wrote to the aforesaid physician, Dr Henry Bellringer. They received a prompt reply stating that in 1968 he had examined several members of the British Royal Family. He had indeed found symptoms of porphyria in one of them. With consummate irony, the elusive proof which Macalpine and Hunter had sought had been available. The porphyria sufferer in the Royal Family was none other than Prince William of Gloucester, then seventh in line to the throne.

In August 1968 HRH the Duchess of Gloucester (the present Princess Alice) asked Dr Bellringer to see her son, Prince William, who was then aged twenty seven. When they met, Prince William explained to Dr Bellringer that three years previously, not long after a diplomatic posting to Nigeria, he had become weak, dizzy and feverish. Both jaundice and malaria were suspected. However he also developed a rash of blisters on his face, his chest, the backs of his hands and, occasionally his back. For the following three years, he continued to have these blisters, which were large and extensive enough to cause scarring. Prince William also noted that, intermittently, for days at a time, his urine was dark.

Dr Bellringer made a tentative diagnosis of variegate porphyria. As William was flying imminently to Japan on another diplomatic posting, there was no time to carry out tests. All that Dr Bellringer could do was advise his patient of his likely condition and give him palliatives, such as cream to protect him from sunlight. Dr Bellringer told the Duchess of Gloucester of his diagnosis and arranged to see William again upon his return.

Two years later, in August 1970, Prince William returned to Britain and was examined at greater length by Dr Bellringer. By then there was extensive blistering and scarring on the Prince's forehead and on the backs of his hands. Prince William confessed that he had not made a conscious determination to avoid exposure to sunlight. On his chest, which had been exposed to sunlight when wearing an open shirt, there was further scarring.

When Dr Bellringer tested specimens obtained from Prince William he found porphyrins 'greatly in excess of normal'.[(36)] Similar tests carried out by another physician replicated these results. A third sample, taken later, gave normal results; however, by this time, the Prince was in remission.

An independent examination was taken for a second opinion by Dr Arthur Rook and his colleagues. They too came to the conclusion that Prince William was suffering from variegate porphyria, in remission. Subsequently Prince William confided in Dr Bellringer that he had received another independent examination in Japan; Professor Ishihara in Tokyo had also come to the conclusion that the Prince had porphyria.

In addition to the detection of porphyrins in the test results, Prince William had shown classic symptoms of porphyria: extreme sensitivity to sunlight, affected skin, muscle weakness, bilious attacks, debilitating weakness and dark urine. With considerable regret, Dr Bellringer wrote in his case notes, 'there can be scarcely any doubt that this is a case of porphyria.'(37)

On August 28th 1972, Prince William of Gloucester was killed in a flying accident. Dr Bellringer commented, 'It had been a great privilege to have been able to serve and know him and so intimately. What a tragic loss.'(38)

The research team of Röhl, Warren and Hunt asked Dr Bellringer whether he had made the diagnosis of porphyria with the Macalpine and Hunter research in mind. Naturally Dr Bellringer was aware of their work; however he replied that he had tried to prevent it influencing him. The symptoms and test results told their own story; he was left with no alternative but to diagnose porphyria. Both of William's parents were descended from Mary Queen of Scots. If one accepts the thesis that the porphyria gene comes through her, then either of William's parents could have infected him unknowingly. In fact there were rumours that William's father, Henry, Duke of Gloucester (1900 – 1974) also had this royal malady.

The researchers obtained further confirmation of Prince William's porphyria from other people, some of whom had worked closely with him. They recalled the porphyria as being inconvenient, rather than problematic. This illustrates two very important points. Porphyria sufferers can experience the affliction to a greater or lesser degree; the lives of Vicky, Charlotte and Feodora were ruined by it, whereas for Prince William it was an irritating condition, his persistent skin rashes and blisters seemingly being the worst symptom. Also, the more we learn about porphyria, the more able we will be to manage it by paying judicious attention to environmental and lifestyle factors.

After his first diagnosis of Prince William, Dr Bellringer wrote to Sir Ronald Bodley Scott, the chief royal physician, alerting him to his concerns. It appears that Sir Ronald was not best pleased with the news. There was little further contact between the two physicians and Dr Bellringer never know whether Sir Ronald screened other members of the Royal Family and, if so, whether fellow sufferers of porphyria were identified.

In 1998, Röhl, Warren and Hunt published their ground-breaking scientific work as *Purple Secret*. Sadly, Dr Bellringer, who had given them the final, crucial piece of evidence, died in 1997, just before publication. He was ninety one. He was well aware of possible controversy and scurrilous bad press in relation to Prince William's porphyria. Out of his respect for the Prince and out of his concern for porphyria sufferers, he overcame his 'anxious thoughts and reservations' to tell his story.[(39)]

Röhl, Warren and Hunt made their findings about Prince William known to several leading porphyria experts who agreed upon a diagnosis of porphyria in remission. The tragic death of the Prince precluded DNA analysis. Nevertheless the agreement of so many independent authorities establishes a verdict of porphyria beyond any reasonable doubt.

Finally Röhl, Warren and Hunt met with Dr Geoffrey Dean, the discoverer of variegate porphyria, who, years previously, had promised 'to eat my hat if the authors [Macalpine and Hunter] can produce convincing evidence that they are right.'[(40)] Reviewing the newly uncovered evidence, Dr Dean also came to the conclusion that Prince William had porphyria. Generously he acknowledged that Macalpine and Hunter may well have been correct in their original assertion of porphyria in King George III.

* * *

With Dr Dean's graceful acknowledgement, we come to the end of our thirty year old story of scientific detection. The title of Ida Macalpine and Richard Hunter's first scientific paper, *The Insanity of King George III: A Classic Case of Porphyria*, was inspired.[41] *Porphyria in the Royal houses of Stuart, Hanover and Prussia*, the title of their next scientific paper with Claude Rimington, was prophetic.[42] And yet their ground-breaking work was so nearly consigned to oblivion. It took the later research team of Röhl, Warren and Hunt to combine the disciplines of history and biology, review the preceding oeuvre, conduct their own field-study and finally, in making contact with the late Dr Bellringer, complete the puzzle.

In many ways, this has been an example of scientific detection at its most rigorous and honest. While we do not have unequivocal DNA analysis of porphyria in the British Royal Family, we do have the professional judgement of expert after expert, from Dr Vannotti on Princess Adelaide to Dr Bellringer on Prince William.

We also have a huge mass of evidence, medical and otherwise, of the existence of porphyria in generation after generation of descendants of the ill-fated Mary Queen of Scots. For all their wealth and social position, the misery of their lives through ill health is heartbreaking. So many of them, it seems, were aware of a sinister, nameless malady in their family.

We inhabit an age where science has driven out the superstition of former times. On this great mass of uncovered evidence, King George was not mad; far from it. He is not an object of scorn; rather he deserves our pity and our respect for enduring a tormenting affliction.

Vicky, Charlotte and Feodora present a triptych of suffering. While we regret their miserable existences, we console ourselves with the thought that greater knowledge of porphyria enables sufferers, such as the late Prince William, to manage their affliction and continue with relatively normal lives.

The astute reader will have realised that there is one name conspicuously missing from our litany of porphyria sufferers. There is one person who links Mary Queen of Scots and King George III with Princesses Vicky, Charlotte, Feodora… and Prince William. If they had porphyria, she too must have had it. The 'royal malady' explains so many intriguing facets of her life. That person is, of course, one of the most famous women who have ever lived – Queen Victoria.

Chapter Two
The Child Prisoner of Kensington

History is all the stories of the world. In the early years of the 21st century we inhabit an era of terrifying uncertainty. For most people, the word 'Victorian' conjures up sepia images of a seemingly changeless time when Britain ruled much of the world and its great empire was presided over by a short, stout, unsmiling lady dressed in severe black. We repress a nostalgic desire to return to the perceived stability of that epoch. Across an intervening century, we view Victorians as though through the lens of a telescope. How far away, how remote they seem.

It is the job of the historian to swap a telescope for a magnifying glass. Although facts are recorded accurately, history is so much more than lifeless facts. The historian takes his reader into a world long vanished and makes it come alive once again, albeit vicariously, on the page. Hagiography is discarded; the statements of the malicious are reassessed. We tease out new meanings, portray, as best we can, the truth of a bygone people, place and time.

As an eminent biographer, Giles St Aubyn, has noted, in 1837 Queen Victoria came to the throne as an unknown girl of eighteen. When she died sixty four years later in 1901, she was the most famous person on earth. In the latter decades of her regime, she had been Queen for longer than most of her subjects had lived. Her longevity helped to lull them, as us, into a comforting illusion of enduring stability.

The reality however was very different. The Victorian era was one of massive social, industrial and political change. Cheap raw materials of coal, iron and labour fuelled vigorous entrepreneurial activity, unbridled capitalism. The winners attained great wealth, while the masses endured grinding poverty and appalling working conditions. Five-year-old children worked fourteen hours a day in mills and factories. There was an almost total absence of protective legislation.

Yet across the social classes there was enormous pride in being English. With the defeat of Napoleon at Waterloo in 1815, two decades of peril had ended. Britain, 'that right little, tight little island' found itself the first nation in Europe.[1] France was exhausted after the Napoleonic wars. Spain was a political irrelevance. Germany was composed of many states, jostling for power. Austria was challenged by Prussia. Russia was slowly emerging as the great threat to all these other countries. However the Duke of Wellington's victory at Waterloo had left Britain in pole position. Soon it would go from being the premier European power to the premier world power. Great tracts of Asia, Africa, the Americas and Australia would fall under its dominion. The British empire would become one of the truly great empires in history.

If the Victorian era was very different from its comforting images, so too was its iconic Queen. Victoria's life was one of more than sixty years of service to the people of Britain and the Empire. She had two decades of married happiness before enduring the most crushing despair. Her steely character was, for many, a nexus of paradox; regal yet humble, imperious yet submissive, formal yet wilful, shy yet outspoken. That character was forged in a childhood, stranger and more perilous than any Victorian novel.

* * *

In the year 1817, just two years after Waterloo, Britain faced a grave succession problem. Although the ailing, half-blind King George had twelve surviving children, seven sons and five daughters, all of them were aged over forty. Of his fifty seven grandchildren, fifty six were illegitimate and thereby ineligible. The fifty seventh grandchild was Princess Charlotte, daughter of the Prince of Wales. Her marriage in 1816 to Prince Leopold of Saxe-Coburg had been hailed with delight as 'a marriage of the heart', rather than the more usual one of political expediency.(2) However a year later, aged only twenty one, she died after forty eight hours of continuous labour, in which she gave birth to a still-born son. In remorse, her physician, Sir Richard Croft, blew his brains out. At that time it was muttered cynically that, while French doctors left patients to die, English doctors killed them.

Lord Liverpool, the then Prime Minister, voiced the national question, 'how will this event operate on the succession to the Crown?'(3) George, Prince of Wales, had been acting as Prince Regent since 1811. Unhappily married, he wanted a divorce, not another union. Thus his chances of producing an heir to the throne were as slight as those of most of his brothers. Shelley termed George III's children 'the dregs of their dull race'.(4) Victoria would later hear disparaging tales of 'my disreputable uncles'.(5) Wellington, the victor of Waterloo, was typically more forthright. The princes were, 'the damndest millstone about the necks of any Government that can be imagined'.(6)

* * *

George III's fourth son, Edward, Duke of Kent, was born in 1767. Disliked by his parents, his unloving, harsh childhood ended prematurely by being sent to Hanover for military training. In the army, he won an undesirable reputation as a martinet. In 1803 he was recalled from Gibraltar, after enforcing military discipline with 'bestial severity'.(7) The garrison had resounded to 'fearful blood-curdling cries of men being flogged by the Duke of Kent's orders, 100 lashes being the punishment for trifling defaults in dress.'(8) More severe offences merited 400, 500 and 700 lashes. One unfortunate earned the maximum then permitted under military law – 999 lashes.

Hangings further reinforced the Duke's ideals of military order. Such inhuman behaviour in any army, at any time, could not fail to incur severe risks of mutiny and murder. World War I and Vietnam would see many instances of officers murdered by men who had grown to hate them. The Duke was a liability. When he returned from Gibraltar, his military career was over. He had no other means of earning a living.

Lack of money had always been the Duke's weakness. From an early age, his mother, Queen Charlotte, had viewed his wants as 'monstrous' and him as epitomising 'imprudence and extravagance'.[(9)] At the age of seventeen, he had begun serious borrowing. In 1816 he fled to France from his creditors. By the following year, he was desperate for money.

Back in 1790 the Duke had formed a liaison with a lady named Madame Julie de St Laurent. For the next twenty seven years, he lived with her. But with ever-mounting debts, social position yet no source of income, a favourable marriage seemed the only viable option. Next-generation heirs to the throne were in markedly short supply; if he provided one, surely his prospects would better. By the 1817 succession crisis, he had already spent a couple of years casting around for a suitable wife. When Madame de St Laurent learned of the death of Princess Charlotte, she fainted. After nearly three decades, her relationship with the Duke would soon be at an end. His undoubted fondness for her would be superseded by self-interest, thinly disguised as patriotism.

In 1818 the Duke married Victoire, Dowager Princess of Leiningen. With this marriage, he regarded his future as assured. He confidently asserted, 'My brothers are not so strong as I am; I have led a regular life, I shall outlive them all; the crown will come to me and my children.'[(10)]

It was imperative that an heir be born on English soil. However, until then, it was equally imperative that the Duke live on the Continent, in relative safety from his English creditors.

Within a year, the Duchess was expecting a child. Ever fearful of his creditors, the Duke remained on the Continent to the last possible time. Finally, in the eighth month of his wife's pregnancy, he made his move. Although the Prince Regent deplored the rashness of the Duchess travelling at such an advanced stage, the Duke was undeterred. He drove a carriage occupied by his wife, his step-daughter, Princess Feodore, and her governess, Louise Lehzen and assorted other persons in a madcap twenty-five-miles-a-day rush for the coast, a highwayman's dream. Luck favoured them. Arriving in England, they made their way to the then tumbledown wreck of Kensington Palace. On May 24th 1819, the Duchess of Kent gave birth to 'a pretty little princess as plump as a partridge'.[(11)] The Duke of Wellington was one of a deputation outside the birth chamber to guard against subterfuge. The child was named Alexandrina Victoria, at first known as 'Drina' or 'Vickelchen' to her mother. The Duke of Kent was fourth in succession to the throne; Princess Victoria was fifth. 'Take care of her,' the Duke was wont to say, 'for she will one day be Queen of England.'[(12)]

Unhappily for the Duke, the arrival of his daughter was not enough to restore his fortunes. In an economy drive, he moved the entourage once again, from Kensington to Sidmouth in Devon. There, in the winter of 1820, he caught a chill and died. Unlike his brothers, whom he had confidently expected to outlive, he had always led an austere life, eating little, deploring drunkenness and rising at 5am. As was said of him, 'he was the strongest of the strong, never before ill in his life, and now to die of a cold, when half the kingdom had colds with impunity…'[(13)] His wife, the Duchess, adrift in a strange country, admitted, 'I am hopelessly lost…'[(14)] The Duke's coffin went to Windsor while the Duchess 'sat in my solitude here, eating my heart out.'[(15)] Her brother-in-law, the Duke of Cumberland, remarked to King George, 'I should have thought he would have outlived us all from his regular habits of life… the poor Duchess & his little girl go to my soul…'[(16)]

The Duke of Kent had died on January 23rd 1820. Six days later, on January 29th, as his body was being escorted from Sidmouth to Windsor, his father, the porphyria-stricken George III, also died, blind, senile and incontinent at the age of eighty two. The Prince

Regent now became King George IV. Although nominally 'the first Gentleman in Europe' due to 'the inimitable grace of his bow and the dazzling quality of his waistcoats,' the unsavoury truth was that he was 'the first bounder in Europe, vain as a peacock, false to his friends and remorseless to those who had offended him.'[17]

In George IV's opinion, his late brother had offended him. He would be no friend to this widow and infant child.

When her father died, Victoria was a day under eight months old. She was bequeathed three legacies. The first legacy was a viable claim to the English throne, the greatest prize in Europe. The second legacy was an upbringing as a lonely child, in what we would now term a one-parent family, with a dysfunctional parent at that. The third legacy was abject poverty. True to form, the Duke had died leaving a plethora of unpaid bills. His daughter, who would ultimately become the most powerful person in the world, was to endure early, formative years of great financial hardship.

Some time earlier, a Captain John Conroy had become military equerry to the Duke. Conroy was able, ambitious and utterly amoral. An Irishman, he was capable of seductive charm when he got his own way and vicious temper when he did not. His family came from county Roscommon in Connaught, a remote province on the west coast of Ireland, bounded by the vastness of the Atlantic. James I was wont to voice his displeasure thus: 'Go to hell or Connaught!' This sentiment might have been expressly coined for Captain Conroy. Conroy's military career had been distinguished by a conspicuous lack of active service. An early assessment by his Commanding Officer is rife with ambiguity. Conroy was noted to be, 'an excellent pen and ink man, possessing great knowledge of horses'.[18] In 1818 the Duke of Kent had written to no less a personage than the Duke of Wellington himself, commending Conroy as 'an officer particularly deserving of your notice.'[19] Perhaps Wellington might place Conroy 'in some position of confidence about his person?'[20] Unsurprisingly he did not. The upshot was that Conroy became ever more disappointed and bitter. The premature death of his father-in-law had nullified the political gains of his marriage of convenience. His wife was described as 'a perfect cypher' with 'below the average' mental powers.[21] He had a brood of six children to support.

When the Duke of Kent died, his distraught widow wrote, '... I am hopelessly lost without dearest Edward, who thought of everything and always shielded me. He was my adored partner in life, whatever shall I do without his strong support?'[22] Into this power vacuum stepped the nimble Captain Conroy, who had been the 'very intelligent factotum' to her husband. The Duchess wrote that he was acting 'as a dear devoted friend of my Edward and does not desert his widow, doing all he can by dealing with my affairs... His energy and capability are wonderful.'[23] Conroy quickly became 'invaluable, I don't know what I should do without him.'[24]

On December 10th 1820, the Duchess of Clarence gave birth to a baby six weeks prematurely. George IV and the Royal Family greeted the news with delight. The 'thorn in their side' of Edward's child coming to the throne was apparently removed.[25] By contrast, Captain Conroy noted sourly, 'We are all on the kick and go. Our little woman's nose has been put out of joint.'[26] Less than three months later, the Clarence baby died from 'an entanglement of the bowels'.[27] The thorn in the side of the Royal Family went back in with redoubled force.

On February 1821, Lord Liverpool raised with George IV the issue of a financial accommodation for the fatherless Princess. 'The royal answer,' wrote Prince Leopold, brother of the Duchess of Kent, 'was that he would be d_____d if he consented to it, that her uncle [i.e. Prince Leopold] was rich enough to take care of her.'[28] Friendless in a strange country, the Duchess' first impulse was to return to Germany. However Leopold insisted that she remain in England, to strengthen her daughter's claim to the throne. The Duchess might yet be Regent of a nation she ill understood; and Leopold, a foreign Prince, might become the power behind the throne. Victoria, who had been conceived as a meal-ticket for her father, was now viewed as a meal-ticket for others.

Accordingly the Duchess returned to Kensington Palace and took up permanent residence. Clearly the King and his surviving brothers stood to gain by the death of Victoria; consequently she was always guarded by a trusted retainer. Initially a nurse slept in her room; later Victoria shared a bedroom with her mother. When she was too old for a nurse, she was entrusted to a German governess, Louise Lehzen. 'Lehzen' as she became known, was thirty five years old when she arrived at Kensington. In the words of Charles Greville, she was 'a clever agreeable woman'.(29) In the ensuing battle for control of Victoria, she would prove to possess unimpeachable loyalty for her young charge.

Prince Leopold may have wanted to become the power behind the British throne; but he had a rival – Captain Conroy. Bereft of a conventional career, Conroy fully intended to make the Duchess of Kent his livelihood. When Charles, Prince of Leiningen, Queen Victoria's half-brother, arrived in England in 1824, at first he found Conroy to be 'a companion as pleasant as he was extremely charming' and accepted his 'unlimited affection' for the Duchess and Victoria.(30) George IV was in poor health and was not expected to last long. The Duke of Clarence was over sixty. For Conroy, it was essential that the Duchess of Kent should manoeuvre a position 'so that... the nation should have to assign her the Regency'. She must achieve two aims – and they must dovetail seamlessly. 'In order to be sure of winning and retaining this strong position... the Duchess of Kent should win for herself the esteem and approbation of the entire nation,' i.e. 'she must acquire popularity and a wide following'.(31) We would, perhaps, now term this a public relations charm initiative. Yet this would be of no account unless the Duchess retained absolute dominion over her daughter Victoria. 'Every effort must be made to keep the education of the daughter completely in the hands of her mother and to prevent all interference... nothing and no-one should be able to tear the daughter away from her.'(32)

To achieve the latter aim, Conroy devised what became known as the Kensington System. Victoria was to be socially isolated from all outside influences which might threaten the power of Conroy and her mother. She was to come into contact with nobody outside a tight circle of acolytes. 'Regulations' were laid down to govern every aspect of her life and turn this ten-year-old fatherless child into a malleable dupe.[33]

To buttress his position, Conroy cynically advanced an argument which, oddly enough, had substance to it. Both the English Royal Family and the Duchess's German family, the Coburgs, were to be kept away from the Princess for the same reason: moral turpitude. It was essential that Victoria be presented as a royal candidate unblemished by the sins of both sides of her family. While pretending to act in concert with Leopold, Conroy worked hard to turn the Duchess against her brother. Conroy, not Leopold, must become sole adviser to the Duchess. Leopold, far away in Germany, was too preoccupied with his own troubles to delve into what was happening at Kensington. For this, he has received censure. As virtually the only utterly reputable member of the Coburg family, Prince Albert later confided to Queen Victoria 'Mama here [the Duchess] would never have fallen into the hands of Conroy, if uncle Leopold had taken the trouble to guide her.'[34] Alas, Prince Leopold, or 'Prince Humbug' as he was known in England for his stiff manners, did not guide her.

While Conroy presented the English Royal Family as enemies of the Duchess, only too ready to remove her child from her, King George IV played straight into his hand. The Duke of Wellington later recorded that the King 'was always talking of taking her child from her' and 'he inevitably would have done but for the Duke [Wellington]'[35] Conroy used the spectre of Victoria's wicked English uncles to frighten the Duchess into submission, by continually insisting that they had everything to gain by her death.

Lehzen survived at Kensington only because she was an outsider. Prince Charles later told of Conroy's strategy, 'of the difficulty and danger of bestowing this post on any English woman, who would necessarily have a political connexion and influential friends.'[36] The lack of such connections would mean that 'the Baroness [Lehzen was later ennobled] being entirely dependent upon the Duchess of Kent, would also conform in all matters entirely with the latter's will.'[37] This was sound reasoning – but it overlooked Lehzen's increasingly obsessive loyalty to her charge.

The Kensington System was a marvel of Machiavellian cunning – yet Conroy made two fatal mistakes. He misread Lehzen's integrity; and, as we shall shortly see, he misread Victoria's determination to be her own woman.

For the rest however, Conroy astutely managed the players on the Kensington stage. Princess Sophia, who lived next door to the Duchess of Kent in Kensington Palace, became very friendly with her. Conroy, who had exchanged his role as the Duke of Kent's equerry for that of Comptroller to the Duchess, lost no time in becoming the unofficial Comptroller to Princess Sophia also. As his son, Edward Conroy, later wrote, ' … she gave him nearly all her large income.'(38) Prince Charles noted that Princess Sophia 'stood in close-linked friendship with Sir John Conroy' and 'was considered by him to be very favourably disposed towards the Kensington System and was used by him whenever necessary and in various ways, for the carrying out of his plan.'(39) Conroy regarded Princess Sophia as 'indispensable' to his plans and tellingly referred to her as his 'spy'.(40)

For Victoria, life at Kensington was spartan. In later years, she reminisced, 'I never had a room to myself; I never had a sofa, nor an easy chair; and there was not a single carpet that was not threadbare.'(41) Food was plain and frugal. She rationalised such hardship as 'a great blessing and advantage to have lived in such very simple and restricted circumstances' and attributed her 'humble tastes' and dislike of 'great palaces' to her early upbringing.(42)

Victoria was brought up in a stifling, claustrophobic regime, surrounded by middle-aged women who watched her every move. Gradually she began to realise that she was different from other children. Being referred to as 'Your Royal Highness' and 'Ma'am' was certainly a vivid contrast to threadbare carpets. Her loss of political innocence came in March 1830, just before her eleventh birthday, when Lehzen inserted an updated genealogical table into one of her history books. Upon discovering it, Victoria remarked, 'I never saw that before.' Lehzen replied tartly, 'It was not thought necessary that you should.' Victoria examined the table and finally remarked, 'I see that I am nearer the throne than I thought.'(43) By degrees, the attitudes of the Duchess and of Conroy began to make perfect, sinister sense.

Inevitably there was speculation that the Duchess and Conroy were lovers. Wellington believed it so; he further asserted that Victoria's 'hatred' of Conroy was due 'to her having witnessed some familiarities' between him and her mother.[44] And yet, for all of her life, Victoria denied such an affair. Given that she shared a bedroom with her mother, she was au fait with her mother's habits, nocturnal and otherwise. And keeping such a secret in the hothouse atmosphere of Kensington would have been well-nigh impossible. Certainly there was flirtation between these two attractive middle-aged figures. But the Duchess showed no inclination towards 'immoral' behaviour. Besides, she cared for Conroy's wife, Elizabeth. And one of Conroy's few redeeming virtues was his devotion to his wife, however insipid she may have seemed to others.

Three months later, in June 1830, Lehzen's genealogical table was rendered out of date when King George IV died and was succeeded by his brother, who became King William IV. To the English people, it was doubtful if William represented any great advance. The Duke of Kent had been packed off for military training at an early age; similarly William had gone to sea at fourteen. His elevation to King, some fifty years later, after a life of relative obscurity, so unbalanced him that, in the words of a later commentator, 'he nearly went mad, and distinguished himself by a thousand extravagances of language and conduct, to the amusement of all who witnessed his strange freaks.'[45] Even after he 'sobered down' he remained something of a 'buffoon'.[46] Physically unprepossessing, he was 'a little, old, red-nosed, weather-beaten, jolly-looking person, with an ungraceful air and carriage'.[47] He insisted upon walking the streets of London unescorted and alone, on one occasion being kissed publicly and embarrassingly by a belle de nuit. When riding in his carriage, he spat out of the windows, and cheerfully offered lifts to total strangers. His behaviour was not quite what one would expect from the monarch of the most powerful nation in Europe.

For Victoria however, the new king's accession marked a sea change – unlike King George, William and his wife, Queen Adelaide, had always been fond of her. In 1821, when Adelaide's second daughter had died, she had written touchingly to the Duchess, 'My children are dead, but yours' lives and She is mine too!'(48) In the same year, the very first letter that Victoria had ever received was from 'Aunt Adelaide' to 'my dear little Heart'.(49)

Scarcely had William been installed on the throne when a letter was received by the new Prime Minister, the Duke of Wellington. Although signed by the Duchess, it was clearly written by Conroy. It proposed that the Duchess be elevated to Dowager Princess of Wales, recognised as Victoria's sole guardian and, if need be, Princess Regent. Wellington was incensed by its audacity and peremptorily told the Duchess to await a parliamentary debate on the matter. When it came, the result was fascinating. Although the Duke of Cumberland, as heir to the throne, possessed the best claim to be made Regent, he was so unpopular that reasons were found to exclude him. With his exclusion, the Duchess was made sole Regent, by an Act of Parliament. The Duchess promptly declared that it was the first happy day she had experienced for ten years. Conroy rejoiced. His dream of becoming the power behind the throne had advanced enormously.

Under Conroy's tutelage, the Duchess was quick to flex her muscles, insisting that Victoria, as heir to the throne, should walk behind the King at his coronation, despite alternative arrangements having already been made. Stalemate swiftly ensued, with neither the Duchess nor the King willing to give in. Ultimately Victoria was the loser, the Duchess banning her from the coronation on the pretext that it would be too tiring for a young girl. She was distraught. William and Adelaide were two of the few relatives of either side of her family to have shown her kindness.

With supreme irony, considering that the coronation had been deemed too tiring, the years 1932 to 1835 saw Victoria embarking upon a series of tours of 'her' country. Ostensibly these were to further her education; in reality they were what we would now regard as a public relations offensive, stage managed by Conroy. As might have been expected, the King was severely unimpressed by the promotion of a 'replacement' ready to step into his shoes; to him, the 'royal Progress' was a 'disgusting affront'.(50) One benefit was that the tours removed Victoria, albeit temporarily, from the stifling claustrophobia of Kensington Palace. For the first time, she glimpsed the quotidian lives of her future subjects. Passing through the midlands' Black Country, which then richly merited its name, she was shocked by the 'other England', a spectre of inhuman desolation. Her Journal noted 'the grass is quite blasted and black' and mentioned 'wretched huts and carts and little ragged children' which they passed.(51) Her humanity was stirred by the sufferings of the common people. For all of her very long life, she would feel an instinctive pity for the downtrodden.

Meanwhile, at Kensington, Conroy's efforts intensified. In 1834 Lady Flora Hastings was appointed to the household as another Lady-in-Waiting. In reality, Hastings quickly became a creature of Conroy, who hoped to replace Lehzen with her in Victoria's affections. This plan was doomed on two counts. Hastings was entirely lacking in rapport with the young princess; and Victoria saw straight through Conroy's ploy. When it became obvious that the plan had failed, Conroy switched tactics, treating Lehzen so inhumanly that any normal governess would have resigned. Alas for Conroy, Lehzen was no normal governess; obsessively devoted to Victoria, she proved immovable.

Despite Conroy's efforts to seal Kensington hermetically, inevitably word of his latest offensive reached the Royal Court. William was enraged. At Victoria's confirmation, he made his feelings toward Conroy abundantly clear by ordering him to leave the Chapel Royal. After the service, the Duchess gave Victoria a letter stating that henceforth Lehzen should be treated more formally. In addition, she hinted that her parental authority would persist until Victoria was twenty one, despite being fully aware that her age of majority was eighteen.

Another 'royal tour' in September 1835 began badly and rapidly became worse. Victoria was loath to embark upon it. She told her mother that she felt too unwell to set out. She added that she wanted nothing to do with a journey of which her uncle William so staunchly disapproved. The Duchess responded with a torrent of emotional blackmail, slyly suggesting that William's disapproval stemmed from selfish motives.

The next day a reluctant Victoria set out for the North of England. With each mile, her vitality ebbed further. She was beset by tiredness, back pains and headaches. After a week's journey, they reached York. By then, a concerned Lehzen regarded her as 'so markedly unwell, in body and soul, that it seemed almost a marvel she did not succumb there'.(52) The Duchess was unmoved.

After a three-week tour, they returned to Kensington. Three days later, they started out again for Ramsgate to meet the Duchess's brother, Leopold. Victoria was still unwell with her mysterious malady. When Leopold departed from Dover, she finally collapsed and was bedridden for five weeks. Her symptoms were back pains, stiffness, poor circulation, lack of appetite and hair loss. Even then, the Duchess and Conroy remained callously unconcerned. Conroy snorted about 'childish whims', while the Duchess reproved Lehzen for exaggerating the situation.(53) Eventually Victoria became delirious. With almost unbelievable callousness, Conroy seized his chance. If he could not win against a helpless teenage girl, he would use her sickness to his advantage. With the tacit support of her mother, he tried to browbeat Victoria into making him her secretary, even going so far as to thrust a pencil into her hand to make her sign the requisite document. As Victoria later observed proudly to Lord Melbourne, 'I resisted in spite of my illness.'(54)

This illness of 1835 has never been properly explained. Various diagnoses were proffered, from 'bilious' fever to blood poisoning. Victoria herself believed that she had contracted typhoid. Her symptoms are, of course, the classic ones of porphyria, probably induced by the terrible stress of her situation. Conroy's rude browbeating, the emotional blackmail of the Duchess, Victoria's feelings that conducting her 'royal tour' was tantamount to betraying her uncle William all contribute to a powerful emotional cocktail.

Her tour of the North of England was a gruelling ordeal of travel and public appearances. The last straw must have been the departure of her beloved uncle Leopold. Although he was of little practical use to her, at least she always knew that he cared for her.

Undoubtedly Queen Victoria's famously steely character was forged by Conroy's attempts to break her. For a lonely, loveless child to be betrayed by her mother and her surrogate father is horrible to contemplate. Always afterwards, she would be on her guard against those whom she could not trust.

In the following year, 1836, William's anger toward the Kensington regime exploded in the most public manner imaginable, in front of Victoria, the Duchess and over a hundred other guests seated at table. When it came to the toast to 'His Majesty's health and long life', William acidly responded that he wished to stay alive for at least another nine months, so that a Regency might be avoided through Victoria's coming of age. The Duchess sat aghast as the King cuttingly spoke of 'a person now near me, who is surrounded by evil advisers and who is herself incompetent to act with propriety in the station in which She could be placed.' He berated the Duchess from keeping Victoria from Court and laid down the law in no uncertain terms. '… I am King… I am determined to make my authority respected…'[(55)] Queen Adelaide was mortified by this dreadful breach of protocol and good manners from the King to his guest. A distraught Victoria burst into tears. With masterly understatement, the Duke of Wellington summed up the entire episode: 'Very awkward by God!'[(56)]

Unfortunately William's rant, however well-intentioned, proved counterproductive. Victoria was further traumatised; and the Duchess was even less inclined to visit the Court. As William's health ebbed and Victoria's eighteenth birthday came ever closer, Conroy grew increasingly desperate. On May 18th 1837, the Lord Chamberlain, Lord Conyngham, arrived at Kensington with a private letter from the King to Victoria. When both the Duchess and Conroy tried to intercept it, Lord Conyngham produced as his authority a handwritten note from the King. When Victoria opened it, she read a comprehensive plan to give her financial independence from the

Duchess and Conroy on her eighteenth birthday, less than one week hence. It would be the end of the Kensington System.

Over the following few days, a salvo of letters flew from Kensington with the Duchess and Conroy furiously trying to stave off disaster. Shockingly, an emotionally exhausted Victoria was coerced into copying out a letter drafted by her two oppressors, expressing her supposed desire for maintaining the status quo. That evening, wretchedly, she dictated a memorandum to the faithful Lehzen stating that the letter had been written under duress. Of course the King had not been taken in. When William saw the spurious document, he said with utter finality. 'Victoria has not written that letter.'(57)

May 24th 1837 was Victoria's eighteenth birthday and her coming of age. Conroy still refused to be beaten. Victoria was continually assaulted with a torrent of blackmail from her mother, her half-brother Prince Charles, and Conroy's acolytes, Lady Flora Hastings and Princess Sophia. Lehzen, her only ally in the household, wrote secretly to King Leopold, assuring him that Victoria was 'fully aware of the wickedness of the Prince [Charles] of Leiningen and his friend Sir John [Conroy]'(58) Even then, Leopold did not seem to grasp fully the severity of the situation. He sent his personal troubleshooter, the eminently capable Baron Stockmar, to Kensington to monitor events. Stockmar wrote that 'O'Hum [Conroy] continues the system of intimidation with the genius of a madman, and the Duchess carries out all that she is instructed to do with admirable docility…'(59)

Conroy's last chance was his Ramsgate private secretary ploy, perhaps combined with a Regency on the grounds of Victoria's tender years and inexperience. An attempt was made to co-opt Lord Liverpool to the private secretary lobby by Conroy who tried hard to convince him of Victoria's unsuitability for the throne. A shocked Lord Liverpool tartly told Conroy that there must be 'no private secretary'.(60) Victoria's views on the subject were abundantly clear. 'Sir John Conroy is Her [the Duchess's] private secretary and neither my Servant, nor Adviser, nor ever was.'(61)

Afterwards, Victoria saw Lord Liverpool in a private meeting. Far from being unsuitable, she particularly impressed him with a skilful exposition of a well-written agenda. Lord Liverpool reiterated King Leopold's advice that immediately Victoria succeeded to the throne, she should send for Lord Melbourne and place her trust in him.

In the last days of William's reign, Conroy's desperation was akin to madness. Stockmar related that, on June 16th, Conroy told the Duchess to 'keep her [Victoria] under duress till she had extorted this engagement [Conroy's appointment as private secretary] from her.' Prince Charles later attested that, at this time, he overheard Conroy telling the Duchess, 'If Princess Victoria will not listen to reason she must be coerced.'(62) Still her spirit remained unbroken, although she was very possibly reaching the limits of her endurance. On June 18th she noted in her journal, 'The poor King, they say, can live but a few hours now'(63) The following day, when told that William was dying, she 'turned pale, burst into tears and continued very much affected'(64)

And then suddenly it was all over. Victoria's Journal entry for June 20th 1837 records, '...my poor uncle, the King, was no more, and had expired at 12 minutes past 2 this morning and consequently that I am Queen.'(65) The years of terrible struggle were at an end. Conroy and the Duchess had lost. The price of victory was a ruined childhood. Emotionally scarred from protracted trauma, the new Queen of England ached for love.

Chapter Three
Queen Albertine

In 1816 Princess Charlotte, daughter of the Prince of Wales, married Prince Leopold of Saxe-Coburg, who was to become Victoria's uncle. In the marriage ceremony, when Leopold promised to endow Charlotte with 'all his worldly goods', she burst out laughing. Poor Leopold had no worldly goods; he was well-nigh penniless.

Charlotte was the favourite niece of Victoria's father, the Duke of Kent, who had interceded with his brother, the Prince of Wales, to make the marriage possible. Many years later, Leopold told Victoria how her 'poor father' had been the 'chief promoter' of his marriage. Charlotte repaid the Duke's favour by directing his attentions to Leopold's sister, Victoire, who became his wife and Victoria's mother. Although, as we have seen, Charlotte died in childbirth at the tender age of twenty-one, the two marriages between members of the English Royal Family and the House of Coburg helped to turn that tiny domain into what Bismarck was to describe contemptuously as the 'stud farm of Europe'.(1)

In 1817 Ernest, the middle-aged eldest brother of Victoire and Leopold, married Princess Louise, the sixteen-year-old daughter of Duke Augustus of Saxe-Gotha-Altenburg. His marriage too was not without financial motivation. In 1818 a son, also called Ernest, was born. In 1819, another son, Albert, arrived. Ernest resembled his father in looks and character, whereas Albert took after his mother. In despair at Ernest's infidelities, in 1822, Louise embarked upon an affair. Ernest insisted upon a separation. Two years later, in 1824,

Louise left Coburg, subsequently divorced her husband, and married her lover. Ernest kept custody of the two boys. From the time of her departure in 1824 until her premature death in 1831, Louise never saw her sons again.

The house of Coburg was infamous for its dissolute ways. Ernest grew up in his father's likeness, whereas Albert grew up as his mother's son. (Although it was rumoured that Duke Ernest was not Albert's father, there is no evidence of this.) In England, Albert's cousin Victoria was growing up fatherless; in Germany, Albert was growing up motherless. Victoria was surrounded by women; Albert was surrounded by men and would always be uneasy with members of the opposite sex. Both children grew up in emotionally unnatural surroundings; as adults, both would be shy and reserved.

The Dowager Duchess Augusta of Saxe-Gotha-Altenburg was the grandmother of both Albert and Victoria, who were born a mere three months apart. From the earliest days of their childhood, she looked forward to a marriage between her grand-children. As early as 1821, she told the Duchess of Kent that 'the little fellow' (i.e. Albert) was the 'pendant' to Victoria.[(2)] This intention was no mere whim; Albert grew up believing that his destiny lay in marriage to his slightly older English cousin.

In 1836, at the height of the Kensington System, King Leopold sent a secret letter to Lehzen to convey the message to Victoria that Albert and he were 'the only two people' who 'cared about her for her own sake'.[(3)] Victoria was then approaching her seventeenth birthday. Owing to the youth of the two cousins, an 'immediate alliance' between them 'was out of the question'.[(4)] Nevertheless the Princess was advised to make a choice for her future and 'firmly anchor herself to it.'[(5)]

Two weeks later, Ernest and Albert arrived in England with their father. Victoria's Journal records that 'Albert… is extremely handsome… the charm of his countenance is his expression… full of goodness and sweetness, and very clever and intelligent.'[(6)] Albert, who was suffering from the after-effects of seasickness and travel weariness was plunged into an interminable round of social events. Within a week, Victoria's stamina had exhausted him. Albert became 'very poorly' and 'turned as pale as ashes' while Victoria nonchalantly recorded that 'all this dissipation does me a great deal of good.'[7] As she was being released briefly from the stifling embrace of the Kensington System, it is almost certain that the 'dissipation' was doing her a power of good.

Albert, an inveterate early riser, admitted that he 'had many hard battles to fight against sleepiness.'[8] Nevertheless he soldiered on, winning the grudging approval of King William who had previously been ill-disposed to the Coburgs. When the time came for the deputation to leave, Victoria cried 'very bitterly'.[9] She gave the Duke of Coburg a letter for her 'beloved uncle' Leopold, thanking him for the prospect of the 'great happiness' which he had delivered to her 'in the person of dear Albert' who had 'every quality that could be desired' to make her 'perfectly happy'.[10]

Victoria subsequently noted that no 'understanding' had been mooted between Albert and herself.[11] For his part, Albert wrote that 'not a word in allusion to the future passed between them' though they 'were very much pleased with each other.' [12]

Three years passed, with little contact between Victoria and Albert. Victoria's status changed from that of being a downtrodden Princess to Queen of the most powerful country in Europe. Three decades later, Victoria recalled that 'the sudden change from the secluded life at Kensington to the independence of her position as Queen Regnant' had 'put all ideas of marriage out of her mind, which she now much regrets.'[13]

However, on April 18th 1839, Victoria 'mustered up courage' to tell her mentor Lord Melbourne, the Prime Minister, that her, 'Uncle's great wish – was – that I should marry my Cousin, Albert.'[14] Melbourne acted as devil's advocate. Was it a wise move to marry her own cousin? He pointed out the Coburgs' unpopularity in Europe. What if Albert sided with his countrywoman and relative, the Duchess, against Victoria?

Together Queen and Prime Minister went through a short-list of other European princes. Victoria haughtily decreed that 'not one' of them 'would do'.[15] When Melbourne observed that traditionally the English had little liking for foreigners, the riposte was swift. Victoria declared that, 'marrying a subject was making yourself so much their equal, and brought you so in contact with the whole family.'[16] In any case, a final decision could be delayed 'for 3 or 4 years'.[17] Meanwhile she 'dreaded the thought of marrying', having become so accustomed to her independence that, 'it was 10 to 1 that I shouldn't agree with anybody.'[18]

Yet when Victoria met the Coburg cousins for a second time, she saw that the plump youth had been replaced by an Adonis. She found Albert 'quite charming, and so excessively handsome, such beautiful blue eyes, an exquisite nose and such a pretty mouth.'[19] Within two days, she was writing to Leopold, '... Albert's beauty is most striking, and he is so amiable and unaffected – in short, very fascinating; he is excessively admired here...'[20] In the more private pages of her Journal she wrote, 'It was with some emotion that I beheld Albert – who is beautiful... my heart is quite going.'[21]

Shortly afterwards, she signalled her intentions to Lord Melbourne, who, in turn, wrote, '...I do not know that anything better could be done. He seems a very agreeable young man, he is certainly a very good looking one, and as to character, that, we must always take our chance of...'[22]

* * *

When Victoria had come to the throne, there were mutterings of 'bad blood'. Generally, both the English and German sides of her family were widely regarded as scandalous; specifically, neither of her parents had been popular. Promoting another Coburg into a position of great influence into the Royal Family might have been considered an act of folly. Given these circumstances, Melbourne's tolerance was to his credit. As it happened, taking a chance on Albert's character was one of the best blind investments in British history. Almost from childhood, he had been groomed to be Victoria's consort. In the three years between his visits to England, he had been training specifically for this role under the auspices of his uncle, King Leopold, and the supremely trusted family adviser, Baron Stockmar.

Certainly Albert's character was an odd one. As a student at Bonn, he was 'the best and most obedient pupil' there had ever been.(23) He started work at five o'clock each morning and never missed a single lecture. To Stockmar, a shrewd judge of character, Albert bore 'a striking resemblance to his late mother… He has the same intellectual quickness and adroitness, the same cleverness, the same desire to appear good-natured and amiable to others.'(24) And yet Stockmar admitted that, where Albert's social skills were concerned, 'there is much to desire.'(25) This was understandable since he had 'been deprived of the intercourse and supervision of a mother.'(26) In familiar company, he could be relaxed. Otherwise 'he appeared formal, measured, and reserved, and, as many thought, cold and stiff.'(27)

The house of Coburg traded in matrimony; Albert was its most marketable asset. He knew full well that his second visit to England could have one of only two possible outcomes. If a suitable deal was not struck, he acknowledged, 'he would be known to have failed.'(28) His status as a marriageable commodity would plummet and he would become 'an object of ridicule'.(29)

Less than a week after he had arrived in England, Victoria requested his presence at a private meeting. As she wrote, 'I said to him that I thought he must be aware why I wished them [Ernest and Albert] to come here, and that it would make me too happy if he would consent to what I wished (to marry me).'(30)

Once again we have a striking contrast between our arch-traditional image of Victoria and the much more interesting reality. In the 1830s a woman is proposing to a man younger (albeit only slightly) than herself; such behaviour would have been considered avant-garde 150 years later.

What were Albert's emotions? Relief certainly, that the outcome was decided and that he had not been found wanting. Satisfaction probably, in that he would fulfil the duty and the destiny decreed for him from childhood. And yet Albert was not a cynical, heartless man, devoid of finer feelings. Far from it.

'We embraced each other over and over again, and he was so kind, so affectionate; Oh! To feel I was, and am, loved by such an Angel as Albert was too great a delight to describe! He is perfection; perfection in every way – in beauty – in everything! I told him I was quite unworthy of him and kissed his dear hand – he said he would be very happy… and was so kind and seemed so happy, that I really felt it was the happiest brightest moment of my life, which made up for all I had suffered and endured. Oh! How I adore and love him, I cannot say!! How I will strive to make him feel as little as possible the great sacrifice he was made; I told him it was a great sacrifice, - which he wouldn't allow…'[31]

To a friend, Albert wrote, 'I think I shall be very happy.'[32] To Victoria, Leopold wrote, 'If you love him and are kind to him, he will easily bear the burden of the position.'[33] For Albert, plunged into the politics of a country he ill understood, the burden began almost immediately. Writing to Stockmar, he expressed his discomfiture that Victoria's mother, the Duchess, 'is not to know of it. [the engagement] But as everyone says, she cannot keep her mouth shut and might even make bad use of the secret if it were entrusted to her.'[34]

In private, Albert and Victoria kissed 'again and again'; he gave her the term of endearment 'vortrefflichste' – superb one.[35] Writing to a German friend, he noted, 'My future lot is high and brilliant but also plentifully strewn with thorns… I shall be untiring in my efforts to labour for the country to which I shall in future belong…'[36] The problem was that neither Albert's new country nor its Queen had any desire for his labour; instead, as consort, his public role was to be purely decorative. Victoria wrote to him to explain why he would not receive a peerage and a seat in the House of Lords. '…the English are very jealous of any foreigner interfering in the government of this country, and have already in some of the papers… expressed a hope that you would not interfere. Now, though I know you never would, still, if you were a Peer, they would all say, the Prince meant to play a political part. I am certain you will understand this.'[37]

In the days before the wedding, Baron Stockmar was in London, reporting the public mood to his master, Leopold, in Germany. 'The ultra-Tories are filled with prejudices against the Prince... They give out that he is a Radical and an infidel... The public is tolerably indifferent as to the person of the bridegroom; but I hear it generally complained that he is too young.'[38]

Albert spent the night before his wedding at Buckingham Palace, the residence of his bride-to-be. Victoria's mother, the Duchess, was not the only one who was scandalised. Even the worldly Lord Melbourne raised his eyebrows. Victoria airily dismissed their umbrage as 'nonsense'.[39] Once again we have an instance of the supremely down-to-earth Victoria behaving in a way that could not have been more 'un-Victorian'.

At the wedding ceremony, out of some 300 guests, virtually the only people whom Albert knew well were his father, his brother and Victoria's mother, his aunt. Florence Nightingale, the future heroine of the Crimea, noted acidly that he was dressed in clothes which seemed 'borrowed to be married in.'[40] Victoria had pruned the guest list almost entirely of Tories, whom she regarded as political enemies. 'It is My marriage and I will have only those who sympathize with me,' she declaimed with ineffable hauteur.[41] The Duke of Wellington was a rare Tory survivor of her dramatic veto. John James Ruskin, father of the famous critic, was probably expressing prevalent sentiments about the couple when he suggested sourly that 'The Queen is but a silly child & seems to have no character' and 'I wish the Boy [Albert] may grow into something better. It is a poor prospect for the Country.'[42] Ruskin Senior could not have been more wrong on both counts.

As with the 1816 marriage ceremony between Leopold and Charlotte, the endowing of worldly goods to the bride struck a decidedly comic note. Although Victoria had the good grace to keep a straight face, doubtless Albert squirmed with embarrassment. It was scarcely his fault that he was penniless. Afterwards Victoria kissed her aunt Adelaide but, chillingly, merely shook hands with her mother.

Victoria, the former lonely child, revelled in her first evening as a married woman. 'Albert sat on a footstool by my side, and his excessive love and affection gave me feelings of heavenly love and happiness, I never could have hoped to have felt before! He clasped me in his arms, and we kissed each other again and again! To be called by names of tenderness, I have never yet heard used to me before – was bliss beyond belief! Oh! This was the happiest day of my life!' Marriage was a 'foretaste of heaven'.[(43)]

There was no honeymoon. Victoria was quick to remind Albert, 'You forget, my dearest Love, that I am the sovereign, and that business can stop and wait for nothing. Parliament is sitting, and something occurs almost every day, for which I may be required, and it is quite impossible for me to be absent from London…'[(44)] Two tables were set, side-by-side in Victoria's workroom, although there was no work for Albert. 'No one could feel more for you in the very trying position you will be placed in than I do,' Victoria sympathised, even as she placed Albert in this 'very trying position' in which he could do little more than blot her paper for her.[(45)]

Lord Melbourne had foreseen the difficulty of reconciling 'the authority of a sovereign with the duty of a wife.'[(46)] Early on, he adjudged, 'The Prince is indolent & it would be better if he was more so, for in his position we want no activity.'[(47)] George Anson, Melbourne's private secretary, who had been seconded to Albert, was quick to protest at this fundamental unfairness. 'If you required a cipher in the difficult position of Consort of the Queen, you ought not to have selected the Prince; having got him you must make the most of him & when he has the power of being useful to the Queen he will act.'[(48)]

Again, to his credit, Melbourne swiftly recanted. Whereas Victoria's wedding guest list was a vivid testimonial to her political bias, in favouring Whigs over Tories, Albert argued for a Royal Household above party politics, concerned only with the greater good of the country. Sensing that Albert was made of better stuff,

Melbourne began sounding him out, initially on foreign affairs. Soon Albert was able to write to his father with a wry mixture of pride and chagrin. 'He [Melbourne] seldom answers me but I have often had the satisfaction of seeing him act entirely in accordance with what I have said.'[49]

Six weeks after the wedding, Victoria awoke 'furious' to discover the first signs of pregnancy, 'the ONLY thing I dread'.[50] She had hoped for 'a year of happy enjoyment' with Albert, 'but... I was in for it at once – and furious I was' with this 'unhappy condition'.[51] Being in splendid health, she quickly recovered and continued with an impressive workload. Although Albert considered himself 'very happy and contented' in his domestic life, he noted sadly that 'I am only the husband, and not the master in the house.'[52] Melbourne advised Victoria to 'by degrees impart everything to him.'[53]

One obstacle was Lehzen, Victoria's former governess. While her loyalty to her charge had proved invaluable in the Conroy machinations, it had long since become blindly obsessive. Acting as controller of Victoria's personal expenditure, Lehzen presided incompetently over an empire of widespread corruption and waste. To Albert's horror, she even retained a private entrance into Victoria's bedroom.

Albert confided to Stockmar, 'Victoria takes everything about the Baroness [Lehzen] so much to heart' that she 'feels she ought to be her champion.'[54] And yet, for Albert, there was an element of fear between the Queen and Lehzen. Albert believed fervently that Victoria 'would really be happier without her.'[55] Certainly he would have been happier without her. '...all the disagreeableness I suffer comes from one and the same person, and that is precisely the person whom Victoria chooses for her friend and confidante.' He bitterly resented the 'Yellow Lady' as he called her. (The unfortunate Lehzen suffered from jaundice.)[56] His secretary, George Anson, informed Lord Melbourne that Lehzen was forever 'pointing out and exaggerating every little fault of the Prince, constantly misrepresenting him, constantly trying to undermine him in the Queen's affections and making herself appear a martyr.'[57] For his part, Melbourne told Victoria that he had 'spoken most seriously' with Lehzen, assuring her in no uncertain terms that if she caused strife 'between husband and wife', she would 'draw down ruin on herself.'[(58)]

On a summer evening in 1840, as Albert and Victoria drove up Constitution Hill, 'a little mean-looking man', with a pistol in each hand, looking absurdly 'theatrical', shot at them. 'My God!' Albert shouted, 'don't be alarmed!'[(59)] He pushed the Queen down, as a second bullet flew over her head. Shouting 'Kill him! Kill him!' Onlookers seized the gunman, a 'half-crazy potboy' named Edward Oxford. Oxford, whom Lord Melbourne described as 'an impudent, horrid little vermin of a man', was sentenced to twenty seven years in a lunatic asylum.[(60)] Victoria later admitted, with masterly understatement, to the then Home Secretary, Lord Normanby, that seeing a gunman taking aim at one 'was not at all pleasant.'[(61)] However she had shown admirable pluck, scoffing at Albert's agitation. The young wedded couple carried on with their visit to the Duchess. Afterwards, they went for a drive in Hyde Park, in Albert's words, 'to show the public we had not... lost all confidence in them.'[(62)] Victoria was four months pregnant; luckily no damage was done.

Following the attempted assassination, rumours flew that Oxford's pistol bore the monogram E.R. (Ernestus Rex) and that, among his belongings, were found letters posted in Hanover. Stockmar was dismissive, arguing that Albert's father would never have contemplated such a foul act; nor would he have been party to such crass ineptitude. Besides, what motive would he have had? Interestingly however, neither Albert nor Normanby believed in the verdict of insanity. Marvellously Lehzen wrote, 'Dere was too much of de method in his madness'.[(63)] She insisted that Oxford should be hanged. The true causation of the bodged assassination attempt remains a mystery. Unsurprisingly, public sympathy for the newly-weds was in abundant supply. In particular, Albert's popularity soared. For the rest of his life, his public status would be on a roller-coaster between reverence and vilification.

With the elaborate and necessary security measures of our own time, the casual attitudes of the royals of a former era seem well nigh inconceivable. (It will be recalled that, as King, Victoria's uncle William strolled freely through the streets of London.) Later in 1840 'the Boy Jones', a seventeen-year-old urchin of 'most repulsive appearance' sneaked into Buckingham Palace, consumed 'soups and eatables' and, at his leisure, 'sat upon the throne'.[64] He was eventually found under a sofa next door to the Queen's bedroom. Shockingly 'the Boy Jones' was merely emulating the antics of an earlier 'Boy Cotton'.

Late on in Victoria's reign, at Balmoral, there would often be only one policeman to guard a remote household containing some of the most powerful people in the world. It is sad indeed to reflect upon the necessary loss of such innocent, easygoing attitudes. Victoria's reign marked a watershed. In all, there were seven failed assassination attempts upon a monarch whose humanity and benevolence stood in stark contrast to so many of her predecessors.

As Victoria's pregnancy advanced, her physician, Dr. Locock, enquired about her attitude to sedation. 'I can bear pain as well as other people,' she assured him tartly.[65] Albert remained unconvinced and suggested that the Queen 'would make a great Rompos.'[66] In the event, Victoria was in labour for twelve hours and gave birth three weeks prematurely. When the baby arrived, Locock told her, 'Oh Madam, it is a Princess.' 'Never mind,' Victoria replied, 'the next will be a Prince.'[67]

The Princess Royal was given the same name as her mother; soon it became abbreviated to Vicky. In an age when men paid scant attention to the welfare of newly born children (and often their mothers), Albert proved a husband whose tenderness was a century and a half ahead of its time. Notwithstanding this, Victoria's attitude to pregnancy remained unchanged. A baby was a 'nasty object'; many children would be 'a hardship and inconvenience' and 'men... seldom think, what a hard task it is for us women to go through this very often.'[68] Alas, with contraception in its infancy, it would be a 'hard task' which Victoria would have to go through regularly.

One outcome of Victoria's pregnancy was Albert becoming 'in fact, tho' not in name, Herr Majesty's Private Secretary' with his own key to the boxes of Cabinet documents.[69] On the domestic front, he found an appalling catalogue of waste presided over by Lehzen, and laid down a stringent programme of cutting costs and increasing revenue. Unlike Victoria, Albert was an early riser, keen to start work each morning. Getting his wife out of bed at eight o' clock and having breakfast at nine o'clock meant a longer and thereby more profitable working day. Unfortunately, soon after Vicky's birth, Victoria succumbed to what we would now term post-natal depression; before long, it was deepened by her discovery that she had become pregnant once again.

Life for the newly married couple was eventful. In February 1841, while skating on the pond at Buckingham Palace, the ice cracked and Albert fell through into the freezing water. While her lady-in-waiting screamed ineffectually, the Queen grabbed her husband and pulled him out, displaying 'much presence of mind and courage…'[70] On May 29th of the same year, there was another assassination attempt when 'a little swarthy, ill-looking rascal' named John Francis tried to shoot at the couple while they were in their carriage.[71] His gun appeared to misfire and he escaped. Victoria fretted about being 'shut up for days' while he was apprehended and preferred 'to run the immediate risk' of going out the following day, even though both Albert and she felt that the assassin would be 'skulking about the Palace'.[72] Albert wrote, 'You may imagine that our minds were not very easy. We looked behind every tree, and I cast my eyes round in search of the rascal's face.'[73] Once again, Francis got close to them. From a mere five paces, he shot at them for a second time, missing as before. He was apprehended and received the same verdict of insanity as had Oxford. Victoria, for one, did not believe a word of his supposed lunacy. She insisted, 'he was not the least mad but very cunning.'[74] For Lord Melbourne, Francis had shown 'a depravity and a malice as unintelligible as it is atrocious.'[75] Oxford, the first would-be assassin, told a warder, 'If I had been hanged there would have been no more shooting at the Queen.'[76]

Almost immediately afterwards, there was another assassination attempt. The diminutive (barely four feet tall) hunchback, John William Bean, fired a pistol, loaded largely with tobacco, at Victoria.

For a fourth time, she escaped unscathed. The crowd, thinking mistakenly that the episode was a joke, shouted good-naturedly, 'Give him back his pistol!' This time, there was genuine doubt as to Bean's intentions. Albert admitted that execution would have been 'judicial murder'.[77] Under newly-introduced legislation, Bean received a mere eighteen months in gaol. When Sir Robert Peel came to see Victoria to discuss improved security measures, he was so dismayed by the perils she faced that he burst into tears.

Writing to his brother Ernest, Albert noted of his wife's second pregnancy, 'Victoria is not very happy about it.'[78] The Queen regarded her first two years of marriage as 'utterly spoiled by this occupation! I could enjoy nothing – not travel about or go about with dear Papa…'[79] She complained about 'the trials which we poor women must go through', while accepting gloomily that things could not 'be otherwise as God had willed it so.'[80] In November, Victoria went into labour once more. 'My sufferings were really very severe,' she noted, 'and I don't know what I should have done, but for the great comfort and support my beloved Albert was to me.'[81]

This time it was a boy, Prince Albert Edward, heir to the throne. He was named after his father and his grand-father, respectively. The problem of having two Alberts in close proximity was solved by referring to the new arrival as 'Bertie'. To her uncle Leopold, Victoria confided her hope that her son would come to 'resemble his angelic dearest Father in every, every respect, both in body and mind.'[82] It was a vain hope. Bertie, the future Edward VII, would resemble his father in few respects.

Acting as consultant to the royal couple, Baron Stockmar expounded his policy on child rearing. Victoria's uncles had brought the monarchy into disrepute and thus the royal couple faced a more difficult position 'than that of any other parents in the kingdom'.[83] Their children must be surrounded by those known to be 'good and pure'.[84] Albert saw it as his mission to make the Prince of Wales 'as unlike as possible to any of his great-uncles'.[85] He refrained from mentioning his brother Ernest, Bertie's uncle, in this litany of sinners.

Albert and Victoria were fearful of 'young and carefully brought up boys mixing with older boys and indeed with any boys in general, for the mischief done by bad boys and the things they may hear and learn from them cannot be overrated.'(86) Perhaps it never occurred to Victoria that Bertie might suffer in the same way (though not as greatly) as she had suffered under the Kensington System. Early on, it was realised that Bertie was 'uncommonly averse to learning' with 'peculiarities' due to his 'want of contact with boys of his own age'(87) When it was suggested belatedly that it might be desirable for him to mix with 'boys of his own age away from home', a group of Etonians was brought to meet him.(88) Albert hovered constantly, 'less they should throw bread pellets at each other or talk lewdly.'(89) One of the group admitted being 'frightened to death' by the constant presence of Bertie's father. 'Other children are not always good,' Bertie once ruminated plaintively. 'Why should I always be good?'(90) Of course the well-intentioned policy of keeping to the 'good and pure' proved ultimately to be an unmitigated disaster. Unfortunately it was a disaster for which Albert, in particular, would pay a dire cost.

* * *

Albert's efforts to eliminate gross waste and bring royal expenditure under control meant an intensification of the conflict with Lehzen. To him, Lehzen had to go: 'the welfare of my children and Victoria's existence as sovereign' were at stake.(91) However he acknowledged fully the deep bond between the two women.

> [Victoria] has never been away from her, and like every good pupil, is accustomed to regard her governess as an oracle. Besides this, the unfortunate experience they went through together at Kensington has bound them still closer, and Lehzen, in her madness, has made Victoria believe that whatever good qualities she possesses are due to her.(92)

Of his wife, he noted:

> Victoria is too hasty and passionate... She will not hear me out but flies into a rage and overwhelms me with reproaches of... want of trust, ambition, envy, etc. etc. There are, therefore, two ways open to me: 1. to keep silence and go away (in which case I am like a schoolboy who has had a dressing down from his mother and goes off snubbed): 2. I can be still more violent (and then we have scenes..., which I hate, because I am sorry for Victoria in her misery, besides which it undermines the peace of the move)...[93]

The conflict came to a head when Vicky, the Princess Royal, fell seriously ill. Albert blamed both Lehzen and Victoria's physician, Sir James Clark, for negligence. (Victoria had a soft spot for 'poor Clark' who had previously displayed incompetence.) Albert wrote a bitter note to his wife, telling her:

> Dr Clark has mismanaged the child and poisoned her with calomel, and you have starved her. I shall have nothing more to do with it; take the child away and do as you like, and if she dies you will have it on your conscience.[94]

As Stockmar noted acidly, 'The nursery gives me more trouble than the government of a Kingdom.'[95] For him, much of the trouble in the nursery came from Lehzen. As long as she remained in the Palace, the royal marriage would be in peril. Finally he gave the Queen an ultimatum. Either Lehzen would go or he would go. Victoria was shocked out of her denial by the plain speaking of this adviser of unimpeachable integrity. Soon afterwards, Lehzen was persuaded to retire on the face-saving pretext of ill-health. For Victoria, her former charge, it was 'for our & her best.'[96] Faithful in her manner to the end, Lehzen departed London with no fuss or farewell, to spare Victoria embarrassment and sadness. Once gone, her former charge had a volte-face. 'I blame myself for my blindness,' Victoria confided to her Journal. 'I shudder to think what my beloved Albert had to go through... It makes my blood boil.'(97)

Lehzen received a generous pension from Victoria; her plan was to live in quiet retirement with her sister in Hanover. However, three months after she arrived, her sister died. For almost thirty years Lehzen lived alone, surrounded by portraits of her erstwhile pupil. For the first few years, Victoria wrote faithfully every week; then the letters became once a month. The two women only met again twice in, 1845 and 1862 respectively. 'Saw my poor Lehzen,' Victoria recorded on the second occasion, 'she is grown so old, we were both much moved.'(98)

In 1870 Victoria would write to Vicky, 'My poor dear old Lehzen is gone to her rest, within less than a month of her 86th birthday! I owed her much and she adored me! Even when she was quite wandering she spoke of me.'(99) She had been 'an admirable governess, and I adored her, though I also feared her.'(100) She 'devoted her life to me, with the most wonderful self-abnegation, never ever taking one day's leave!'(101) Although she could be 'rather trying', due to her 'mistaken idea of duty and affection', she had never been motivated by 'personal ambition' but simply believed 'that no one but herself was able to take care of the Queen.'(102) '...the Queen owed her so much, that she did not wish her faults to be brought forward (as they are quite forgotten now)'.(103) It was said that, on her deathbed, Lehzen's last word was, 'Victoria'.(104)

The departure of Lehzen spelled an easing of the troubled relationship between Victoria and her mother. Victoria blamed Lehzen for being 'so foolish – not to say more – ' as 'to confound her very right opposition to Sir John, with my love and affection for my dearest Mama.'(105) Thinking that she had missed 'a mother's friendship... when a girl most needs it' made her 'wild'.(106) Albert proved the perfect intermediary with the Duchess. He knew how bitterly she resented her banishment and how much she craved attention. His 'species of good-natured banter' was 'exactly suited to her warm heart and simple nature.'(107) Apart from Stockmar, she was the only person near to the Court with whom he could reminisce about Coburg. Deprived of his own mother from an early age, in the

Duchess, he found a surrogate mother. By 1861 Victoria could write with satisfaction, 'But thank God! That [the friction between daughter and mother] is all passed long, long ago, and she has forgotten it, and only thought of the last very happy years.'[108]

Towards the end of 1841, Albert's secretary, George Anson, noted that 'Her Majesty interests herself less and less about politics.'[109] Victoria's post-natal depression after the first birth had intensified into a more lasting malaise. It is tempting indeed to speculate whether this was connected to her porphyria. With her fondness for food and her liking for cold air, Victoria was managing the condition instinctively. Yet only a few years previously, she had declared repeatedly her dedication to the business of government; now, although still in her early twenties, she was tiring of it.

The burden was taken up by Albert, who simply worked even harder. In 1840 he had been underemployed; within three years, he was shouldering an enormous load. Always discreet and self-effacing in his duties, he refused nevertheless to be reduced to a cipher by Victoria, who could be decidedly troublesome. In the words of one social commentator:

> They do say, however, that, Queen though she be, he [Albert] will not allow himself to be, in matrimonial phrase, 'managed,' – that when it is necessary, he resists her firmly, though kindly, and I think it is the best security for their future happiness.[110]

On April 25th 1843, a third child was born to Victoria. This time the labour period was far less than it had been with Vicky or Bertie. In her Journal Victoria noted that, 'The only person who was there to whom the child could be shown was Lord Liverpool.'[111] George Anson recorded that:

> It is a disappointment to both the Queen and the Prince that the child is not a boy; and I think there was a general wish in the country that the succession should have been strengthened by another male descendant; but there is time enough for that yet.[112]

It is dubious whether Anson really knew, within a few hours of the birth, that the baby's sex was a matter of 'disappointment to both the Queen and the Prince.' However his chauvinism (the word was not coined until 1870) perhaps reflected a more general feeling. In a Council meeting held on the same day, Prince Albert received 'addresses of congratulation and condolence from both houses.'(113)

Victoria recorded that, 'My beloved Albert who had watched so tenderly over me the whole time, had many people to see and such numbers of letters to write.'(114) One of those letters was to Lord Melbourne, the former prime minister, who had been Victoria's first mentor, after the dreadful Conroy years. The three year political partnership between Victoria and Melbourne has been termed 'one of the romances of history'.(115) By 1843, Melbourne was in personal as well as political decline, having suffered a stroke the previous year. As with Lehzen, he had been devoted to the Queen. He missed her 'every hour of the day, missed her more even than he feared he was going to and more with every month that passed.'(116) Some years before, when they had discussed children's names, Melbourne mentioned that the name Alice was a beautiful one. To his delight, Victoria's second daughter was christened Alice. In spidery writing, he wrote from Brocket Hall, 'I cannot sufficiently express my gratitude for the early communication of this auspicious intelligence'.(117) To Leopold, Victoria wrote, 'Our little baby, who I really am fond of for she is so very forward for her age, is to be called Alice, an old English name…'(118) Alice, as we shall see, would be forward, not only for her age but for the age in which she lived. She would save her mother's sanity; and she would save the British monarchy.

* * *

In 1844 Albert and Victoria suffered their first serious loss, when Albert's father, Duke Ernest, died from his dissipated lifestyle at the age of sixty. Previously the Duke had been an embarrassment. 'Always money, money, money,' Albert had noted grimly.[119] However, in death, Victoria's remote and unprepossessing father-in-law became 'our dearest Papa'.[120] Regret was blown up into a minor orgy of mourning. 'God has heavily afflicted us,' Victoria told Ernest's brother, her uncle Leopold, 'we feel crushed, overwhelmed, bowed down by the loss of one who was so deservedly loved, I may say adored, by his children and family; I loved him and looked on him as my own father; his like we shall not see again… I have never known real grief till now, and it has made a lasting impression on me.'[121] The Royal Court, gloomy enough at the best of times, adopted black as its official colour. Steeped in sadness, Victoria admitted to Leopold, 'One loves to cling to one's grief.'[122] Her words were to prove prophetic beyond measure.

By the end of the following year, 1845, Victoria was slackening her grip upon the reins of power and Albert was hastening to act in her stead. As one commentator noted:

> …and as he likes and she dislikes business, it is obvious that while she has the title, he is really discharging the functions of the Sovereign. He is King to all intents and purposes.[123]

Shortly afterwards, the failure of the potato crop in Ireland and the resulting famine plunged Sir Robert Peel's government into crisis. Peel wanted to repeal the protectionist Corn Laws and import cheaper grain into the country to alleviate the starving masses. He was opposed by vested interests, not least in his own party. Appeals for cross-party support went unheeded, even by such luminaries as Wellington who loftily referred to the 'fright' given to Peel over some 'rotten potatoes'.[124] The prime minister was left with little option but to tender his resignation.

Albert was horrified by the scale of the famine. Other European countries had suffered from the potato blight and had taken extraordinary measures to relieve the suffering. Was it not possible to take 'energetic means' to replace the 'usual food' of the 'poorer class'?[125] Public opinion agreed with Albert; vested interests continued to say otherwise. Following Peel's resignation, the government struggled to form a Cabinet. Peel met with Albert and Victoria, who asked him to continue. Although 'much moved' by their entreaty, Peel told Victoria, 'There is no sacrifice that I will not make for your Majesty except that of my honour.'[126]

In an effort to help Peel, Albert attended a Commons debate on the Corn Laws. Lord George Bentinck sharply rebuked him. His presence gave:

> the semblance of a personal sanction of her Majesty to a measure which, be it for good or for evil, a great majority, at least of the landed aristocracy of England, of Scotland, and of Ireland, imagine fraught with deep injury, if not ruin to them.[127]

Albert never again entered the House of Commons. The famine continued. Although some English landlords willingly spent fortunes trying to subsidise their starving tenants, thousands died and many more thousands were forced to flee to America on ships not fit for cattle. Albert and Victoria were forced to watch helplessly as the country depopulated. Belatedly a relief organisation was formed; Victoria was the first benefactor. But it was the end of Peel's career and it was a salutary lesson to the royals of the depth of vested interests. When they visited Ireland some years later, they found an absence of animosity towards them personally. Nevertheless the potato famine stands as a lasting affront to civilised behaviour. Widespread starvation could not fail to aid the causes of Irish nationalism and English republicanism. The rancid smell of Wellington's 'rotten potatoes' persisted for decades.

1848 was a year of political upheaval across much of Europe. The Prince of Prussia fled to Belgium. The French King, Louis-Philippe, sought refuge in England, where the bursting of financial bubbles caused misery. Paris demonstrations had their counterpart in Chartist meetings in London. Supporters of political change saw their ranks swollen by the hungry and homeless. A Chartist mass meeting was organised for April 10th. A petition with over one million signatories was to be presented to the House of Commons.

Two days earlier, Victoria and Albert decamped to the country. Sir James Graham felt that the departure of the royals 'will look like cowardice in her personally, and as indicative of a sense of danger which ought not to be manifested.'(128) On the evening before the rally, Albert's equerry sounded out popular opinion by the simple expedient of walking quietly through the streets of the capital. He reported thus:

> Her [the Queen's] reputation for personal courage stands so high, I never heard one person express a belief that her departure was due to personal alarm.(129)

London braced itself for revolution. 150,000 special constables were created. Government offices were closed and guarded. The key method of communication, the telegraph system, came under strict military control. Gunboats cruised up and down the Thames. Bridges were patrolled.

In the event, only 20,000 demonstrators turned out. Their leaders were told by the Police Commissioner that, while they were entirely free to hold their meeting, the demonstrators would not be allowed to march across the Thames bridges. Agreement was reached and the Chartist leaders asked their supporters to disperse. The petition was taken to the Home Office.

Earlier, Leopold (who had his own political problems) had written to Victoria, 'The human race is a sad creation, and I trust the other planets are better organised and that we may get there hereafter.'(130) To him she confided:

> an uncertainty in everything existing, which (uncertain as all human affairs must be) one never felt before. When one thinks of one's children, their education, their future – and prays for them – I always think and say to myself, 'Let them grow up fit for

> whatever station they may be placed in – high or low.' This one never thought of before, but I do always now.[131]

Victoria's children and grand-children would fit stations high and low; some would come to terrible ends.

In 1848, the year when Europe trembled, England stayed firm. The Chartist protest had been civilised, relatively good-natured, certainly non-violent. However sympathetic Victoria was to the sufferings of the hungry and dispossessed, she felt in her marrow that Chartism was not the way forward:

> I maintain that Revolutions are always bad for the country and the cause of untold misery to the people. Obedience to the laws & to the Sovereign is obedience to a higher Power, divinely instituted for the good of the people, not the Sovereign, who has equally duties and obligations.[132]

Towards the end of 1849 Albert and Victoria had their second major loss when Viscount Melbourne finally died at the age of sixty nine. Whatever his deficiencies as a Prime Minister, he had been a good friend and mentor to Victoria upon her accession to the throne. Escaping the vicious cruelty of Conroy for the humanity and savoir-faire of Melbourne had helped Victoria make the transition from beleaguered Princess to triumphant Queen. She had much for which to thank Melbourne. Her naming of Alice was a gracious touch. Alice would grow to become the very embodiment of humanity.

In the following year, Albert's private secretary, George Anson, dropped dead at his wife's feet. He was only thirty seven. The diligent and loyal Anson had come to be far more than a trusted employee for Albert. Victoria wrote that he had been 'almost the only intimate friend he [Albert] had in this country, and he mourns for him as a brother.' 'The blow is painful and the loss immense,' Albert told Stockmar. Victoria 'sobbed and cried all the afternoon.'[133] For the previous year, Anson had been suffering acute headaches and Albert had given some of his crushing workload to two other helpers. But, had Albert and Victoria stopped to consider it, Anson's death held a dreadful warning. Albert's workload had expanded massively. His solution was to work even harder. Delegation was alien to his nature. Chronic overwork may not have been the sole cause of Anson's death; however it was certainly a prime contributor to it. Anson's workload paralleled that of Albert.

The following year, Sir Robert Peel's horse stumbled and fell on the slippery surface of Constitution Hill. Peel was trapped underneath it. He died, in severe pain, three days later. He was sixty two. Victoria owed a great debt to Melbourne; Albert owed a similar debt to Peel, who had become almost a 'second father' to him. Peel had recognised Albert 'as one of the most extraordinary young men he had ever met' and helped to ensure that his talents were well used.[134] Victoria wrote sadly to Leopold that Albert 'felt and feels Sir Robert's loss dreadfully.'[135] She had 'extreme admiration' for Peel's 'unbounded loyalty, courage, patriotism, and high-mindedness.'[136] She was 'in a constant flood of tears,' at losing 'not merely a friend but a father'. Writing to the Duchess of Kent, who was abroad, Albert broke the sad news:

> Since you left us, blow after blow has fallen upon us... And now death has snatched from us Peel, the best of men, our truest friend, the strongest bulwark of the throne, the greatest statesman of his time! You know the whole extent of our loss; and such a frightful death![137]

In 1848, in an attempt to boost domestic trade, Victoria issued a decree that guests at her drawing-rooms should wear clothes made in Britain. It was a brave if doomed edict, as continental visitors showed a marked preference for Parisian fashions. Futile though the gesture was, it set Victoria, and especially Albert, thinking of ways to promote British trade and thus make British jobs more secure. In an age when many members of the aristocracy still sneered at those 'in trade', Victoria did not. And Albert, who had begun his service in England by cutting costs in his wife's household, was eminently pragmatic. His interest in promoting technology and industry, combined with his visits to several exhibitions, gave him the idea of a Great Exhibition, to be held in London, which would be an international showcase for British products and services.

Albert quickly discovered what every true innovator discovers – resistance on all sides from those terrified of change. The Corn Laws had given him a sour experience of protectionism; he soon received further disagreeable experiences from other protectionists alarmed at free trade. Capitalism was all very well for oligarchies and capitalist cartels; but why should its opportunities and rewards be shared with the common man?

And where would such an exhibition be held? Albert suggested Leicester Square. Too small. Well then, why not Hyde Park? Conservationists were outraged. All 'the vagabonds of London' would flock to 'our pleasant Park', which would be permanently disfigured by 'a vast pile of masonry'.(138)

Finally a gigantic conservatory, a 'Crystal Palace' of ribbed glass was designed. It could be dismantled afterwards. There was no need to cut down trees; instead they could be enclosed. And yet the critics still refused to be silenced. The entire edifice would collapse in a storm. The crowds of people inside would infect each other with illness and cause epidemics. 'The excommunicated of all lands', already in London, would use 'this rubbishy Exhibition' as cover to attack visiting dignitaries.(139) Albert's rational approach to problem solving carefully assessed each stated problem and either rejected it as spurious or came up with a suitable solution. At times his patience was tested to its limits. The Crystal Palace seemed akin to a 'second Tower of Babel [which] would draw upon it the vengeance of an offended God.'(140) Given the assassination attempts upon Victoria, would the exhibition be safe for her – or, indeed, for anyone? Huffing and puffing, *The Times* hastened to assure all that, 'Where most Englishmen are gathered together, there the Queen of England is most secure.'(141)

The project was innovative; so too was the choice of creator. Joseph Paxton was employed as the Duke of Devonshire's gardener. He possessed no formal qualifications whatsoever; predictably there were howls of protest. It has been claimed that his amazing design was 'more of a work of art than most of the exhibits'.[142] Certainly it conformed admirably to the two fundamental criteria of good design: fitness for purpose and aesthetic delight. This, of course, did not stop critics such as John Ruskin vilifying it as a 'cucumber frame between two chimneys'.[143]

The Crystal Palace, the triumph of Paxton's genius and Albert's patronage, rose to the sky. It was three times the length of St Paul's Cathedral. On one of Victoria's visits, she listened with delicious amusement, to the ultimate accolade, delivered by the Duke of Devonshire. 'Fancy one's gardener having done all this.'[144]

When the project was first mooted, Victoria had written in her Journal, 'I do feel proud at the thought of what my beloved Albert's great mind has conceived.'[145] But, as the weary weeks and months wore on, her mood changed, as did his. The day before the opening, she visited the site to preview it. Writing in her Journal afterwards, she noted, 'My poor Albert is terribly fagged. All day some question or other, or some difficulty, all of which my beloved one takes with the greatest quiet & good temper.'[146] Albert himself was more concise. 'I am more dead than alive from overwork.'[147]

The success was overwhelming:

> The sun shone & gleamed upon the gigantic edifice, upon which the flags of every nation were flying... The glimpse through the iron gates of the Transept, the moving palms & flowers, the myriads of people filling their galleries & the seats around, together with the flourish of trumpets, as we entered the building, gave a sensation I shall never forget, & I felt much moved... The tremendous cheering, the joy expressed in every face, the vastness of the building, with all its decorations & exhibits, the sound of the organ... & my beloved Husband the creator of this great 'Peace Festival', uniting the industry & art of all nations of the earth, all this, was indeed moving, & a day to live forever. God bless my dearest Albert, & my dear Country which has shown itself so great today...'[148]

The Crystal Palace, seemingly a creation of the Arabian Nights, was 'astonishing, a fairy scene. Many cried, and all felt touched and impressed with devotional feelings.'[149] Over the next six months, more than six million visitors attended. Despite the plethora of earlier fears, there were no contagious diseases, no outbreaks of violence, no attempted assassinations. It was reported that, 'those who abused it most vehemently now praise it as much.'[150] No less a personage than Gustave Flaubert noted dryly, 'A very fine thing, despite being admired by everyone.'[151] For Victoria, who faithfully visited the exhibition several times a week and showed keen interest in the displays:

> It was such a time of pleasure, of pride, of satisfaction & of deep thankfulness, it is the triumph of peace & good will towards all, - of art, of commerce, – of my beloved Husband – & of triumph for my country.[152]

Every objection seemed to have been overcome, every problem seemed to have been resolved. When the issue had been raised of birds and their droppings disfiguring the exhibits, the doughty Duke of Wellington had chipped in with a piece of blunt advice. 'Try sparrow-hawks Ma'am.'[153]

At last the enormous triumph of the Great Exhibition came to an end. On the day before the final closing, Victoria made her last visit. Everything was being dismantled.

'The canvas is very dirty, the red curtains are faded, and many things are very much soiled, still the effect is fresh and new as ever, and most beautiful... I could not believe it was the last time I was to see it... It made us all very melancholy.'[154]

The following day, some 50,000 people arrived for the closing ceremonies. Victoria wrote:

> How sad and strange to think that this great and bright time has passed away like a dream... I feel as if it were doing my dearest Albert an injury that it should be gone by...[155]

The Great Exhibition, a monument to Free Trade and a triumph of innovation over innate conservatism was, perhaps, Albert's greatest gift to his adopted country. Yet it came at a great personal price. The gruelling, unrelenting workload would have destroyed the health of the most robust of persons. And Albert's health had never been robust.

Chapter Four
Another Death in the Blue Room

The Great Exhibition marked the end of the first part of Victoria's reign. It also, perhaps, marked the apogee of the partnership between Albert and Victoria. Both cousins were in their early thirties. The formerly downtrodden Victoria, who had barely escaped the clutches of Conroy, had become an assured monarch with well over a decade's experience on the throne. Albert, the penniless foreign princeling, had proved his worth to his adopted country. With the Great Exhibition, he had shown himself the friend to commerce and industry.

Ironically the triumphant public relations initiative of the Great Exhibition was not matched by a similar public relations initiative on the part of the royals. Albert, with his stiff Teutonic manner, so obviously lacked the 'common touch'. It did not help matters that he spoke German within the confines of his family. His diary was written in German. Culturally he remained German. Instead of Victoria converting him to British manners, he was converting her to German ones. He was not becoming more English; she was becoming more German.

At the beginning of her reign, Victoria had thrown herself with gusto into the business of government. A decade later, exhausted by chronic post-natal depression, she had wearied of it. By contrast, Albert, who had begun by being denied any useful role, had displayed unsuspected enthusiasm coupled with an obsessive work ethic. In comparison to Kings George III, IV and William IV, he was doing a superb job. Yet it was all too easy for the media to portray Albert as a vaguely sinister foreign figure manipulating their beloved Queen.

Although the weight of responsibility, coupled with an unrelenting workload, had aged Albert prematurely, to Victoria he remained the Adonis of their wedding day. By contrast, she had become increasingly shrewish, especially where pregnancy and children were concerned. For her, 'one becomes so worn out and one's nerves so miserable' from near-continuous pregnancy which made life 'wretched'.[1] The births of her eighth and ninth children, in 1853 and 1857 respectively, were assisted by the 'soothing, quieting and delightful beyond measure' benefits of 'blessed chloroform'.[2] Clergymen led the choruses of protest; characteristically Victoria was unperturbed. Her ready acceptance of chloroform in childbirth helped to legitimise such painkilling medication. Undoubtedly this resulted in the alleviation of unnecessary suffering among a population long conditioned to accept the vagaries of 'God's will'. For the first time in history, the dreary Biblical dirge, 'in sorrow thou shalt bring forth children' could be laid aside. For this, Victoria deserves great credit. It should be noted that she acted personally as a guinea pig for what was then leading-edge (and relatively untested) pharmaceutical innovation.

Although the media image of Victoria and Albert as doting parents was a minor public relations triumph, the reality was one of relative disinterest on the part of the Queen. Certainly the first-born children, Vicky and Bertie, had received what we would term 'quality time' from their parents. However child followed child, in what resembled a royal 'production line'. Prince Leopold, Victoria's haemophilic eighth child, was described by his mother as 'common looking' and 'ugly'.[3] Increasingly there was less interest and less time for the newcomers being bathed or put to bed. Although, to later generations, the Queen's confession seems shocking that personal time with the 'younger ones' was 'once in three months perhaps', she was simply following the mores of her class and her era.[4]

There is no doubt though that Victoria was scarcely the maternal type. A letter to her from Albert reveals:

> It is indeed a pity that you find no consolation in the company of your children. The root of the trouble lies in the mistaken notion that the function of a mother is to be always correcting, scolding, ordering them about and organising their activities.

With masterly understatement, he continues, 'It is not possible to be on happy terms with people you have just been scolding.'[(5)] Lady Lyttelton remarked that, although the Queen was fond of her children, she was 'severe in her manner, and a strict disciplinarian.'[(6)] Bertie, in later life, proffered the tentative opinion that 'we were perhaps a little too much spoken to or at.'[(7)] Victoria displayed no such polite restraint. There were times, she confided, when she regarded her eldest son with 'unconquerable aversion.'[(8)] 'He is my caricature,' she observed tartly on one occasion, 'that is the misfortune.'[(9)] In Hanoverian looks and character, Bertie was all too reminiscent of her outlandish uncles. If she should die, her beloved Albert would be cast aside for this 'caricature'.

With good reason, Victoria viewed pregnancy as intrinsically unfair to women. It was easy to extrapolate such unfairness to men (the cause of pregnancy) and children (the outcomes of pregnancy). Without warning, she would flare up due to what Albert would regard as a 'miserable trifle'. The 'distressing scene' which so often followed, would appal Albert and place considerable strain upon the royal marriage. Assiduous in everything he attempted, Albert tried to act as an impromptu marriage counsellor. Unfortunately the roles of husband and marriage counsellor conflict; he had limited success.

Vicky, the Princess Royal, was seen as academically the most able child. By contrast, Bertie was viewed as backward and thereby a disappointment to both parents. Albert, who planned study regimes for his children, was forced to devise remedial programmes for Bertie. Predictably they increased the academic pressure upon him. His frustration would explode in periodic outbursts of rage at his tutors. The irony was that Bertie, the future King Edward, possessed from his early days the 'common touch' of easy friendliness which his father so conspicuously lacked. For all of Albert's reforming zeal, he never realised that, for children to find their true way in life, their individual talents must be unearthed and cultivated. Measuring their progress against a conventional template, however well meaning, is a well-trodden path to disaster.

Alice, the third child, grew up in Vicky's shadow. While Bertie was viewed as academically hopeless, Alice was viewed as academically 'slow'. She too was subject to a strict study regime and she too was forced to endure dreaded, periodic inspections. The reality was that she was 'slow' only when compared to the superior performance of Vicky. And, although Alice did not possess Bertie's easy manner, she had other, more unusual gifts, which would blossom with maturity. From the earliest age, she displayed acute sensitivity to the physical and emotional well-being of others. Outwardly so dissimilar in character to Bertie, she shared a deep and enduring friendship with her older brother. Well aware of his deep unhappiness due to his impossible situation with their parents, Alice showed tact beyond her years in smoothing over family squabbles.

Understandably parental hopes were pinned on Bertie and Vicky. Each succeeding child became more and more of an insurance policy. With a decided surplus of royal children, the succession fears of 1817 had receded. The supposed Coburg 'bad blood' of both Victoria and Albert had turned good. Victoria's monarchy was far superior to those of her uncles and grandfather. Yet the warning signs were becoming increasingly evident. In matters of state, Victoria was no longer pulling her weight. Albert was destroying his health with overwork. Although his private secretary, George Anson, had paid for such overwork with his life, the lesson was quickly forgotten. Exhausted by his professional life, Albert was equally exhausted by the emotional demands of his wife. Victoria's troubled childhood had left her with emotional abscesses. For all of her life, she would give out mixed messages. She would dominate… and she would yearn to be dominated. She would ache for Albert's love, and yet her vagaries of mood would run him ragged. Her post-natal depressions accentuated her malaise. And her porphyria, however well managed, cannot have helped. Victoria loved her husband passionately, yet her emotional demands added to a burden which grew heavier with each passing year.

* * *

In 1850, the eighty-one year old Duke of Wellington, hero of Waterloo, and exemplar of a fast-vanishing generation, suggested that he should relinquish his post as Commander-in-Chief of the army and that Albert should take it up. Wellington gave his opinion to Victoria that:

> It was of the utmost importance to the stability of the Throne and Constitution, that the command of the Army should remain in the hands of the Sovereign, and not fall into those of the House of Commons.(10)

It was a view with which Victoria concurred. Albert's reply to the venerable statesman was a vivid expression of his perception of his role. He noted that his 'most peculiar and delicate' situation as consort means:

> that the husband should entirely sink his own individual existence into that of his wife – that he should aim at no power by himself or for himself – should shun all contention – assume no separate responsibility before the public, but make his position entirely a part of hers…(11)

With a formidable array of duties, he must regretfully 'discard the tempting idea of being placed in command of the British Army.'(12)

Although Albert failed occasionally to 'shun all contention', (e.g. his decidedly un-Teutonic opposition to duels), his depiction of his role was accurate. Nonetheless it failed to prevent a spate of lurid rumours. He was a Prussian spy. He was a land speculator who had abused his position as instigator of the Great Exhibition to make a financial killing buying land in South Kensington. He was a contender for Wellington's place as Commander-in-Chief. The latter charge was, of course, particularly ironic, considering Wellington's offer and Albert's refusal.

Albert's diligence, hard work and essential goodness were disguised by his stiff demeanour, a legacy of his native country and his own woman-less, troubled childhood. Undoubtedly he was the victim of racism, accentuated by xenophobia. Englishmen were realizing that the glories of Waterloo were already three decades hence; the Europe of the mid-nineteenth century was a different and frighteningly insecure place. Albert was a convenient hate object. Even his Great Exhibition support for the merchant classes could be twisted into a supposed attack upon older vested interests. Predictably the Tory press was the most vociferous in its criticism of Albert, who:

> has been in the habit of meddling improperly in public affairs, and has used his influence to promote objects of his own and the interests of his family at the expense of the interests of this country... he is German and not English in his sentiments and principles... he corresponds with foreign princes... he thwarts foreign policy... when it does not coincide with his own ideas and purposes.(13)

In vain Victoria protested that, 'In attacking the Prince, who is one and the same with the Queen herself, the throne is assailed.'(14)

Matters reached a head at the beginning of 1854 when news was announced that 'a certain powerful foreign influence behind the Throne' was one of 'two Personages of the highest rank' who 'were secretly conveyed to the Tower, under a military guard, by order of the Government, and have been lodged in safe custody to await their trial on a charge of high treason for conspiring against the safety of the Realm.'[15] A well-meaning bystander was heard to say, 'Poor young man; we hope he may not be executed.'[16] Wearily Albert remarked to Stockmar, 'We might fancy we are living in a madhouse.'[17] Lord Aberdeen who had misread the hate campaign against Albert simply as 'contemptible exhibitions of malevolence and faction'[18] realised belatedly the danger to the monarchy and the constitution. In the Lords and the Commons, he spoke of Albert's 'unimpeachable loyalty to the Crown and to the Country' and offered the pious hope that the torrent of malicious lies would be terminated 'at once and for ever'.[19] Writing of the event, Victoria noted the 'immense concourse of people' who had turned out to assess the veracity of the rumours.[20] The 'immense mischief' was laid to rest by a 'triumphant' refutation; the relieved masses were 'very friendly'.[21] Although the attacks against Albert continued, their tempo was diminished.

* * *

One of the more lurid rumours had asserted that Albert was a Russian agent, in league with the Czar. For years, Russian expansionism had threatened Europe. In 1853 Turkey came under attack. The Black Sea was the naval gateway to the Mediterranean. The Czar's claim of protection to Turkish Christians was a blatant pretext for intervention which fooled nobody. If the Russians captured Constantinople, the barbarian would be at the gate. Victoria wrote to the Czar reminding him of his visit to England nine years previously. She expressed the hope that political differences might be settled amicably. Alas, on the occasion of the Czar's English visit, while Victoria had admired his 'fixed principles of duty, which nothing on earth will make him change,' she had also adjudged shrewdly, 'clever I do not think him.'[22] By degrees, it became obvious that conciliation was not going to work. When Lord Aberdeen mentioned his 'terrible repugnance' for war 'in all its forms', Victoria squashed futile appeasement by telling him bluntly, 'This will never do.'[23]

There was one unexpected benefit: the Czar proved a much more potent hate object than did poor Albert and the vicious attacks upon the Prince dwindled. No-one:

> now thinks of anything but of the coming war and its vigorous prosecution. The national blood is up, and those who most earnestly deprecated war are all for hitting as hard as we can now that it is forced upon us.[24]

War was declared on March 28th 1854. An Anglo-French force left for the Black Sea for what was widely viewed as a brief military expedition to teach the Russian bear a lesson. 27,000 men departed from England; many of their weapons had been used on Wellington's campaigns, more than forty years previously. Logistical backup was almost entirely absent. Supplies of food, clothing and medicine reached the Crimea with painstaking slowness. There was little provision for the care of casualties, whether from war or sickness. In short, like many another naively conceived military campaign before and since, the Crimean War was a disaster ready to escalate. When Lord Raglan warned the government that the army was not prepared for fighting in winter, he was informed blithely that the Crimea had a climate which was 'one of the mildest and finest in Europe'.[25] Men died in droves due to cholera, typhoid, dysentery, exposure, frostbite...

Victoria had played a full part in the diplomatic initiatives undertaken before the onset of war. Prussia, in supporting the Czar, had given popular credence to Albert's supposed role as German national turned Russian agent. The King of Prussia was the brother-in-law of the Czar; securing his neutrality was a diplomatic coup which redounds greatly to Victoria's credit.

From the onset of the conflict, Victoria 'never regretted more' that she was 'a poor woman and not a man'.[26] The War Minister, Lord Panmure, noted to the Commander-in-chief, Lord Raglan, 'You never saw anybody so entirely taken up with military affairs as she is.'[27] She suffered 'agonies of suspense and uncertainty from hour to hour' but was buoyed up by tales 'of such gallantry, such devotion, such courage under privations.'[28] To her, the soldiers were 'her own', even her 'children'.[29] She signed the commission of every officer. She asked that wounded soldiers should be told that 'No-one takes a warmer interest or feels more than the Queen. Day and night she thinks of her beloved troops.'[30]

With characteristic energy, Albert threw himself into the war effort. His enemy was the stifling bureaucracy which sent men to fight and die without adequate support. The Royal Archives have fifty bound volumes of his war letters and memoranda. He created a royal commission, subsequently known as the Patriotic Fund, which raised and distributed over £1,000,000 for the relief of distress to those, such as widows and orphans, left bereft. Soon Victoria found herself engaged in writing letters of condolence to aforesaid war widows, a sad duty which she never shirked. She busied herself knitting scarves and gloves for the beleaguered soldiers. She set a stern example and insisted that her daughters and her ladies-in-waiting followed it.

The Crimean war went from bad to worse. The Charge of the Light Brigade has entered legend as an instance of heroism twinned with military incompetence. After the dreadful carnage of Inkerman, Victoria's cousin, the Duke of Cambridge, fell victim to what we would now term post-traumatic stress disorder. When the Queen saw him in London, he was 'ill and much broken'[31], an object of pity not scorn. To Victoria's horror, media coverage of the war erred both on the side of arrant defeatism and the deliberate covering up of inconvenient truths. She viewed bragging 'of victories not yet achieved' as 'in very bad taste and unworthy of this great country'.[32] In particular, she was 'disgusted' by *The Times*' coverage.[33] Albert, who had long endured unwelcome attention from the same publication, went further. He opined that 'soon there will not be room enough in the same country for both the Monarchy and *The Times*.[34] Although censorship was debated,

Victoria felt that it would be counterproductive. However she made no secret of her disquiet. Her stinging media criticism was not confined to the British press:

> The French show their usual vivacity in pressing so hard for decision upon what is to be done with Sebastopol when taken. Surely we ought to have taken it first...[35]

Although resigned to the conflict, in principle, Victoria had been against the war. As the litany of incompetence grew ever longer, her instincts were proved sound. She took no pleasure in the fact. Her great concern with the suffering seemed to rouse her from her lethargy about the business of government. Always conscious of being a woman and thereby disbarred from military business, she nevertheless described an episode of the Anglo-French war council as 'one of the most interesting things I ever was present at...'[36] Given the untimely demise of her father's army career, her fascination is ironic.

The long-forgotten Crimean war has bequeathed us at least one legacy of enduring worth: the Victoria Cross. Albert's draft of the Royal Warrant made the honour for 'officers or men', without distinction. It commemorated 'some signal act of valour or devotion'. For the following 150 years, the Victoria Cross would stand, and still stands, as an accolade to the bravest of the brave. As long as civilisation endures, the many acts 'of valour or devotion' remain as vivid testimonies to the human spirit.

For every Victoria Cross holder there were, of course, many who had lost their lives; others were broken in body and spirit. The redoubtable Florence Nightingale brought a new standard of medical care to the terrible field hospitals of the Crimea; in so doing, she practically invented the profession of nursing as we now know it. Back in England, Victoria was assiduous in visiting the wounded, the sick, the lame, the amputees. Some of the wounds were shocking; the Queen never flinched. Many of the soldiers were working-men who would never again toil at their former trades. Victoria, who had grown up in circumstances of relative poverty, was concerned 'to try and get some employment for those who are maimed for life.'[37]

British and French losses in the Crimea were matched by levels of Russian fatalities – a grim precursor to attrition rates in future conflicts. The Czar Nicholas II went to his deathbed unrepentant. Magnanimously, Victoria told Princess Augusta, 'Although the poor Emperor has died as our enemy, I have not forgotten former and more happy times.'[38] She asked Augusta to 'express to the poor Empress [Augusta's sister-in-law] as well as to the family, my heartfelt condolence.'[39]

Years before, Victoria had danced with the Czar's son, who became Alexander II. Initial hopes of making peace with Alexander were soon dashed, then replaced with protracted diplomatic manoeuvres, conducted via Prussian and Austrian intermediaries. Finally peace was achieved – a thin, unsatisfactory peace. Victoria admitted that, after such enormous suffering, 'peace rather sticks in my throat'.[40] The war, which had cost so many lives, had achieved little. Russian expansion would bide its time; the Balkans would continue to be a cauldron of ethnic conflict. A later historian, Lord Esher, was 'amazed' to discover how influential Victoria and Albert had been in limiting the damage due to the ill-favoured Crimean adventure.[41] He concluded, 'They were the real ministers of the Crown.'[42]

* * *

On June 26th 1857 Victoria presented the first batch of Victoria Crosses. One conflict had ended, yet already another had begun. On the same day, news of the Indian mutiny arrived. India was a powder keg which had finally exploded. The catalyst was a rumour that mutton used for greasing cartridges was to be replaced with bullock or hog fat. The latter substances, containing beef and pork respectively, were anathema to practising Muslims and Hindus. Defilement meant spiritual debasement and social ostracism. Penny-pinching by arms suppliers was to result in widespread massacres and a lasting rupture in Anglo-Indian relations. The carnage of the Crimea was replicated in India; this time however, civilians, including many women and children, were butchered. Victoria was haunted 'day and night'.[43] A bitter letter to her Prime Minister noted that, 'The Queen must say that the Government incur a fearful responsibility towards their country by their apparent indifference.'[44] The Cabinet remained apathetic. 'We are constantly digging our spurs in their sides,' Albert despaired.[45]

As the tide of war turned, Indian atrocities were replaced by British ones. Lord Canning, the Governor-General, railed against 'rabid and indiscriminate vindictiveness' being displayed by 'many who ought to set a better example'.[46] For this, he was vilified. Victoria regarded the public mood as 'too horrible and really quite shameful!'[47] People were 'judging of things from a distance, and not understanding them, and not waiting for explanations.'[48] Lord Canning concurred. There was, perhaps, some excuse for those 'whose hearts have been torn by the foul barbarities inflicted upon those dear to them.'[49] But, Lord Canning assured the Queen, 'the cry is raised loudest by those who have been sitting quietly in their homes from the beginning'[50] Victoria shared his 'feelings of sorrow and indignation' and hoped that, 'to the nation at large – to the peaceable inhabitants, to the many kind and friendly natives who have assisted us... these should be shown the greatest kindness.'[51] Victoria gave Canning vital support when he was being vilified.

The lesson of the mutiny was clear: rule of the country must be wrested from the East Indian Company. In 1858 Victoria signed the document to take royal control of 'that enormous Empire which is so bright a jewel of her Crown' and 'a source of great satisfaction and pride'.[52] Wisely she had argued earlier that the document be re-drafted to 'breathe feelings of generosity, benevolence, and religious toleration'.[53] She insisted upon having changed a passage referring to her power to modify Indian customs and religions. Had the government learned nothing from the mutiny? Instead was inserted:

> the deep attachment which Her Majesty feels to her own religion, and the comfort and happiness which she derives from its consolations, will preclude her from any attempt to interfere with the native religions.[54]

Lord Canning congratulated her for these sentiments. Victoria felt that bringing Indian rule under direct control might make it possible to 'draw a veil over the sad and bloody past'.[55]

* * *

In 1858 Vicky, the Princess Royal, was married at the tender age of seventeen to Prince Frederick William, in line to the throne of Prussia. Albert wrote to her, 'I am not of a demonstrative nature and therefore you can hardly know... what a void you have left behind in my heart.'[56] Albert cherished the notion of a pan-Germanic Europe, a nexus of relationships between friendly states, where war would be replaced by the ties of trade and commerce. Perhaps his vision anticipated our present European Union; certainly it was far ahead of its time. Prussia saw military intervention (i.e. war as 'diplomacy by other means') as the way to manage politics. In Berlin, many looked askance at marriage to an English Princess. Why had the heir to the throne gone outside the country to marry a future Queen, even one of three-quarters German descent?

Prussians were not the only reactionaries. For so many years Albert had given loyal service to England, a country which had rewarded him with no official title whatsoever. Weary of incessant squabbling within Parliament, Victoria finally issued Letters Patent on Albert's behalf. Writing to his old mentor, Stockmar, Albert noted that *The Times* was 'sneeringly approving'.[57] Wryly he wrote to his step-mother, 'I now present myself before you as an entire stranger, 'Prince Consort''[58]

Vicky's marriage stirred up Victoria's mixed thoughts upon the subject. While being 'with a husband one worships' was a 'foretaste of heaven', the 'yoke of a married woman' held 'sufferings and miseries and plagues' – principally the consequences of repeated pregnancy. 'I think our sex a most unenviable one,' she noted dourly.[59]

Undeterred, Vicky soon found herself pregnant. Victoria, who was accustomed to exert iron control over her children, attempted to control Vicky by distance, via correspondence. When Albert found out, via Stockmar, Victoria received a missive from her husband, who castigated:

> your fidgety nature, which makes you insist on entering, with feverish eagerness, into details about orders and wishes which, in the case of a Queen, are commands, to whomever they may be given. That is your nature, it is not against Vicky, but is the same with everyone and has been the cause of much unpleasantness for you.[60]

Albert declared:

> It is the dearest wish of my heart to save you from these and worse consequences, but the only result of my efforts is that I am accused of want of feeling, hard-heartedness, injustice, hatred, jealousy, distrust, etc. etc.'[61]

Almost in desperation, he concluded:

> I do my duty towards you even though it means that life is embittered by 'scenes' when it should be governed by love and harmony. I look upon this with patience as a test which has to be undergone, but you hurt me desperately and at the same time do not help yourself.[62]

In autumn 1859, a heavily pregnant Vicky caught her foot in the leg of a chair and fell badly. When her child was born four months later, she suffered terribly. The baby had to be taken out of her body with forceps. Whether from movement in the womb from the chair accident, the rigours of forceps delivery, or medical malpractice, the future Kaiser William was born with a withered left arm. It is believed by some that his over-compensation for his affliction engendered his military belligerence, a contributory factor to the onset of World War I.

By then, William's uncle, Bertie, would have ruled as King of England. The Edwardian era, a coda to Victorianism, would come to resemble a twilight world, vanished forever amid tattered Flanders poppies. The young Bertie remained sadly underrated by both his parents. 'I own I think him very dull' Victoria had earlier noted heartlessly to Vicky.[63] Paradoxically she acknowledged that his social talents (so different from Albert's) were 'remarkable'.[64] With no doubt unconscious humour, she opined that Bertie could be:

> lively, quick and sharp when his mind is set on anything, which is seldom… Usually his intellect is of no more use than a pistol packed at the bottom of a trunk if one were attacked in the robber-infested Appenines.[65]

To Victoria, children were often tiresome and invariably a disappointment. A psychiatrist might wonder whether she was projecting feelings of worthlessness from her miserable Conroy-ridden childhood onto her own children. We tend to think fondly of Victoria as maternal, surrounded by children. Often she was surrounded by children; yet she was rarely maternal, as we now understand the term.

* * *

In February 1860, Albert and Victoria celebrated their twentieth wedding anniversary. Writing to Stockmar, Albert recalled him standing in the wedding Chapel, surrounded by British strangers. To his old mentor, he reflected poignantly, 'We have gone through much since then, and striven after much that is good; if we have not always succeeded, the will was at least good...'[66] With equal poignancy, Victoria wrote, 'I wish I could think I had made one as happy as he has made me. But this is not for want of love and devotion.'[67] Victoria's 'beloved and perfect Albert had raised monarchy to the highest pinnacle of respect, and rendered it popular beyond what it ever was in this country.'[68] Albert's popularity had risen to its zenith with the huge success of the Great Exhibition; thereafter, through no fault of his own, it had diminished. Subsequent threats in the Crimea and India had engendered a sense of patriotism, the 'Dunkirk spirit' of the following century. The personal standing of Albert and Victoria had benefited from such patriotism. Yet did the monarchy truly enjoy 'the highest pinnacle of respect'? In government, political parties came and went with frightening alacrity. The robber-baron capitalism of the Victorian era created chasms between rich and poor, fomenting social discontent. Newspapers had unprecedented power. The political passivity of generations working the land had been replaced by urban dwellers, far more aware of current events and far more likely to harbour resentment.

Meanwhile Albert carried on working himself into a state of exhaustion. It was as though he had to prove his worth again and again: to Victoria, to his adopted country, to himself. The supposed Coburg 'bad blood' must be made good. Victoria continued to eschew most of the business of government. Bertie continued his playboy existence. And Albert worked on. Two decades of gruelling effort had aged him prematurely. He was balding, overweight and moved more like a man in his sixties than one in his forties. His gums ached incessantly. He suffered from having to endure the cold, draughty rooms, which Victoria so loved and which probably benefited her porphyria. In October 1859, the Prince Consort had been forced to take to his bed with acute stomach pains. In a letter to Vicky, Victoria made light of his ailment. 'Dear Papa was a little indisposed with his old enemy, but it was not a very bad attack, without sickness or shivering.'[69] To Stockmar, Albert confided that he was 'rallying from a gastric attack... The only new symptom I had was a violent cramp at the pit of the stomach, which lasted very sharply for two hours at noon, several days running.'[70] Stockmar, who had been a doctor, wrote back to Albert recommending a more relaxed lifestyle, geared towards prevention, not cure. Bluntly he noted that Albert's description of his ailment 'has disquieted me, and made me very sad.'[71]

For decades, Stockmar had given unfailing loyalty to the Coburgs; now he was in his seventies and in failing health. Also in poor health was Albert's stepmother, the Dowager Duchess Marie. In 1860 it was decided that Albert and Victoria should travel to Coburg to visit Stockmar and Marie. Vicky would cross Germany to meet them there. En route, they received the news that Marie had died. When they met Vicky in Coburg, she was 'in the deepest German mourning, long black veils...' From Victoria, there was, 'A tender embrace, and then we walked up the staircase... Could hardly speak, I felt so moved, and quite trembled.'[72]

Shortly after Marie's funeral, Albert was involved in a near-fatal accident. While driving a carriage, his four horses bolted. Out of control, they raced for two miles until they arrived at a level crossing by a railway track. There was a wagon waiting on the track and a bar across the road. Albert had no choice but to leap for his life. One of the horses was killed; the others raced on. Although badly bruised and shocked, it was typical of Albert that his first concern was to help the coachman of the wagon he had hit. When the runaway horses reached Coburg they were recognised and the alarm was raised. Help soon arrived. Both Victoria and Stockmar were mortified. Although Albert made light of the accident, coming so soon after the death of Marie, it seemed a bad omen. Nevertheless he continued with his massive workload. Victoria noted that there were 'constant dispatches' and consequently 'Albert [was] too busy to go out.'[73]

Despite his own decline, Stockmar was more perturbed about Albert. He knew from constant correspondence, how low the Prince Consort had sunk. Marie's death and the accident with the runaway horses had served to lower his spirits further. 'God have mercy on us!' Stockmar told Albert's brother, Ernest, 'If anything serious should ever happen to him [Albert], he will die.'[74]

At Coburg, Ernest went for a final walk with Albert. When they reached a particularly memorable place, 'Albert stood still, and suddenly felt for his pocket handkerchief.'[75] Thinking that Albert's wounds were weeping, Ernest turned to him. To his dismay, Ernest found that, 'tears were trickling down his cheeks… he persisted in declaring that he was well aware that he had been there for the last time in his life.'There was nothing to say. Side by side, the two brothers walked back to the chateau. Shortly afterwards, Albert left Coburg forever.

* * *

The glorious Autumn weather of only a few weeks previously had turned with a vengeance into cold, interminable downpours. Although continuing to make light of his situation, Albert was dangerously ill with cramps and headaches. Unusually, Victoria became feverish with a sore throat and a heavy cold. By the time they reached Verviers, Victoria recorded, 'I could hardly walk when we got out and with difficulty got up stairs… Dr. Baly found my throat very bad, that I had much fever; so I was ordered to remain lying down in my room and to see no one.'[77] It was six weeks after they reached home before Albert felt fit to start working properly again. 'My attack was the real English cholera,' he wrote to Vicky.[78] So called 'English cholera' involved diarrhoea and stomach cramps lasting up to a week – not the two months which Albert had suffered.

It was as though, by degrees, Albert was releasing his hold on life. At first glance, Victoria's relative equanimity about his condition resembles heartlessness; doubtless there were also elements of denial. But her determined positivism was a refreshing antidote to Albert's equally determined fatalism.

> Papa never allows he is any better or will try to get over it but makes such a miserable face that people always think he's very ill. It is quite the contrary with me always; I… never show it, so people never believe I am ill or ever suffer. His nervous system is easily excited and irritated, and he's so completely overpowered by everything.(79)

Albert, it must be said, was not 'so completely overpowered by everything' that he neglected his self-imposed duties.

Ever paradoxical, as 1860 ended, Victoria paid tribute. 'My precious husband cheered me & held me in his dear arms saying 'We must have trust, & we have trust that God will protect us.''(80) On February 10th 1861, Victoria had been married for twenty-one years to 'that most perfect of human beings, my adored Husband!'(81) Certainly the twenty-one years had contained many stormy passages. However much Victoria may have deplored her 'foolish sensitivity & irritability', it was an inevitable part of her personality.(82)

Only months after the death of Albert's stepmother, the Dowager Duchess Marie, Victoria's mother, the Dowager Duchess of Kent, took a turn for the worse. At seventy-four, she was crippled by erysipelas; her strength was ebbing. When Vicky's grandfather-in-law, King Frederick William IV of Prussia, had died in January, Victoria told Vicky, 'I have never even yet witnessed a death bed.'(83) On March 16th, she went to her mother's bedroom to see her alive for the last time. 'I sat on a foot stool, holding her dear hand… I felt the end was fast approaching, as [Doctor] Clark went out to call Albert… Fainter and fainter grew the breathing. At last it ceased… The clock stuck half-past nine at the very moment.'(84)

When Victoria went into the Duchess's sitting room 'to weep and pray', she saw the 'work basket… and the little canary bird, which she was so fond of…' It was too much for her.(85) Albert, who was in great distress himself, asked Princess Alice to 'comfort Mama'.[86] To Alice, this became 'a vorbedeutung [portent] of what was to come.'[87]

* * *

From her earliest days, Victoria had an ambivalent relationship with her mother. During the terrible years when Conroy had tried firstly to mould, then break her, she had come to view her mother as a member of the enemy camp. Lehzen's death and Albert's discreet facilitation had reconciled daughter with mother to some extent. However, when Victoria came to sort out her mother's effects, she was astounded to discover that the Duchess had saved every possible memento of her childhood. 'Not a scrap of my writing – or of my hair has ever been thrown away…'[88] It was impossible to doubt the inference; the Duchess had always loved her. Even with their reconciliation, had Victoria somehow fallen short in her duty and affection to her mother?

Under the stress of such thoughts, Victoria's mind collapsed. She inhabited a state of almost woeful ecstasy. She would sit in her mother's room, kept exactly as it had been when the Duchess was alive. To outsiders, it appeared that her mourning was excessive. Lord Clarendon scoffed that she 'was determined to cherish her grief & not be consoled.'[89] She wrote of 'The blank – the desolation… come back with redoubled force, and the weeping, which day after day is my welcome friend, is my greatest relief.'[90]

> To lose a beloved mother is always terrible, but when you consider that this mother has lived for no one and nothing but me, that for 41 years I have never been separated from her for more than three months, that she was the gentlest, most tender and loving creature that one can ever imagine,' [thus] 'how immeasurable is my loss and grief.[91]

Ironically this 'poor orphan child' was incapable of being comforted by her own children, who were 'a disturbance'.[92] She cut herself off from her family; for three weeks, she dined alone. Albert was 'well nigh overcome' with work.[93] The previous month, Sir George Couper, the comptroller of the Duchess's household, had died and Albert had taken over his duties, in addition to everything else. Now he also had to deal with the administration of the Duchess's estate. Victoria withdrew from public appearances, leaving her husband to bear the brunt. 'Am ill, feverish, with pains in my limbs, and feel very miserable,' his diary noted.[94] Be that as it may, the business of government must go on. In addition to a myriad foreign policy considerations, the onset of the American Civil War had put a question mark against the supply of cotton to the textile mills of Yorkshire and Lancashire. The last thing the government needed was another economic crisis.

It took Victoria almost six months to recover. At times, 'the grief and yearning' were almost unbearable.[95] Without appetite, she felt 'stupefied' and 'stunned'.[96] There were constant headaches. She could barely endure 'the least noise or talking'.[97] Even the crunching of her carriage wheels on the gravel was infuriating to her. All of this sounds uncommonly like an attack of porphyria brought about by the stress of her mother's death. When Vicky queried her mother's protracted mourning, Victoria replied, 'You are right, dear child, I do not wish to feel better… The more others recover their spirits – the more trying it becomes to me.'[98] 'I could not and would not [recover].'[99] Lord Clarendon felt that she was so 'determined to cherish her grief' that she was practically resentful of those who wished to help her.[100] 'I hope this state of things won't last,' he confided, 'or she may fall into the morbid melancholy to which her mind has often tended and which is a constant cause of anxiety to Prince Albert.'[101] Albert struggled to get Victoria 'to take things as God sent them'.[102] She took little heed of his advice but paid tribute to his devoted care. 'My dear husband has been a veritable angel of goodness to me in this terrible time.'[103] These sentiments were echoed by one of her Ladies-in-Waiting, Lady Augusta Bruce, who had never seen 'such tenderness, such gentleness, such tact as His – Oh! He is one in millions – well might She love Him as She did.'[104] Albert's love was to come at a terrible cost.

* * *

Victoria had described Bertie's intellect memorably as 'of no more use than a pistol packed at the bottom of a trunk if one were attacked in the robber-infested Appenines.'[105] Nevertheless he was the heir to the throne and his abilities, such as they were, must be deployed to best advantage. The previous year, he had been packed off on a tour of Canada and the United States. His easy, relaxed social manner had made him a huge success with society hostesses and the general public alike. However Albert would not give him any credit; he spoke disparagingly of 'our hero'.[106] If much desired approval from his father was lacking, at least Victoria was proud of him. He had been 'immensely popular' and 'really deserved the highest praise… all the more as he was never spared any reproof.'[107]

Subsequently Victoria co-opted Vicky for a trawl of European princesses, to select a suitable wife for Bertie and, most probably, a future Queen of England. A further strand of Bertie's rehabilitation from playboy to aspirant monarch was a stint in the army, with ten weeks to be spent in Ireland. As part of a public relations offensive, Albert and Victoria would visit Ireland at the same time, to inspect Bertie leading his troops. Such a visit would achieve several aims: it would impress the Irish, who had given the royals such an unexpectedly enthusiastic welcome back in 1849, after the Potato Famine. It would be a convincing show of public unity between the Queen, the Prince Consort and the Prince of Wales. And, perhaps most importantly, it would be a statement that the Queen had arisen from her grief and was back on form.

Unfortunately, while the Irish visit was sound in theory, it was hopelessly flawed in practice. Albert was on the verge of physical collapse. Victoria's mind was still profoundly affected by the death of her mother; ugly rumours were consigning her to padded cells. And a plan to promote Bertie one officer grade each fortnight was as unrealistic as had been Albert's study plan for him when he was a few years old. When it became obvious that Bertie was not up to a military progression that might have taxed the abilities of an Alexander the Great, it was time for damage limitation. The plan for him to command a battalion was changed to one of taking charge of a company of Grenadier Guards. Victoria, who felt 'weak and very nervous', managed to scrape through the visit.(108) Albert sank lower.

The Irish visit was notable for another episode, which was to have an unexpectedly devastating consequence. In his rehabilitation, via supposed military prowess, from playboy to aspirant monarch, it was decided that Bertie be kept well away from his fellow officers. Understandably, they resented such a decree; equally understandably, they viewed it as a challenge. Previously it had been stressed to Bertie's Equerries that nothing 'approaching to a practical joke' should ever be permitted.(109) Now, as a practical joke, Bertie's fellow officers contrived to smuggle a young lady named Nellie Clifden into his bedroom. Nellie was amenable; Bertie was both charming and appreciative. Had the episode remained secret, no great harm would have been done. Unfortunately it did not remain secret.

Albert and Victoria had gone to their refuge in Balmoral to recover. 'Johnny Brown', that 'invaluable Highland servant' 'takes the most wonderful care of me', Victoria noted.(110) On their last day trip of the holiday, in the Cairngorms, they scaled 'a precipitous place, which made one dread anyone's moving backwards'.(111) As they made ready to go, 'Albert wrote on a bit of paper that we had lunched there, put it into a Seltzer-water bottle, and buried it there, or rather stuck it in the ground'.(112) Was it another leave-taking? Brown, with his bluff Highlandman's courtesy, tendered his good wishes for them as they departed for London. Ominously he added his desire that 'above all, you may have no deaths in the family.'(113) Victoria was still grieving for her mother. Writing to Vicky, she confided, 'I feel now to be so acquainted with death – and to be so much nearer that unseen world.'(114)

On their return to Windsor, Albert buried himself once more in his paperwork. Duty had long since become obsession He gulped down his meals so that he could return to work. At Windsor and at Buckingham Palace, he raced down the corridors, to save precious seconds. His constant refrain was, 'I have no time, I must write letters.'(115) He would not delegate; thus, his time was stolen by a constant stream of trivia. 'Ask the Prince' was the stock solution to every problem. In 1859 Victoria had confided in Vicky, 'My greatest of all anxieties is that dearest Papa works too hard... [He] wears himself quite out by all he does.'(116)

Thus Albert was in no fit state to receive the news that his cousin, Prince Ferdinand, had died of typhoid. Shortly afterwards he received further news that another cousin, King Pedro V, had also died. Both Victoria and he were shocked.

Hard on the heels of these grim pieces of news came the 'horrifying' revelation from Lord Torrington to Albert about Bertie's dalliance with Nellie Clifden. In the Victorian age, as in all others, many fathers have greeted their sons' foibles with indulgence. Albert was not such a father. 'Papa was too perfect for this world,' Victoria told Vicky.(117) His 'face of woe and sorrow' bore eloquent testimony to the devastating blow to his 'pure, noble, heavenly spirit.'(118) Some of 'the disgusting details' of Bertie's dalliance were deemed too indecent for Victoria's ears.(119) Melodramatically she wrote in her journal that never again would she be able to look at her son 'without a shudder'.(120) 'With a heavy heart' Albert wrote to his son, 'upon a subject which has caused me the greatest pain I have yet felt in this life.'(121) 'This person' had the power 'to break your poor parents' hearts.'(122)

In retrospect, it is easy to see that Albert's over-reaction drained him of the last of his emotional energy. Bertie's brief encounter was as nothing compared to the excesses of some of his ancestors. But for Albert, desperate to preserve the sanctity of the monarchy, his son's behaviour must have appeared the ultimate betrayal. At one stroke, twenty years of continuous effort seemed to have been wasted. It could not have come at a worse time. Albert's health was broken. He was physically and mentally exhausted from two decades of over-work. Ever since the visit to Coburg, one disaster had followed another – the deaths of Duchess Marie, the Duchess of Kent, Prince Ferdinand, King Pedro. Victoria's bouts of post-natal depression had deepened into guilt-ridden grieving. Albert had suffered the trauma of the near-fatal accident with the runaway horses. His work had expanded still further, first with managing the Duchess of Kent's finances after her comptroller, Sir George Couper, had died, then with managing her estate after she, in turn, had died. And always the business of government remained, an ever-harsher taskmaster. The American Civil War was the latest foreign crisis; there had been so many others – the Potato Famine, the Crimean war, the Indian mutiny. Always there would be further ones unfolding. At his wit's end, Albert told Victoria:

> I do not cling to life; you do; but I set no store by it. I am sure that if I had a severe illness I should give up at once, I should not struggle for life. I have no tenacity of life.[(123)]

The pressure never let up. The young Prince Leopold, who had inherited haemophilia from Victoria, suffered a terrible bleeding attack. A visit, in foul weather, to Sandhurst to inspect the recently completed Staff College, left Albert soaked and chilled. Again in dire weather, he forced himself to confront Bertie, whose sojourn in Cambridge was a typically vain attempt to lend an academic string to his bow. Albert's letter to his son had been well-nigh hysterical; yet when he saw Bertie in the flesh, it was obvious that this supposed demon was, in fact, mortified. Bertie was forgiven. But Albert remained at 'a very low ebb' due to 'much worry and great sorrow',[(124)] on the verge of physical collapse. At this time an incident concerning a Union warship threatened to escalate into full-blown war between Great Britain and the United States. While this may have been in line with the desires of certain politicians, it was anathema to Victoria and

Albert. Earlier Victoria had reproached Vicky for referring to 'those horrid Yankees'.[125] She tersely reminded her daughter of Bertie's rapturous reception in the United States, attributing this not to his charm but 'principally from the (to me incredible) liking they have for my unworthy self...'[126]

Early on the morning of December 1st 1861, Albert got up out of bed and staggered into his study. He worked feverishly at a face-saving solution for the diplomatic impasse, a way to avert war. By 8.00am, the time he normally roused Victoria, he had finished the draft and brought it to her to read. 'I am so weak, I have hardly been able to hold the pen,' he whispered.[127] Later Victoria was to write in the margin of the document, 'This draft was the last the beloved Prince ever wrote...'[128]

Over the next few days, Albert's condition worsened still further. He could not sleep; he could not keep food down. Incredibly his physician seemed unperturbed. When a concerned Lord Palmerston asked Victoria to get another opinion, she replied loftily, 'In addition to Sir James Clark, the Queen has the advantage of the constant advice of Dr. Jenner, a most skilful Physician...'[129] Writing to Vicky, Victoria regarded Dr Jenner as 'a great friend of our poor Dr Baly. He is extremely clever, and has a pleasing clever manner.'[130] In her Journal she wrote:

> Dreadfully annoyed at a letter from Lord Palmerston suggesting Dr Ferguson should be called in as he heard Albert could not sleep and eat. Very angry about it... Good kind old Sir James... reassured me and explained to Dr Jenner too that there was no cause whatever for alarm – either present or future. It was not likely to turn to a low fever. My Darling himself was in apprehension of a low fever. This they assured me he need not be...[131]

On December 6th, Sir Charles Phipps wrote a confidential letter to Lord Palmerston:

> ...everything connected with the subject [of the Prince's health] requires much management. The Prince himself, when ill, is extremely depressed and low, and the Queen becomes so nervous, and so easily alarmed, that the greatest caution is necessary. The suggestion that it could be desirable to call in another Medical Man would I think frighten the Queen very much, and the Prince already is annoyed with the visits of the three who attend him. [the third person was Mr Brown, the Windsor Apothecary] You will easily believe with how much diffidence I hesitate to act on any suggestion of yours – but I sincerely believe that to ask to call another Doctor would do more harm than good. The mere suggestion upset the Queen and agitated her dreadfully, and it is very essential to keep up the spirits both of Her and the Prince.[132]

By this time, Victoria's 'stiff upper lip', her determined positivism, was wearing thin. Albert was left to his own devices, getting out of bed when he could, even though at times he was almost delirious. Always he was accompanied by his third-born child, the eighteen-year-old Princess Alice, who, although without previous experience, acted as an extremely effective head nurse.

On December 7th, Dr Jenner told Victoria 'in the kindest, clearest manner' that a distinctive pink rash on Albert confirmed a verdict of 'gastric fever', i.e. typhoid.[133] Victoria's 'heart was ready to burst'.[134] Airily she was informed that the disease would run its course in a month. Others had survived; why should not the Prince survive also? There were no 'bad symptoms', as she noted in her Journal.[135] Interestingly there were no other cases of typhoid at Windsor or, indeed, at Sandhurst.

Clark, the senior physician, knew that Albert had an obsessive fear of typhoid. He laid down a decree that the word must never be mentioned in Albert's presence; the patient was to be told simply that he had a 'feverish cold'.[136] Similarly Victoria's spirits must be raised, lest Albert read his peril in her demeanour. Phipps endorsed this policy. Writing to Palmerston, he noted that 'The Prince himself, when ill, is extremely depressed and low...' No little management was needed to prevent the Queen 'from breaking down altogether.'[137] It was a kindly meant tactic, which would backfire by leaving Victoria unprepared for the worst.

On Sunday, December 8th, Victoria was informed that Albert seemed better. He asked Alice to play 'A Mighty Fortress Is Our Friend' on the piano. Afterwards she continued with some of his favourite German tunes. He requested that the sofa be moved closer to the window, so that he could watch the clouds high above. Thinking that he had nodded off, Alice covered him with a blanket. Unexpectedly he opened his eyes. 'Were you asleep?' she asked.[138] He gave a wry, gentle smile and replied, 'No – but my thoughts were so happy that I did not want to drive them away by moving.'[139]

That evening Albert changed his bedroom to the Blue Room, the 'King's Room', where the two previous monarchs, George IV and William IV, had died. The significance of his move could not have been more ominous. Nevertheless his physicians continued to interpret each development in a positive light.

The following day, envoys arrived from Lisbon, where they had been offering condolences on the death of Prince Ferdinand. Heedless of the risk of typhoid, Albert insisted on seeing them. Once again Lord Palmerston begged Victoria to solicit alternative medical opinion; once again she refused. By now, Albert's mind was drifting; he held Victoria's hand and called her 'Liebes Frauchen' (dear little wife).[140] Wearily Palmerston noted, 'If it is unavoidable that the highest interests of the nation be sacrificed to personal and professional jealousy, there is no help for it and so it must be.'[141]

On December 10th, Albert was too feeble to play any part in dressing himself. Despite the physicians' blithe assurances, it was obvious to those close to him that his condition was deteriorating. Belatedly two other doctors, Thomas Watson and Sir Henry Holland, were called in; they supported the conclusions of Clark and Jenner. Holland considered Albert's delirium as 'of no consequence, though very distressing'.[142] Although 'fortunate in the doctors', Victoria reluctantly acknowledged that it was necessary, 'to satisfy the public to have another eminent doctor to come and see him [Albert], which I own distressed me much… however I submitted.'[143] Lord Clarendon's opinion of Holland and Clark was far different; the pair of them, he declared, were 'not fit to attend a sick cat'.[144]

On the morning of December 11th, Albert managed to sit up in bed. He raised an unwelcome glass of medicine and wryly toasted his aide, 'Your very good health, [General] Grey.'[145] Victoria wrote, 'he gets sadly thin. It is a dreadful trial to witness this, and requires all my strength of mind and courage not to be overcome – when I look at him…'[146]

On December 12th, Albert's temperature had risen. His breathing was rapid. He shuddered with chills. He coughed up a great deal of phlegm. He was slipping in and out of delirium, one moment worrying about absurd trifles, the next imagining he could hear the birds singing in his childhood haunts at Rosenau. He asked Alice whether the news of his condition had been conveyed to Vicky in Berlin. 'Yes,' Alice replied. 'I told her you were very ill.'[147]

'You did wrong,' Albert reproached her. 'You should have told her that I am dying. Yes, I am dying.'[148]

Previously Albert had tried unsuccessfully to convey the same message to Victoria, who had burst into tears. He seemed to want to confide something of import to Alice. She pulled her chair closer to his bed. He tried to speak but she could not understand.

On the morning of Friday, December 13th, Dr Jenner told Victoria that the patient was in a stable condition; she could take a break from the bedside and have a morning walk. Any respite was short-lived however. The previous day, without asking for the Queen's permission, Alice had summoned Bertie. By late afternoon, it was obvious that the entire family needed to be present. Belatedly Jenner showed disquiet. Two medical bulletins had previously been issued to the public, suggesting merely that Albert was suffering from a fever. Dr Clark issued a third bulletin, with the fateful words, 'the symptoms have assumed an unfavourable character during the day.'[149]

Albert had eaten no solid food for many days; instead he had been kept sedated with nips of brandy every half-hour. In Victoria's words, 'The breathing was the alarming thing, it was so rapid. There was what they call a dusky hue about the face and hands, which I knew was not good.[150] Albert made as if to arrange his hair. He folded his arms. It was 'just as he used to do when well and dressing... Strange! As though he were preparing for another and greater journey.'[151]

Outside the sick-room, Victoria dissolved into tears and hysteria. Recovering, she returned and sat calmly by the bed. Albert held her hand and kissed her. A message was sent to Lord Palmerston. 'I deeply grieve to say that the Prince's disease has taken a very unfavourable turn, and that the Doctors are in the greatest anxiety – they have even fears for the night.'[152]

December 14th dawned with hope. Albert's condition seemed to have improved; some of the gauntness had left his face. There was a tinge of radiance about his features, a memory of his former beauty. Victoria would always remember how 'his face [was] lit up by the rising sun' with 'his eyes unusually bright, gazing as it were at unseen objects.'[153] One of the physicians suggested that 'there was ground to hope the crisis was over' and Victoria telegraphed such a message to Vicky.[154] Later however, a message was sent to Palmerston, 'the hopes of the morning are fading away...'[155] Dr. Watson told Victoria, 'He is not worse, the pulse keeps up.'[156] Then his professional composure cracked. He admitted to being 'very much frightened, but [I] don't and won't give up hope.'[157]

Albert's bed had been moved from the window to the centre of the room. The innocent pleasure of gazing at clouds was over. He was surrounded by his family, by members of the household and by the physicians. For days, Princess Alice had spent nearly every waking minute by his side. Her father's breathing became alarmingly rapid. Victoria whispered, 'Es ist kleines Frauchen' ('It is your own little wife!')[158] She leaned over and asked her husband for 'einen Kuss'.[159] He kissed her for the last time. Then he slipped out of consciousness. With a dreadful calmness, Victoria held his icy hand. Then, suddenly her façade crumpled. She ran from the room and burst into tears.

Alice stayed with her father until his breathing changed. 'That is the death rattle,' she whispered.[160] She went out to fetch the Queen.

When Victoria came back and looked at Albert, all false hope was gone. She knelt by his side, clutching his icy hand as life ebbed from his body. Finally he took a drawn-out, gentle breath, then another. Suddenly, 'all, all was over'.[161] 'Oh, yes, this is death!' Victoria murmured, 'I know it. I have seen it before.'[162] She kissed her husband's 'dear heavenly forehead' and cried bitterly, 'Oh! My dear Darling'[163]

She collapsed upon his cold, lifeless body, calling him 'by every endearing name' she could remember from their former life, then sank to her knees 'in mute distracted despair, unable to utter a word or shed a tear!'[164] In an agony of grief, she was escorted from the room.

Chapter Five
An Unexpected Saviour of Sanity

For Victoria, the emotionally scarred survivor of Conroy's brutal Kensington Method of attempted mind control, her cousin Albert had been the perfect soul mate. 'Albert… is beautiful…' she had written.[1] Long after his beauty had faded, he remained beautiful to her. Yet originally she had 'dreaded the thought of marrying'.[2] Once free of Kensington, she had revelled in her independence as monarch and felt that, '…I shouldn't agree with anybody.'[3]

Albert had begun their marriage declaring ruefully that 'I am only the husband, and not the master in the house.'[4] Initially his help was unwanted, both by Victoria and by Lord Melbourne, the then Prime Minister. Undeterred, he went on to become the perfect partner, unfailingly industrious and unremittingly professional. Hundreds of bound volumes in the Royal Archives pay enduring testimony to his prowess. Victoria, the self-willed, had come to depend upon him, 'for all and everything'.[5] Without Albert, 'I did nothing, moved not a finger, arranged not a print or photograph'.[6] Albert became her 'Lord and Master'.[7] With great pride, she had told Vicky, 'I never admit any other wife can be as happy as I am, for I maintain Papa is unlike anyone who lives or ever lived and will live.'[8] To Leopold she had written that, 'a purer, more perfect being than my beloved Albert, the Creator could not have been sent into this world.'[9] She felt unworthy of 'one so great and perfect.'[10] When Vicky had written her a letter asking her to kiss 'beloved Papa's hand', she had replied that she would prefer 'to fall at his feet'.[11] 'What a pride it is for me to be his wife.'[12] Marriage, once 'dreaded', had become a 'foretaste of heaven'.[13]

In 1840, the Duchess of Bedford, one of the Ladies of the Bedchamber, had declared that, while Victoria was 'excessively in love' with Albert, he 'was not a bit in love with her.'[14] This impression is contradicted by a vast amount of evidence. Lady Palmerston maintained that it was 'quite impossible for any two people to be more happy.'[15] While Albert had admitted that he was not of 'a demonstrative nature', a letter to Stockmar in 1844 tells a very different tale.[16] He refers to Victoria as 'the treasure on which my whole existence rests. The relation in which we stand to one another leaves nothing to desire. It is a union of heart and soul.'[17] In 1851, when separated for a single night, he had written to Victoria:

> You will be feeling somewhat lonely and forsaken... and I too feel the want of only one person to give a world of life to everything around me. I hope to fall into the arms of this one person... your faithful and loving A.[18]

On the first morning of their married life, Victoria told Lord Melbourne that 'she never thought she could be so loved' as she was by 'dearest, dear Albert.'[19]

Nevertheless, for Victoria, marriage had never been easy. In 1871 she wrote to Princess May, upon her engagement, that marriage:

> should not be looked upon lightly or as all roses. The trials in life in fact begin with marriage, and no one should forget that it is only by mutually giving way to one another, and by mutual respect and confidence as well as love , that true happiness can be obtained.[20]

In 1893 she wrote to Princess Victoria of Hesse:

> So many girls think that to marry is merely to be independent and amuse oneself – whereas it is the very reverse of independence

> – 2 wills have to be made to act together and it is only by mutual agreement and mutual yielding to one another that a happy marriage can be arrived at.[21]

Victoria had begun her marriage thinking largely of amusement and independence. Learning 'the very reverse of independence' was a harsh lesson with which she struggled for over twenty years.

One difficulty had been repeated pregnancy, coupled with chronic bouts of post-natal depression. When her youngest daughter, Beatrice, married, Victoria remarked acidly that 'no girl could go to the altar if she knew all'.[22] There was 'something very dreadful in the thought of the sort of trap she is being led into.'[23] For the Queen, the 'unhappy condition' of pregnancy would always be 'horrid news'.[24] It was a 'shadow side' of marriage.[25] She warned Vicky that it was 'a complete violence to all one's feelings of propriety (which God knows receive a shock enough in marriage alone).'[26] '…nine times over for eight months' she had been 'pinned down – one's wings clipped – in fact at the best only half oneself…' '… the poor woman is bodily and morally the husband's slave.' '… selfish men would not bear for a minute what we poor slaves have to endure.'[27] Even her beloved Albert was, she believed, not entirely exempt from 'despising our poor degraded sex – for what else is it, as we poor creatures are born for man's pleasure and amusement.'[28]

However scathing were Victoria's views on the 'shadow side' of marriage, in all nine of her pregnancies, Albert had been the most devoted of husbands. 'The Prince's care and devotion were quite beyond expression.'[29] They were 'like that of a mother, nor could there be a kinder, wiser or more judicious nurse.'[30] Nothing was too much effort. Always there had been 'a sweet smile on his face.'[31]

If Victoria detested pregnancy, she detested bringing up babies no less. Breast-feeding aroused 'insurmountable disgust'.[32] She never failed to reproach her daughters and granddaughters for 'making cows of themselves'.[33] For her, babies had an 'animal existence'.[34] 'I don't dislike babies,' she remarked on one occasion, 'though I think very young ones are rather disgusting.'[35] 'I have no tendre for them till they have become a little human; an ugly baby is a very nasty object – and the prettiest is frightful when undressed – till about four months; in short as long as they have their big body and little limbs and that terrible frog-like action.'[36]

So much for babies; children fared little better. 'ALL the numerous children are as nothing to me when he [Albert] is away; it seems as if the whole life of the house and home were gone...'[37] Victoria 'found no especial pleasure or compensation' with her children; 'only very exceptionally' was it possible for her to find 'intimate intercourse with them either agreeable or easy.'[38]

Albert had held very different views, treating children with a great degree of affection. With his children, he could relax and forget, albeit temporarily, the burdens of state. 'He is so kind to them and romps with them so delightfully,' Victoria wrote.[39] 'What a joyous childhood we had,' Princess Alice reminisced to her mother. 'No other children were so happy; and so spoiled with all the enjoyments and comforts children can wish for.'[40]

For Albert, family life had been a decidedly mixed blessing. Seemingly born to endure tribulations, his life had never been easy. He had long grown accustomed to racism and contempt in his adopted country. Once Lord Alfred Paget, the cosseted 'son' of Lehzen, had proclaimed loudly within Albert's hearing that 'foreigners are inferior and Germans are dregs.'[41] Nevertheless, for over twenty years, this particular foreigner had applied a Teutonic diligence to serving the Crown. Ultimately it cost him his life. The Japanese have a word, karõshi, to describe death from overwork. Although there may have been several causes to Albert's premature demise, undoubtedly chronic overwork was one.

Insidiously Albert had become trapped between the remorseless burden of overwork and the remorselessly demanding character of his wife. He once remarked, 'To me, a long closely connected train of reasoning is like a beautiful strain of music.'[42] Problems would be traced back to first principles; rational solutions would emerge through diligent application of reason. All this proved of no avail when dealing with his wife. Victoria readily confessed that, by contrast, she was 'too passionate', 'too fervent' and possessed an 'irascible temper'.[43] These combined in 'heaping up large stores of combustibles', which exploded regularly.[44] Two decades after the death of her husband, she could still record, 'How sadly deficient I am, and how over-sensitive and irritable, and how uncontrollable my temper is when annoyed and hurt.'[45]

Albert had impressed upon Victoria that 'your great task in life is to control your feelings.'[46] That 'great task' had blighted their marriage, however loving it was in other respects. And it would prove life-long in nature. Albert had admitted to feeling 'completely cowed'; there was a 'perpetual terror of bringing on the hereditary malady' of George III and his offspring.[47] He watched his wife's mental health as 'a cat watches at a mouse hole'.[48] Now that he was gone, who was there to watch at the mouse hole?

Albert's death had come as the culmination of a series of deaths: those of his mother, the Dowager Duchess Marie, Victoria's mother, the Dowager Duchess of Kent, and his cousins, Prince Ferdinand and King Pedro. The death of the Duchess of Kent had proved immensely damaging to Victoria's mental health and augured ill for the future. Describing herself as a 'poor orphan child', rather than the monarch of the most powerful country in the world, she 'was determined to cherish her grief & not be consoled.'[49] Her sanity had 'trembled in the balance.'[50] Tellingly she had informed Vicky, the Princess Royal, 'You are right, dear child, I do not wish to feel better…'[51]

With the hindsight of a century and a half, the psychological pressures upon Victoria are apparent. Her appalling childhood at Kensington Palace had left her emotionally scarred, alternately dependent and distrustful. Marriage gave her joy, tarnished by savage bouts of post-natal depression, eroding much of her initial fascination with the business of government. The 'hereditary malady' of George III and his offspring, i.e. porphyria, left her prone to sporadic attacks, triggered by trauma such as Conroy's brutality and the demise of her mother. The death of Albert, her husband, lover and protector, left her exposed psychologically – and constitutionally.

What was the true cause of Albert's death? The official medical diagnosis was 'typhoid'.[52] It is ironic that Albert, who proved such an able reformer and who had transformed the Queen's Scottish estates into a model of sound management, was at risk from 'the noxious effluvia' of the Windsor drains.[53] In the words of a contemporary royal insider, 'There are more stinks in royal residences than anywhere else.'[54] It now seems likely that Napoleon was poisoned unwittingly by arsenic in his wallpaper. Did Albert suffer a similarly macabre death from poor sanitation?

The typhoid diagnosis rests uneasily with the fact that no other member of the Windsor retinue succumbed to this disease. Although Victoria had an almost naïve confidence in the royal doctors, such confidence was not shared by others, such as Lord Palmerston. Lord Clarendon had declared trenchantly of Holland and Clark that they were 'not fit to attend a sick cat'.[55] Clarendon was in no doubt that the negligence of Albert's doctors had been a contributing factor to his death.

> Holland and Clark are not even average old women, and nobody who is really ill would think of sending for either of them. Jenner has had little [experience of] practice... Watson (who is no specialist in fever cases) at once saw that he had come too late to do any good.[56]

What is the truth? In 1831 Albert's mother, Princess Louise, died of cancer at the age of thirty. It may be that Albert also was prone to cancer. He had a long history of suffering from painful inflammation of the gums, which could have been due to an excess of hydrochloric acid in his stomach. Three causes of such excess are Crohn's Disease (regional enteritis), peptic ulcers and carcinoma of the stomach. The first two ailments are associated with high-stress lifestyles; as we have seen, Albert suffered from chronic overwork and the demands of caring for a psychologically scarred, postnatally depressed wife whom he loved dearly. Relevant symptoms, such as physical and psychological exhaustion, are consistent with Albert's medical history, as are fever, cramps and vomiting. With her brisk, no-nonsense approach to life, Victoria viewed Albert's medical situation as emanating from too little 'pluck'.(57) 'He died from want of what they call pluck,' she adjudged.(58) 'Some people rally much better than others: it is all pluck.'(59) In reality, it seems likely that the Prince Consort suffered from the most serious of conditions from which there was little medical recourse, then or now. The only salvation might have been a relaxed, undemanding lifestyle. Such a lifestyle was incongruent with his stern sense of toil and duty. It was incongruent with the remorseless demands due to being so close to the centre of power of the British Empire at its zenith. And it was incongruent with the tumultuous emotional character of his wife.

During Albert's final illness, Victoria's mood had swung from glacial calm to heartbroken outbursts. During her previous outpourings of grief upon the death of her mother, Albert had chastised her for 'giving way so completely'(60) Heedful of his advice to preserve her equanimity in the immediate aftermath of his death, she struggled for composure. 'Now you see I am calm,' she insisted.(61) 'I am profiting by his advice, I am doing what he wished.'(62) Sir Charles Phipps noted how 'wonderful' was Victoria's calmness during the evening of her husband's death.(63) Her calmness persisted into the next day when she made two further visits to the Blue Room where Albert lay 'beautiful as marble', surrounded by flowers.(64) Her doctors cautioned her, at the risk of infection, not to touch the corpse. As ever, she displayed utter confidence in them and contented herself with embracing the clothes in which the body was to be dressed. Her doctors' exhortations for caution ignored the inconvenient fact that the Queen had held and kissed her husband many times in his fatal illness.

For Lord Clarendon, the death of the Prince Consort was possibly avoidable, certainly tragic and undoubtedly cataclysmic. Writing to the Duchess of Manchester, he confided:

> You know, just as I do what the real relations were between him and her, and how different they necessarily were from those of

> any other man and wife; for no other woman has the same public responsibility or the same motive for being absolutely guided by... her husband.[65]

A distraught Phipps asked rhetorically of Lord Palmerston, 'What will happen? Where can she look for that support and assistance upon which she has leaned in the greatest and least questions of her life?'[66]

On the evening of Albert's death, Victoria was adamant that, 'They [her subjects] need not be afraid. I will do my duty.'[67] However admirable her resolve, this bold statement ignored glaring inconsistencies. For many years of pregnancy and post-natal depression, her devotion to duty had been intermittent. Undoubtedly she could rouse herself to formidable efforts when dealing with calamities such as the Crimean war and the Indian mutiny. Otherwise she had been content to allow her husband to shoulder much of the burden of state. In the depression of grief, was it likely that she would carry the same workload which had killed Albert?

'Where can she look for that support and assistance...?' The Prince of Wales had never lacked compassion. On his father's deathbed, Bertie had clasped his mother crying, 'I will be all I can to you.' The Queen kissed him repeatedly, saying, 'I am sure, my dear boy, you will.'[68] But Victoria, who had guarded the throne so jealously from her husband at the onset of her marriage, would guard it still more jealously from her eldest son. Neither of his parents had ever shown much confidence in Bertie's abilities; and it would always be convenient for Victoria to regard the Nellie Clifden episode as a prime contributor of her husband's death. Perhaps the sad truth is that, to Albert, Bertie was all too reminiscent of the 'bad blood' of the Coburgs and that, to Victoria, he was all too reminiscent of her 'wicked' uncles.

'Where can she look for that support and assistance...?' Two days after Albert's death, Lord Granville wrote to Lord Canning.

> The loss to the country is great: To the Queen it is irretrievable... Perhaps the grief at the Duchess of Kent's death has been a

> preparation for her. Still her future is fearful. Having given up [for] twenty years, every year more, the habit of ever deciding anything, either great or small, on her own judgment, the situation is immense for her to conduct the affairs of her family, her Court and of the Country. And who has she upon whom she can lean?[69]

Had Granville but realised it, the answer was at hand. The following day it would become evident when he was 'sent for' to attend to official business at Windsor.[70] The person who sent for him was the hitherto shy, retiring and self-effacing second daughter of the Queen – the eighteen-year-old Princess Alice.

* * *

For over a hundred years after her poignantly young death, Princess Alice remained the 'forgotten daughter' of Victoria and Albert. The third of their nine children, her memory has been obscured by the superficially more vibrant memories of her two elder siblings, Bertie, the Prince of Wales and Vicky, the Princess Royal. Bertie became King Edward VII; Vicky was the mother of Kaiser William II. Alice and certain of her descendants would prove equally pivotal to British history.

To his father, the wayward but good-natured and fundamentally decent Bertie may have seemed an unwelcome throwback to Coburg and Hanoverian rakes. Conversely, to her father, Alice may have evoked associations with the mother he never knew, the ill-fated Princess Louise. As a child, Alice had been 'charming, merry and amiable', though 'always occupying a subordinate place to her very gifted and distinguished sister'[71] And yet there was an 'almost waif-like quality' about her, 'a certain sadness in the fine lines of her angular face' with 'deep-set dark eyes… more often cast down as if in solemn thought.'[72] Photographs of her show a faun-like aspect. There is something ethereal about her.

Born in 1843, Alice was five when Europe exploded into fits of revolution in 1848. At the ages of six and seven, she was by her mother's side when the Queen was attacked while travelling in her carriage. She was eleven at the onset of the Crimean War and fourteen at the outbreak of the Indian mutiny. Her letter of sympathy to Lady Canning, wife of the much-criticised Governor General, is remarkable in its maturity and understanding. The brutal vagaries of world politics had cut short her childhood.

From the onset, there had been an especial bond between Alice and her father. As a child, he was especially protective of 'poor dear little Alice'.(73) At twelve, he found her, 'still very delicate and nervous'.(74) What Albert was detecting was an extraordinary sensitivity in his second daughter, a sensitivity which resonated with his own deeply private inner nature. Although on the best of terms with her siblings, Alice's character was quite different; it was in stark contrast to the Queen's egocentricity. In her early years Alice, perhaps surprisingly, formed another deep attachment with her brother Bertie, who yearned for understanding and sympathy. Always Alice's sensitivity would be employed unstintingly in the care of others. It found its deepest expression through her avocation of nursing, then a barely respectable occupation for any woman, least of all a princess.

In the winter of 1860/61, Alice had made almost daily visits to the Duchess of Kent in Frogmore, in Windsor Great Park. There she would tend to her ailing grandmother and play the piano for her. When the Duchess died and Victoria was prostrate with grief, the Prince Consort gave his daughter a new mission with the simple words, 'Go and comfort Mama.'(75) Victoria later commented: 'Dear good Alice was full of intense feeling, tenderness and distress for me.'(76)

On December 3rd 1861, as her father entered his final illness, Alice had noted with percipience.

> Poor Mama is very unhappy about it – but not worried. But she has no idea how to nurse him, although she would so gladly do

> everything. One must get used to it when one is young... I have to listen to my dear parents' mutual complaints – I only hope I am really useful to them, for I do want to do everything for them, if it were possible...[77]

Alice had played the piano for her dying grandmother; she played it again for her father. As his illness progressed, it seemed as if father and daughter shared an unspoken secret knowledge of what fate had already decreed. Their spirits seemed more intimately linked even than those of the Prince Consort and the Queen herself as they held hands on the edge of an eternity into which one would disappear. It was as if all other mortals, however important, had become temporarily incidental.

One onlooker thus described the quiet dominance of Albert's nurse:

> The Princess Alice's fortitude has amazed us all. She saw from the first that both her father's and mother's firmness depended on her firmness and she set herself to the duty. She loved to speak openly of his condition and had many wishes to express. He loved to hear hymns and prayers. He could not speak to the Queen of himself, for she could not bear to listen, and shut her eyes to the danger. His daughter saw that she must act differently, and she never let her voice falter, or shed a single tear in his presence. She sat by him, listened to all he said, repeated hymns, and then when she could bear it no longer, would walk calmly to the door, and rush away to her room, returning with the same calm and pale face, without any appearance of the agitation she had gone through.[78]

Faced with the Queen's denial, Alice had thrown away all hesitation and taken unchallenged command. On her own initiative and without her mother's knowledge she had telegrammed Bertie at Cambridge. When he arrived at Windsor, he was appalled and grief-stricken and ready to do anything that might help. 'But the suppression under which he had been brought up had destroyed his initiative and it was Princess Alice who took the lead.'[79]

Of her father's death, Alice wrote:

> My heart is quite broken and my grief is almost more than I can bear... Oh God that it should have been my beloved, adored father lying there dead, his hands so cold and stiff – I felt as though I had been turned to stone – when I saw him draw his last breath, and saw the pure great noble soul leave its earthly dwelling... I expected that He would leave us, but I could not take it in. He was too good, too great for this wicked world. God has freed him from everything that still afflicts us. His will be done.'[80]

Albert's death defined the second half of Alice's all too brief life. Afterwards it was noted that 'In every way open to her, did the Princess try to walk in her father's footsteps and so to honour his memory.'[81]

During her father's illness, Alice had displayed 'a fortitude beyond her years' and had, 'without suspecting it, passed her first exam in nursing which was to become her destiny.'[82] Nevertheless it might have been impossible for the same Alice who had accompanied her father to the very fringe of eternity to be the principal agent for coaxing her mother back with safety to the realities of time. It was not, however, the same Alice but a very different one who steeled herself for this forbidding task. She had been utterly transformed by her experiences at her father's bedside. Lord Clarendon mentioned her 'strength of mind and judgment, as well as tenderness.' But Lady Augusta Stanley was the first to notice how, quite suddenly, she seemed to be 'a different creature'.[83] Her fiancé, Louis of Hesse, hurried over from Germany to find an Alice he had never known before and, sadly, would never comprehend.

If Alice had shown during her father's illness 'a fortitude beyond her years', she now displayed all the qualities that a successful nurse most needs. At this critical juncture, Queen Victoria was in need of the most difficult and important of all types of nursing – that fragile type wherein the patient is not aware of being nursed. Anyone looking after old or infirm relations (and relations are of course even harder to look after than strangers) will confirm the need for an infinitely subtle psychological approach, often exhausting but invariably vital. Alice was providentially gifted in this regard; never were her gifts more needed than during the grim vigil of that first night after her father's death. She wondered afterwards how she and her mother came through the ordeal with their sanity unimpaired. She had her bed moved next to the Queen's, in an apartment near the Blue Room. Victoria could find solace neither in sleep nor in tears. Alice sent for Dr Jenner and a mild opiate served to blunt minutely but sufficiently the razor-like edge of tragedy then threatening to sever the Queen's powers of resistance. Alice's vigil by her mother's side lasted for three bitter days. Few doubted that, if her spirit had broken during this crucial triduum, the spirit of the Queen would have done so also. It is terrifying to imagine what might have ensued in such an eventuality. The Queen's sanity was balanced on a needle point.

Alice had two self-imposed duties: the first was to save her mother's sanity; the second was to be the agent of the Queen's duties over official matters that could not be shelved. Lord Granville was not the only one to be 'sent for'. Sir Charles Phipps, formerly Albert's private secretary and now Keeper of Her Majesty's Purse, transacted all business through Alice. Communications from ministers and household alike passed through Alice's hands for Victoria's signature. The young Princess could not have fully realized at the time the magnitude of the burden she was taking on, still less the delayed action it would have on her nervous system in later years.

The Times, which had so often castigated her father, commented approvingly:

> It is impossible to speak too highly of the strength of mind and self-sacrifice shown by Princess Alice during these dreadful days. Her Royal Highness has certainly understood that it was her duty to be the help and support of her mother in her great sorrow: and it was in a great measure due to her that the Queen has been

> able to bear with such wonderful resignation to the loss that so suddenly and terribly befell her.[84]

The destiny of the most powerful country in the world lay in the slender hands of an eighteen-year-old girl. Sir Theodore Martin has noted that:

> The knowledge of this fact and it was a fact – sank deeply into people's minds. It was never forgotten and from that day the name of the Princess Alice has been a cherished household word to all her countrymen and women.[85]

Knowing what we do of Queen Victoria's extraordinary temperament, it is safe to say that no member of her family at any stage in his or her life was assigned a burden quite like that borne by Alice during this period. Its stifling intensity might have proved too much for a tough and experienced matron, let alone a relatively untried girl of eighteen. The nights were unspeakable, with Queen Victoria sobbing uncontrollably until exhaustion induced a brief and uneasy sleep as dawn approached. And Alice shared every prolonged paroxysm and every renewed outburst. Perhaps only someone who has nursed his or her own mother through a period of acute nervous distress can have some idea of what Princess Alice suffered and of what she achieved. The effect upon the 'nurse' is draining and exhausting beyond all description; the attitude of the patient is wholly demanding and overpowering. And the patient's recovery depends ultimately upon one person only. This person must carry all the strain, though the supreme irony is that the patient must be allowed to believe that he or she is doing all the suffering. Thus did Queen Victoria ride out the first, fierce onslaught of the horror, not unmixed with remorse, that assailed her with the approach of Christmas 1861. And thus did Princess Alice act as the channel through which such initial horror worked itself out of her mother's tortured soul. During this twilight three-day interlude, the Queen's pulse could scarcely be felt. It was the most critical juncture of her life. Several years later, Alice confided to her mother, 'How you suffered was dreadful to witness. It tore my heart to pieces.'[86]

The first vital breakthrough occurred on 18th December when Victoria crossed the park to Frogmore to choose a site for Albert's mausoleum. Leaning heavily on Alice's arm she walked round the gardens until she found what she thought would be the most suitable spot. Alice's fiancé, Louis of Hesse, was a spectator of this melancholy promenade. He was a chief mourner at the funeral five days later. Bertie, as untried as Alice, consulted his uncle, the Duke of Cambridge, and chose Monday, December 23rd. It was vital to avoid the Christmas festivities. Nine days was a brief span to organise a state funeral; nevertheless Bertie managed it. His father had shown so little confidence in his eldest son; ironically it took his funeral to demonstrate competence in Bertie. Two days before the funeral, Dr Jenner filed a death certificate, declaring the cause of the Prince Consort's death to be 'typhoid fever, duration 21 days.'(87) There was no autopsy. Inevitably professional eyebrows were raised and searching questions were asked in the British Medical Journal and in the Lancet.

Equally ironically, in death Albert received belatedly the respect he had so clearly deserved in life. Lord Torrington wrote 'I am inclined to think that more real sorrow was evinced at this funeral than at any that has taken place there [at Windsor] for a vast number of years.'(88) Disraeli commented, 'With Prince Albert we have buried our Sovereign. This German Prince has governed England for twenty-one years with a wisdom and energy such as none of our Kings have ever shown.'(89) Disraeli's estimate of Albert seems scrupulously fair. So many monarchs before him had tarnished their crowns. Effectively an uncrowned King, he had given his life for his adopted country. Nobody could have done more.

On the day after Albert's funeral, Victoria wrote to her uncle Leopold what purported to be a dedication of the remainder of her existence:

> I am... anxious to repeat one thing, and that one is my firm resolve, my irrevocable decision... that his wishes – his plans – about everything, his views about every thing are to be my law!

> And no human power will make me swerve from what he decided and wished... I am also determined that no one person, may he be ever so good, ever so devoted among my servants – is to lead or guide or dictate to me. I know how he would disapprove of it. And I live on with him, for him; in fact I am only outwardly separated from him, and only for a time.[90]

In life, the Queen had enjoyed a passionate yet tumultuous relationship with Albert. In death he would become a tragic hero, whom the fates had seized cruelly from her. Remorse that her constant emotional demands were a contributory cause of his death was subsumed by denial. More pressing were her 'agonies of longing for her husband'.[91] 'I am, alas! not old and my feelings are strong and warm; my love is ardent.'[92] She ached for human contact. In the immediate aftermath of the Prince's death, she told Vicky that 'sweet little Beatrice comes to lie in my bed every morning which is a comfort. I long so to cling and clasp a loving being.'[93] For her part, Vicky reflected sadly, 'Poor Mama has to go to bed, has to get up alone – for ever. She was as much in love with Papa as though she had married him yesterday.'[94]

Each night the Queen knelt at Albert's side of the bed before laying her head on her own pillow. Each night she cried herself to sleep clutching 'his dear red dressing-gown'.[95] A cast of Albert's hand was in the bedroom. In each of their homes, the detail of his dressing room and study was preserved. Unused linen was changed. Unused towels and nightclothes were replaced daily. Each morning, hot water was brought in for shaving.

Victoria's future stretched ahead of her – a bleak, empty purgatory of 'awful loneliness'.

> The two creatures who loved me most and to whom I was dearest on earth are gone: my dear mother and my Adored Angelic Husband, and I miss them so terribly. There is no one left to hold me in their arms and press me to their heart.[96]

Victoria was a passionate woman who dreaded 'belonging to no one any more.'[97]

> Truly he [Albert] was my entire self, my very life and soul, yes even my conscience if I can describe it thus... I only lived through him, my heavenly angel! Surely there can never again be such a union, such trust and understanding between two people.[98]

As a child, the young Princess had faced terrible loneliness at Kensington. For two decades as Queen, she had loved and been loved. The return to loneliness – the loneliness of the crowd, which is infinitely worse than the loneliness of solitude – was well nigh unendurable. At times, it seemed utterly unreal. She was 'constantly expecting to find the Prince – whether out walking or coming into the room and hearing his footsteps.'[99] She was an 'utterly broken and crushed widow of forty-two', in her innermost being, a 'deserted child'.[100]

A myriad nostalgic memories returned to mock her. At 'our very own' house of Osborne on the Isle of Wight, 'how happy' they had been.[101] She had written, 'And never do I enjoy myself more, or more peacefully, than when I can be so much with my beloved Albert and follow him everywhere.'[102] When they had walked together in the woods, Albert would whistle to the nightingales 'in their own peculiar long note' and they would reply.[103] In the long, long afternoon of her life, Victoria could never again hear the song of the nightingale 'without fancying she hears him, and without the deepest, saddest emotion.'[104]

* * *

Somehow Victoria endured her first winter of grief. It left her devastated. She was 'thin and worn', beset by headaches, cold and weakness and barely able 'to move one leg before the other'.[105] A visitor was horrified to find her as 'rigid as stone and the picture of desolate misery.'[106] Again it seems likely that she experienced, unwittingly, an attack of porphyria brought on by the stress of grief. Alice struggled to persuade her mother to attend to public business, in particular to receive Lord Palmerston, the Prime Minister, with whom she had a distinctly uneasy relationship. It took the combined efforts of Alice and a visit from her uncle, King Leopold, at the end of January, to accomplish this. When Palmerston braved the Solent in a gale to visit her at Osborne, Victoria was unnerved not by memories of their former animosity but by his decency, humanity and sympathy for her plight. 'He could in fact hardly speak for emotion,' she noted with surprise.[107] Accepting that it was premature to discuss government business in detail, he raised one question of grave national import – the necessity, for the continuity of the monarchy, that Bertie be married as soon as possible.

Palmerston also mooted the delicate subject of Bertie engaging upon further official tours. At home, Bertie had been imprisoned in the role of naughty child by his parents. Yet his triumphant reception in America had shown how his affability could translate into popular acclaim. Unfortunately for the Prince of Wales, his father had never viewed affability as meriting equivalent importance to the more conventional academic subjects. In an age when the cult of royal personality was becoming ever more prominent, this was a severe mistake.

Mutually painful as was this meeting between Victoria and Palmerston, it must be considered the second vital breakthrough in her recovery. There was unanimity between Queen and Prime Minister on what Victoria termed 'the difficulty of the moment', i.e. Bertie.[108] Almost wonderingly she recorded, 'I… would hardly have given Lord Palmerston credit for entering so entirely into my anxieties.'[109]

Prior to their meeting, Victoria had received an assurance from Palmerston that the diplomatic incident with the United States which had so preoccupied the Prince Consort had been resolved. Albert's last proposal, written as he was slipping ever further into his fatal illness, had proved a face-saving escape from the diplomatic impasse. It may very well have prevented escalation into an economically ruinous and bloody war between the two nations of Britain and America. Albert's last official act testified both to his diplomatic prowess and consummate sense of duty.

The saving of the Queen had come at a terrible price for Alice. In the words of one commentator, 'She looks thin and worn and speaks very sadly; and this deep sorrow has evidently changed her from a child to a woman very suddenly, but it has also drawn her out and improved, deepened her mind and character.'[110] Though neither mother nor daughter knew it, both had reached the halfway point in their lives. One would be famously long; the other would be poignantly short.

Yet despite Alice's timely intervention and all her tender ministrations, the outlook remained bleak. Lord Clarendon wrote that the Queen:

> does not seem to improve & her only relief in thinking of her desolate future is Her conviction that She shall & must die soon. She is worse off than ordinary persons with relations & friends who in time bring change & comfort – but she is isolated & the best thing for her is the responsibility of her position & the mass of business wh: She cannot escape from & wh: during a certain portion of the day compels her to think of something other than the all embracing sorrow.[111]

There also remained the problem of the 'P of W', which amounted to 'monomania & nothing can move her upon it.'[112] Palmerston was not alone in his delicate lobbying for an expansion of Bertie's role. John Delane, the editor of *The Times*, pitched in with the suggestion that Bertie's trips abroad, particularly to Egypt and the Holy Land, had given him the ability 'to greet the friends of England in his own country.'[113] He might, perhaps, be able to perform 'many public or semi-public duties' in lieu of the sovereign.[114] Delane's patriotic appeal went unheeded. The sovereign showed no interest in reigning over her kingdom. She also showed no interest in allowing her son to exercise authority.

On February 10th, the anniversary of her wedding, Victoria wrote, 'She feels her Darling Husband very, very near today! But she knows not where He is! She lives in a dream! All dreams here are so unreal!'[115] Immortalising 'that pure angel' in stone was to prove as fraught a subject as a similar creation for Diana, Princess of Wales, more than 130 years later. Lord Clarendon found himself saddled with the 'disagreeable task' of serving upon a committee to decide upon a suitable memorial for Albert.[116] As he admitted candidly, his relevant qualifications were nil. He had no more competence 'than for leading the orchestra at the Opera House' and feared the prospect of 'a disgraceful Monument [being] erected.'[117] Nor did he have any more confidence in the artistic sensibilities of his Queen. She had 'no more notion of what is right & pure in art than she has of the Chinese grammar.'[118] Her desire for an obelisk placed an immediate and unwelcome restriction upon the committee. The project ran into a funding crisis when regional towns withheld revenues raised originally for their own uses. Clarendon dreaded towns up and down the country becoming festooned with images of 'the late Consort in robes of The Garter upon some curious and non-descript animal that will be called a horse, & Albert Baths & Washhouses…'[119]

On March 15th Victoria laid the foundation stone for a memorial at Frogmore. To her, Windsor was otherwise 'a living grave' and her greatest wish was to lie in death with Albert in the Frogmore mausoleum.[120] Lord Torrington noted that 'The Queen looked very nice; to my eye she looked like a young girl and showed great nerve.'[121] Perhaps she had been energised, albeit temporarily, by doing something that she wanted to do, rather than by enduring passively an endless grief.

In the same month, Lord Clarendon visited Victoria at Osborne. Various subjects were discussed. However poor Clarendon was

Queen Victoria replica by Sir George Hayter. Oil on canvas, 1863. (original 1838).© National Portrait Gallery, London

Princess Victoria with her mother the Duchess of Kent and Strathearn. Line engraving by William Skelton after Sir William Beechey. Published 1823. © National Portrait Gallery, London.

Sir John Conroy circa 1830. Oil on canvas by Henry William Pickersgill. Photo by Hulton Archive/Getty Images.

Prince Albert. Watercolour on ivory laid card by Sir William Ross. Signed and dated 1839. Royal Collection Trust © HM Queen Elizabeth II 2012

Christian Friedrich, Baron Stockmar. After John Partridge (1790-1872). © The Bridgeman Art Library.

Queen Victoria, Prince Albert and the Princess Royal, Vicky, 1840-1843.
Oil on canvas titled *Windsor Castle in modern times* by Sir Edwin Landseer.

Princess Alice, Grand Duchess of Hesse photographed by Camille Silvy. Hand-coloured albumen carte-de-visite, 4th July 1861. © National Portrait Gallery, London

Albert Edward, Prince of Wales (later Edward VII). Engraved by G. Cook and published in London by Virtue & Co.

As Well as can be Expected. Queen Victoria, Prince Albert, et al.
Lithograph by an unknown artist, 1840s.

Sir William Jenner. Carte-de-visite, photographed by Herbert Rose Barraud, London.

Sir Henry Ponsonby leaving Flete to catch the train to Osborne. The carriage is a Brougham.

Queen Victoria by Samuel Cousins, Hand-coloured mezzotint, after a portrait by Lowes Cato Dickinson. Published by Dickinson Brothers, 1871. © National Portrait Gallery, London.

discomfited as the Queen referred repeatedly to 'the Prince's opinions and acts as if he was in the next room'.[122]

> [It was] difficult not to think that he was so, for everything was set out on his table, the blotting book open with a pen upon it, his watch going, fresh flowers in a glass, etc., etc.,; just as I have seen them all a 100 times.[123]

Gladstone, the Chancellor of the Exchequer, also visited her in March. He was as uneasy as had been Palmerston and Clarendon. The Queen questioned him about the shortage of cotton due to the American Civil War, exacerbated by domestic industrial action. Manchester, a noted centre of radicalism, had seen mill workers boycotting cotton imported from the Confederate States in support of President Lincoln's policy of the abolition of slavery. The boycott brought great hardship to the workers' families. Lincoln described it as 'an instance of sublime Christian heroism which has not been surpassed in any age.'[124]

Inevitably Victoria steered the conversation to her former husband for '...if ever woman had loved a man, she had fondly loved the Prince.'[125] Among his many attributes had been 'personal beauty'.[126] On receiving this unwonted confidence, Gladstone's uneasiness stiffened into embarrassment. It was as though his Queen was speaking with a confidant, not her Chancellor. Unperturbed, she continued. In the absence of her husband, she would do her best as monarch but 'she had no confidence in herself' and her mind was not 'gifted with... elasticity.'[127] Gladstone found himself in an awkward position. Retreating into stuffiness, he responded that, 'Over-confidence was a vice; and lack of it was often a virtue.'[128] Although Victoria noted of the encounter that Gladstone had been 'kind and feeling', the Chancellor reproached himself for not having spoken more of 'the language of hope'.[129]

Shortly afterwards, Gladstone made a speech in Manchester in which he gave generous praise to the former Prince Consort. Writing to thank him, again Victoria blurred hopelessly the boundaries between professional and personal. He was shocked to learn of his sovereign that:

> Her only wish is to go soon to her own darling again. Every day seems to increase the intensity of a sorrow which nothing, nothing can alleviate, as there never was love and devotion like hers! Every source of interest or pleasure causes now the acutest pain. Mrs Gladstone, who the Queen knows is a most tender wife, may, in a faint manner, picture to herself what the Queen suffers.[130]

Gladstone, who clearly lacked the personal touch when dealing with his distraught monarch, responded again in an unhelpful fashion. 'Unable to see into the future, we believe, Madam, that He [God] can choose for You the best of these [alternatives]; and that He will.'[131]

Such stiffness and stuffiness were not what Victoria wanted. Disraeli showed a very different approach. Writing to Victoria a year later, he imparted confidences that were far more to her liking:

> The Prince is the only person whom Mr Disraeli has ever known, who realized the Ideal. None, with whom he is acquainted, have ever approached it. There was in him a union of the manly grace and the sublime simplicity of chivalry, with the intellectual splendour of the Attic Academe… [His] plans will become systems, his suggestions dogmas, and the name of Albert will be accepted as the master type of a generation of profounder feeling, and vaster range, than that which he formed and guided.[132]

With the death of the Prince, Victoria adjudged that she was 'changed from a powerful sovereign… into a weak and desolate woman.'[133] Although 'I try to feel and think I am living on with him and that his pure and perfect spirit is leading me and inspiring me,' such inspiration was elusive.[134] Six months after Albert's death, the Queen's interest in government business remained sporadic. For her ministers, this was partly unwelcome… and partly welcome, in that it freed them of the interference she had exercised formerly. In the midst of a political discussion with Clarendon, Victoria broke down utterly, clutching her head in her hands, tapping her forehead and crying, 'My reason! My reason!'[135] The message was unmistakable and the alarmed Clarendon backtracked swiftly. Was the madness of George III, the 'Hanoverian malady' breaking through? The Sovereign was certainly in 'a highly nervous state' and 'while talking of the state of her mind, her eye and manner became excited'.[136] '. . . three times at Balmoral she had thought she was going mad.' Governmental change 'would be more than her reason could stand.'[137]

Through personal sacrifice, Alice had saved the Queen's sanity; But it remained precarious. Alternatively was the Queen so in love with her grief that she was inventing convenient excuses for malingering? Clarendon was unsure; but he dared not put a hypothesis to the test. Today, with knowledge of Victoria's porphyria, her conduct may be viewed in a much more understanding light. At the time, all that her ministers knew for certain was her unwillingness to rule. Assuredly this gave them tactical advantages in the day-to-day business of politics. As surely, it raised the most grave of reservations about the future of the monarchy.

Chapter Six
The Monarchy in Peril

In the 19th century, it was customary to commemorate the dead to a degree which we would now find excessively morbid. In England and Scotland, a room was often set aside and dedicated permanently to the deceased. In many parts of the Continent, peasant widows wore black for the rest of their lives. As well as preserving rooms as if Albert continued to use them, Victoria decreed that her entire Household dress in mourning. Black crêpe, broadcloth and bombazine became much in evidence. However, after a year of enforced misery, morale had slumped to such a degree that the Queen was forced to relent. The 'semi-mourning' colours of grey, mauve and white were permitted. Nevertheless, for most of the 1860s, it was incumbent upon royal servants to appear with black crêpe bands on their left arms.

In many ways, large and small, Victoria arranged the tableau of her life to accommodate her memories of Albert. At Windsor, there had been two guest books, one for the Queen, the other for the Prince Consort. The latter was left as it had been. The ever-perceptive Disraeli noted the pathos of grief where '… visitors write their names… as before – calling on a dead man.'(1) At Osborne, Victoria commanded the naval base at Portsmouth to cease gunnery practice. The faint booming of the guns across the Solent proved too painful to her. (This may have been a porphyria sufferer's hypersensitivity to noise.) At Osborne, the Queen engaged in another contemporary tradition of mourning. She began an album consolatium, in effect a scrap-book of literary passages commemorating grief. Its 182 pages were quickly filled.

Victoria was, perhaps, the first media Queen. Newspapers, devoured by an increasingly urban populace, had created massive interest in the lives of the royals. Formerly Albert had appeared in a variety of guises, such as penniless princeling, Prussian spy and prisoner in the Tower. His death elicited mass sympathy; Victoria received condolence letters by the sack-load. In an age when most people died young, inevitably many of these letters came from people acquainted intimately with death. Others however, were wide of the mark. One over-zealous clergyman advised his Sovereign, 'Henceforth you must remember that Christ Himself will be your husband.'[2] Upon reading this stern admonition, Victoria's grief was over-ridden temporarily by her characteristic common sense. 'That is what I would call twaddle,' she burst out. 'The man must have known that he was talking nonsense. How can people like that comfort others or teach anybody?'[3]

Many of Victoria's subjects were troubled by her grief; conversely, she was mindful of their tribulations. At Hartley colliery, there was a mining disaster. Men were trapped underground; their source of livelihood became their tomb. The Queen kept in close contact with the rescuers. When it became evident that the men could not be saved, she issued a statement, 'that her tenderest sympathy is with the poor widows and mothers, and that her own misery makes her feel all the more for them.'[4]

In May 1862, when Victoria returned to Balmoral for the first time since the death of the Prince Consort, she found that '...everything, even down to the smallest detail, is somehow associated with him and his memory.'[5] Writing to the Princess Royal, she exclaimed, 'Oh! Darling child, the agonising sobs as I crawled up with Alice and Affie! The stags' heads, – the rooms – blessed, darling, Papa's room – then his coats – his caps – kilts – all, all convulsed my poor shattered frame!'[6] When the Duke of Argyll arrived on an official visit, Dr Robertson, the Factor, advised him that the Queen had endured 'a day of the deepest waters'.[7] Despite this warning, Argyll was disconcerted to find that his monarch had been struck dumb temporarily and could only shake her head in a parody of communication. Was this yet another manifestation of porphyria?

At Balmoral Victoria lost no time in visiting one of her tenants whose bedridden husband had also died the previous winter. The peasant woman reminisced sadly for what could never be again. 'And we both cried: she cried and I cried.' Then, remembering the status of her visitor, 'I controlled myself as soon as I could, and asked her pardon for crying.'(8) Unperturbed, her Queen replied. 'But, oh! I am so thankful to cry with someone who knows exactly how I feel.' After some moments of reflection, she added. 'You saw your husband's death coming, but I – I did not see – it was so sudden!'(9)

Once again we have an example of Victoria's selectivity of attention and memory acting to preserve her from guilt. Herein also may be a clue as to her unquestioning acceptance of the highly dubious medical opinions of the royal doctors. Victoria's explanations of Albert's demise were various. One bizarre account had her husband catching a fever from having ventured too close to an excavation of 'old earth' at Crystal Palace.(10) And, of course, there was also 'that dreadful business in the Curragh' (i.e. Bertie's dalliance with Nellie Clifden) to fall back on.(11)

With nine children, it was generally expected that the Queen would turn to her sons and daughters as a replacement for her lost love, her lost life. This did not happen. Rather did her children have to play their part, while keeping to their allotted places, supporting their mother and complying with her every whim, if only because there could be no substitute for him. Victoria had spent the first two months of grief in self-imposed seclusion, with Alice by her side. Thereafter she became restless. Alice was forced to follow her mother to Windsor in March, back to Osborne in April, to Balmoral in May, and then to Osborne again in June. In April, she had turned nineteen, a birthday which, as Victoria wrote to Lord Tennyson, 'should have been so happy, for the arrangements for her marriage were almost completed, was the saddest I remember.'(12)

In fact the arrangements for Alice's forthcoming marriage to Louis of Hesse were frustrated precisely because of Alice's exhausting schedule of constant attendance of her mother in ever-changing locations. The following month, Victoria wrote, almost in a spirit of grim satisfaction, 'The Angel of Death still follows us. The Grand Duchess of Hesse has just died and so now Alice's marriage will be even more gloomy.'[13]

Earlier Victoria had 'intended Prince Albert's mausoleum to be no 'Sterbezimmer', no death chamber, but a bright monument to his living glory. Not so the room prepared for Princess Alice's marriage seven months after her father's death. Here was a Sterbezimmer indeed.'[14] A small dining-room at Osborne was converted for the marriage ceremony, which took place on July 1st 1862. The Queen, dressed in black and wearing what her youngest daughter, Beatrice, called her 'sad cap', sat in an armchair removed from the proceedings, yet still dominating them.[15] Poor Alice had a black trousseau. The Archbishop of York kept the service to a minimum and the whole cheerless occasion – the saddest royal wedding for many a long year – was over by 4pm. The guests returned to London. For Vicky, her sister's wedding had been, 'like a funeral'.[16] It augured ill for the success of her marriage. Two months earlier, Lord Clarendon had written of Alice in admiration tinged with sadness:

> There is not such another girl in a thousand. I never met with one who at her age had such sound principles, so great judgment and such knowledge of the world, yet she has been boxed up in a gilt cage all her life and has not had the advantage of interchanging ideas as other girls have. I wish she had better prospects before her but she is going with a dull boy to a dull family in a dull country and I have a presentiment that she won't be happy.[17]

With two of her three eldest children married, the Queen turned to the pressing business of getting the almost twenty-one-year-old Bertie to the altar and thereby out of harm. When Princess Alexandra (Alix) of Denmark was earmarked as the most suitable candidate, Vicky was entrusted with the unenviable task of explaining away Bertie's dalliance. The Queen suggested a cover story which came perilously close to farce. 'Wicked wretches' had compromised the 'poor innocent Boy' and landed him in 'a scrape'. However 'both of us' had forgiven him. Alix would be his 'SALVATION'. He would make a 'steady husband'.[18]

Unsurprisingly the cash-strapped Danes were not deterred by Bertie's high jinks and Victoria was soon conducting negotiations for another royal marriage, distorted by grief. 'I had alone to say and do what, under other, former happy circumstances, had devolved on us both together.'[19] The 'quiet [and] ladylike' Alix was informed by her future mother-in-law that she would enter a 'sad house'.[20] Although Alix had 'a beautiful refined profile', Victoria could not refrain from commenting acidly to Vicky:[21] 'Are you aware that Alix has the smallest head ever seen? I dread that – with his [Bertie's] small empty brain – very much for future children.'[22] Popular rumours that the Queen would abdicate in favour of Bertie and Alix were wide of the mark. If anything, Victoria seemed intent on bestowing upon Alix the same disfavour as she had about Bertie. When Lord Granville tried to help Bertie's development by asking him to preside over a Literary Fund dinner, his mother's riposte was swift and scathing. The Prince of Wales was, 'too young and inexperienced… upon no account [should he] be put at the head of any of those Societies or Commissions, or preside at any of those scientific proceedings, in which his beloved great Father took so prominent a part.'[23]

On May 9th 1863, Victoria took the couple to the mausoleum at Frogmore and joined their hands before Albert's tomb. 'He gives you his blessing!' she intoned dramatically.[24] The following day they were married. As with Alice's wedding, the Queen was determined that the event should be as drab and cheerless as possible. Preparations for what should have been a triumphant state occasion were amateurish and botched. Once again Victoria sat apart in her widow's weeds, casting a conspicuous pall over the proceedings. When the chorale, which had been composed by Albert, began, '[the Queen] gave a look upwards, which spoke volumes'.[25] She eschewed the family luncheon. When the guests had departed, she returned to the Mausoleum to pray beside Albert's tomb.

Bertie's wedding had been as inappropriate as Alice's. At least Alice had escaped to Germany, albeit into the company of 'a dull boy' and 'a dull family'. A month after the wedding, Lord Stanley voiced a general disquiet:

> Much talk in London about the extraordinary way in which the Queen undertakes to direct the Prince and Princess of Wales in every detail of their lives. They may not dine out, except at houses named by her: nor ask anyone to dine with them, except with previous approval or unless the name of the person invited is on a list previously prepared: and the Princess, after riding once or twice in the Park, was forbidden to do so again. In addition, a daily and minute report of what passes at Marlborough House is sent to the Queen. The parties most concerned make no complaint, but others do for them, and the whole proceeding is ill-judged.(26)

The Queen seemed determined to ignore the bitter lessons of Bertie's upbringing. The way to develop the Prince of Wales was to display confidence in him and to give him tasks of increasing importance. Albert's strength had been his intellect; his weakness was dealing with people unlike him. Bertie's strength was dealing with people of all temperaments; his weakness was, perhaps, his less than stellar intellect. Yet Albert had allowed himself to be trapped by his intellect. He insisted upon tracing problems back to his beloved first principles; he would not delegate. He revered trains of logical thought, which so many others simply disregarded. Certainly Bertie was no devotee of first principles and trains of logical thought. Yet he had decency, commonsense and worldliness. He could have been surrounded by clever, honest advisers of the Baron Stockmar type.

Victoria's refusal to give Bertie suitable experience of learning how to rule derived from her conviction that he did not conform to the kingly template established by the Prince Consort. In this, she was absolutely correct. Bertie did not fit the template. Intriguingly, the person whose character resonated most deeply with that of Albert was Alice but, of course, Alice was a mere Princess and therefore of no account when it came to the innermost sanctum of power. However gifted Albert had been, there are other ways to rule. It might be argued convincingly that Bertie was cut from much better cloth than kingly predecessors such as George III and George IV.

With her ever-selective memory, Victoria seemed to have forgotten how jealously she had clung to power in the first few months of her marriage. If Albert had become arguably first among equals, he had begun from a distinctly unequal position. At least Albert had been given a chance to show his mettle. Victoria was determined to give Bertie no such chance. She railed to Vicky:

> I fear [that Alix] will never be what she would be had she a clever, sensible and well-informed husband, instead of a very weak and terribly frivolous one! Oh! What will become of the poor country if I die! I foresee, if B. succeeds, nothing but misery...[27]

It is characteristic of autocrats that they do little to encourage succession. To many autocrats, a strong successor is a feared rival. Lack of succession tends to be one of their greatest weaknesses. Often their lifetime achievements become undone in the immediate aftermath of death. In her grief, Victoria's clasp on life was tenuous. Preparing Bertie for power would have been a prudent step; she did not take it.

The refusal to groom Bertie for public life also missed a huge public relations opportunity. The death of the Prince Consort had elicited mass sympathy. However the Queen of England seemed to be settling into the role of professional mourner. People tire of mourning. They yearn for colourful pageants. Bertie's wedding should have been such a pageant. His marriage, with the prospect of royal children, further heirs to the throne, stirred the public imagination. People wanted to see Bertie. With his easy, good-natured manner, he would have been as popular at home as he had been abroad. His popularity would have helped to ensure the popularity of the royal family and, thereby, the monarchy at a time when monarchies were coming under threat. Sadly it was not to be.

* * *

On the evening of Albert's death, Victoria had insisted, 'They [her subjects] need not be afraid, I will do my duty.'[28] Nevertheless, for almost two years after Albert's death, she made no significant public appearances. It was as though she had lost the will to live. In 1862 she admitted to being 'naturally much occupied with leaving this world.'[29] In 1863 she confided that her life would 'end more rapidly than any of you think; for myself this would be the greatest, greatest blessing…'[30] Many years later, she confessed to Vicky that, in the terrible early years of her widowhood, suicide had beckoned. 'I too wanted once to put an end to my life here, but a voice told me for His sake – no, 'Still Endure''[31] 'Still Endure' became her motto. 'God in mercy willed it so! I was to live…'[32]

The Queen endured. Yet she was permanently psychologically scarred by the events of December 1861. For nearly forty years she would continue to dress in the drab, shabby black of the professional widow. Her comfort in ritual became obsessive. Towards the end of her life, it was noted that, 'there seems a curious charm to our beloved Sovereign in doing the same thing on the same day year after year.'[33]

For Victoria, the 1860s were prolonged nervous breakdown. In the summer of 1863, she confided to her uncle Leopold that she was in thrall to 'violent nervous headaches' and 'complete prostration'[34] These symptoms were caused by 'overwork, over-anxiety and the weight of responsibility and constant SORROW and craving and yearning for the ONE absorbing object of my love…'[35] She was 'wasting away', 'failing in power, in memory, a wreck.'[36] Her pulse raced, noise was agonising for her, 'the slightest agitation or worry' was too much for her.[37] In short, she was exhibiting symptoms of porphyria, almost certainly triggered by the stress of her husband's death and her subsequent grief.

In the autumn of 1863, Victoria broke her seclusion to unveil a statue of the Prince Consort in Aberdeen. Typically she was disregarding his wishes. 'If I should die before you,' he had once implored, 'do not raise even a single marble image in my name.'[38] As with the two royal weddings, she was determined to make the affair as dour as possible. Loyal Scots subjects were told not to put up welcome banners, nor to play musical instruments, nor even to cheer their monarch. Victoria described the day as 'sad & trying & painful'.[39] Appropriately rain fell in torrents.

The visit to Aberdeen, which should have been a public relations coup, was a public relations disaster; if anything, it emphasised the Queen's continued retreat from public life. *The Times* noted tartly that two years was ample time for 'unavailing regrets and in dwelling upon days which cannot be recalled.'[40] However, by then, Victoria had become addicted to grief. Previously she had written, 'For me, my very misery is now a necessity and I could not exist without it.'[41] For the rest of her life she would exhibit a morbid obsession with 'coffins and winding sheets' and all the other paraphernalia of death.[42] At Frogmore, she hung the keys to the mausoleum around her neck and never seemed happier than after a visit to its gloomy shades.

Inevitably there was widespread speculation as to the Queen's mental condition. When Prince Alexander of Hesse paid a visit in 1863, he came with the secret promise that he would report to his sister, the Tsarina, whether the English Queen was 'all there or not.'[43] Unexpectedly he confirmed that he had seldom encountered anyone more sane.

In November 1863, Gladstone, then Chancellor of the Exchequer, felt that he detected 'the old voice of business' in the Queen.[44] If so, it was fleeting. December passed and the monarch entered her third year of mourning. Public sympathy was exhausted; the newspapers lobbied for the return of the monarch to public life. The obvious venue for such a return was the opening of Parliament. Victoria engineered a letter to the Prime Minister stating that her doctors, 'after consultation, are very decidedly of opinion that, with a due regard to the preservation of her Majesty's health, it would be undesirable that her Majesty should undertake such duties.'[45]

Despite her maladies, Victoria still retained an acute instinct for political danger. Early in 1864, she warned Earl Russell, the Foreign Minister, not to align Great Britain with Denmark in the so-called Schleswig-Holstein affair. In essence, Denmark had control of territories with predominantly German populations. Prussia wanted to wrest possession. The detail of the various arguments was famously complicated. In Lord Palmerston's celebrated epigram, there were only three men in England who had ever understood the Schleswig-Holstein issue. The first person was Prince Albert, who was dead. The second person was Mellish, an obscure clerk in the Foreign Office, who had gone raving mad. The third person was Lord Palmerston himself, who had most inconveniently forgotten it.

Whatever the legal rights of Denmark to Schleswig-Holstein, it is an English trait to support the underdog. Left to its own devices, tiny Denmark stood no chance against the military might of Prussia. Public opinion was in favour of sending the navy to protect Copenhagen. Lords Palmerston and Russell, Prime Minister and Foreign Secretary respectively, were in accordance with public opinion. Victoria was not. Her stated logic was one of national self-interest. 'Lord Russell knows,' she admonished sternly, 'that she will never, if she can prevent it, allow this country to be involved in a war in which no English interests are concerned.'[46] The navy must be returned to home ports. Denmark would not be protected. There would be no role for Britain beyond that of peaceful mediation.

Victoria viewed her intervention as akin to Albert's last professional action in staving off a possible war with America. The reality was very different. Behind the stated favouring of neutrality, lay a stolidly pro-German stance. In conversation with Lord Torrington, a useful means of access to *The Times*, she insisted that Prussia 'will take nothing' and that it was vital for Great Britain 'to keep well with the adopted country of her daughter.'[47] In reality, Prussia had every intention of taking all it could lay its hands on. As to the 'adopted country of her daughter', Victoria might equally have stressed the need to protect the country of her daughter-in-law, Alix. She did not. Instead she lamented. 'Oh! if Bertie's wife was only a good German and not a Dane!'[48] If Victoria's pro-German stance was another supposed homage to Albert, it was badly misplaced. Albert had yearned for German-inspired European peace. He would have been horrified by gunboat diplomacy on the part of an increasingly bellicose Prussia.

The Schleswig-Holstein affair, pitting daughter against daughter-in-law, was the first of many instances in which Victoria's children and grand-children would find themselves on opposing sides in major political and military conflicts. The public remained unaware of Victoria's intervention; her Prussian sympathies were well known and would probably have inspired cynicism as to her motives.

At around this time, a letter was received by *The Times*, ostensibly from the Queen, justifying her withdrawal from public life. Was it a hoax? The editor, John Delane, recognised the handwriting as being that of Victoria. Wisely he published the letter as a missive from 'The Court'.[49] The text was contentious:

> An erroneous idea seems generally to prevail and has latterly found frequent expression in the newspapers, that the Queen is about to resume the place in society which she occupied before her great affliction: that is she is about again to hold levees and drawing-rooms in person, and to appear as before at Court balls, concerts &c. This idea cannot be too explicitly contradicted.[50]

Although the Queen insisted that she 'will not shrink, as she has not shrunk, from any personal sacrifice or exertion, however painful', there were 'higher duties' than 'mere representation' with its accompanying 'work and anxiety'.[51] Certainly she would appear in public when 'any real object is to be attained' but 'more the Queen cannot do and more the kindness and good feeling of her people will surely not exact from her.'[52]

As an exercise in public relations, Victoria's letter was counter-productive. Lord Clarendon commented that it 'produced a very painful impression, and is considered very infra dig.'[53] Popular opinion was expressed vividly in a humorous handbill stuck by some wag onto the wall of Buckingham Palace. 'These extensive premises to be let or sold, the late occupant having retired from business.'[(54)]

For yet another year, Victoria refused to open Parliament, using the familiar excuses of 'great fatigue' and 'shattered nerves'.[(55)] She seemed least unhappy when 'retired from business' and out riding on her pony, accompanied by John Brown, 'that excellent Highland servant'.[(56)]

Brown had been a favourite of Prince Albert. With his gruff, no-nonsense manner, he had an almost unique ability to get beneath the carapace of Victoria's grief. She recorded gratefully, 'he is so devoted to me – so simple, so intelligent, so unlike an ordinary servant, and so cheerful and attentive...'[(57)] And yet, 'It is the return home with that silent room nearby, and fagged to death with work, which is fearful indeed!'[(58)]

Most people made the facile equation that public absence equalled dereliction of duty. They simply refused to believe that their Queen was 'fagged to death with work'. In December 1863, *The Times* made another effort to rouse the monarch from seeming torpor:

> The living have their claims as well as the dead; and what claims can be more important than those of a great nation, and the Society of one of the first European Capitals... every honour that affection and gratitude could pay to the memory of the Prince Consort had been offered...[(59)]

The Queen must 'think of her subjects' claims and the duties of her high station, and not postpone them longer to the indulgence of an unavailing grief.'[(60)] It continued with the veiled threat that, 'for the sake of the Crown as well as of the public,' it was 'impossible for a recluse to occupy the British throne without a gradual weakening of that authority which the Sovereign has been accustomed to exert.'[(61)] Although Victoria was perturbed, her royal hauteur would not allow her to be dictated to by a mere newspaper.

* * *

The end of the American Civil War was followed immediately afterwards by the assassination of President Lincoln in April 1865. Lord Russell, the Foreign Secretary, suggested that Victoria send a private letter to his widow. Thus 'a very good effect would be produced in conciliating the feelings of the United States.'[(62)] Predictably Victoria wrote, 'No one can better appreciate than I can, who am myself utterly broken-hearted by the loss of my own beloved husband, who was the light of my life... what your sufferings must be.'[(63)]

In Europe, the Schleswig-Holstein affair had given Prussia an easy victory. Albert had dreamed of a Germany united peacefully under the auspices of a benign Prussia; he had dreamed of German-inspired peace in Europe. By contrast, Otto von Bismarck wanted Prussian mastery of Germany and German mastery of Europe. War was his political weapon. The summer of 1865 saw a seven-week conflict between Prussia and Austria. Inevitably Austria's allies were dragged into the conflict. One of those allies was Hesse, where Alice lived. Vicky's husband Fritz and Alice's husband Louis found themselves on opposing sides. Another easy victory for Prussia augured ill for the peace and stability of Europe. Alice fled with her daughters to Windsor, coming under the protection of a mother who already owed her considerable debts yet would never understand her or show her very much sympathy.

Only Victoria's enthusiasm for preserving the memory of 'my own beloved husband' remained intact.[(64)] In August 1865, on the anniversary of Albert's birthday, she made a special journey to Coburg to unveil yet another statue that he would not have wanted. In stark contrast to previous outings, the Queen insisted upon full formality. 'I was anxious for this day to do all possible honour to my beloved's memory.'[(65)] Bells rang, drums beat, military salutes were given. Albert's statue 'stood there, in all its beauty, so sad and grand.'[(66)] For Victoria, it was an 'indescribable moment...'[(67)]

Soon afterwards, Lord Palmerston, 'that strong determined man' died.[68] Although their relationship had been fraught, the Queen conceded that, overall, 'he had behaved very well.'[69] Certainly he had treated her protracted grieving with great consideration. Russell succeeded him, while Clarendon became Foreign Secretary. Victoria knew that Russell's government would be temporary and that the next government would probably view her withdrawal from public life with far less sympathy.

1865 ended with the death of Victoria's uncle Leopold. For all Leopold's frailties, as mentor, he had served her well since the dark years of Kensington. With two of her closest props abruptly removed and her future uncertain, she was forced to heed Russell's entreaties to open Parliament in the new year. Bluntly she told him that what he was asking for was tantamount to an 'execution'.[70] Would it really help Russell to have 'the spectacle of a poor, broken-hearted widow, nervous and shrinking, dragged in deep mourning, alone in State as a Show?'[71]

Nevertheless, in early February, she made her way to the Houses of Parliament. Dressed in her customary black, she sat in silence, staring ahead, as the Queen's speech was read out by the Lord Chancellor. The occasion was an 'ordeal'.[72] Afterwards she felt 'terribly shaken, exhausted, and unwell from the violent nervous shock.'[73]

The Schleswig-Holstein intervention had coupled personal bias with supposed national self-interest. The opening of Parliament was entirely about personal self-interest. Daughters needed to be married; another son was coming of age. Dowries were required for the former and an annuity for the latter. The government of the day must be buoyed up so that funds for both would be forthcoming. Albert had always urged that the monarchy be above party politics. Victoria had her own political prejudices and her own need of money.

In 1866 Victoria received sympathy from a most unexpected quarter, when, to her immense surprise, John Bright, the Radical M.P., spoke up for her at a Reform meeting:

> I am not accustomed to stand up in defence of those who are possessors of crowns; but I could not sit here and hear that

> observation [disparaging comment about the Queen] without a sensation of wonder and pain. I think there has been… a great injustice done… in reference to her desolate and widowed position. And I venture to say this, that a woman – be she the Queen of a great realm, or be she the wife of one of your labouring men – who can keep alive in her heart a great sorrow for the lost object of her life and affection, is not at all likely to be wanting in a great and generous sympathy with you.(74)

Victoria was immensely touched by Bright's humanity and consideration. So many 'ignorant and unfeeling people attacked her for not going out in the world.'(75) To receive this sincere and public expression of sympathy from such a staunch political opponent was well nigh bewildering. She never forgot Bright's intervention. He was exemplifying the traditional British virtues of decency and fair play at a time when these seemed to be in short supply. Had Victoria but known it, five years hence, her fate would be decided by those same traditional virtues of decency and fair play.

* * *

Political insecurity on the continent was mirrored by political insecurity in Britain. The chasm between the nouveau riche 'haves' and the unemployed 'have-nots' was becoming perilously wide. Mass attention focused on the over-ripe problem of electoral reform. Even Victoria conceded that 'wretched reform' was inevitable. Once more preoccupied with raising funds (this time for an increase in the amount granted for the Albert Memorial in Kensington Gardens), she found a champion in Benjamin Disraeli, the new Chancellor of the Exchequer. Thus did Disraeli, the coming man, endear himself to the Queen.

For Victoria, the 1860s dragged on. In 1867 she complained to Lord Derby of 'the want of consideration shown… for her health and strength. ...ere long' it would lead to a 'complete breakdown of her nervous system.'[76] In her opinion, public appearances were unnecessary. She spent her time 'working and drudging... from morning till night and weighed down by the responsibility and cares of her most unenviable position, and with the anxieties consequent upon being the widowed mother of so large a family.'[77] Ominously she continued, 'Often has she wished that the time might come when she could go to that world 'where the wicked cease from troubling and the weary are at rest.''[78]

Visiting foreign dignitaries fared poorly, although Victoria received grudgingly both the Sultan of Turkey and Empress Eugénie. 'Greatly relieved the visit was over,' she summed up tersely the departure of the latter.[79] When Lord Derby pressed her to receive the Czar of Russia, she gave a tart reply, 'The Queen is UTTERLY incapable of entertaining any Royal personage as she would wish to do, except those who are very nearly related to her, and for whom she need not alter her mode of life.'[80] Her 'mode of life' meant seclusion, combined with regular visits to Osborne and Balmoral, with the minutiae of daily existence enforced rigidly to her whim.

Although Victoria had complained repeatedly to Derby about the demands made upon her health and strength, ironically his powers failed first. In early 1868, at the age of seventy-five, he stood down in favour of Disraeli. Whereas Derby had little idea how to treat Victoria, the wily Disraeli knew exactly how to handle her. For Derby, there was a puzzling absence of 'sympathy or regret' in the Queen's acceptance of his resignation.[81] His son's comments about Victoria's manner reveal Derby's sadness.

> He [Derby] talked to me of the Queen's way of writing to him, about which he was at first very sore: but I think he now understands her nature. She is civil to persons in power under her, whose good will contributes to her comfort (and not always to them): but [she] sees no reason for wasting civility on those who can no longer be of use to her.[82]

Disraeli understood that unbridled flattery was the sure way to Victoria's heart. Tendering his 'devotion', he noted that it would be 'his delight and duty, to render the transaction of affairs as easy to your Majesty as possible...'[83] Warming to his theme, he continued, '...he ventures to trust that, in the great affairs of state, your Majesty will deign not to withhold from him the benefit of your Majesty's guidance.'[84] Unsurprisingly, Victoria noted in a letter to Vicky, 'The present Man will do well...'[85] She continued, '[he] will be particularly loyal and anxious to please me in every way. He is vy peculiar, but vy clever and sensible and vy conciliatory.'[86] Within a month, Disraeli had insinuated himself ever deeper into her graces. 'He is full of poetry, romance & chivalry. When he knelt down to kiss my hand wh he took in both his – he said: 'In loving loyalty & faith''[87] This was drama of the kind that Victoria adored.

Disraeli continued to serve his 'gracious mistress'[88] and to exert maximum political advantage from the tacit support of a sovereign who was supposed to be above party politics. Hounded by the Liberals and defeated in the Commons, he needed every advantage that he could lay his hands upon. Victoria became regarded as being both pro-Prussian and pro-Tory. In many quarters, Disraeli was considered to be a wild card, a likely political liability to his party. And, shockingly, he had to endure the same bitter racism as Albert, before him. To the Marquess of Salisbury, he was, 'the Jew' who had circumvented protocol to enthral the Queen and make her his puppet.[89] 'Matters seem very critical – a woman on the throne, & a Jew adventurer [who] has found out the secret of getting around her.'[90]

Unfortunately for Disraeli, there were limits as to how far even he could get around Victoria. When the Queen went to Scotland, it meant government by remote control. 'Carrying on the Government of the Country six hundred miles from the metropolis doubles the labour,' he noted wryly.[91] Compulsory visits to Balmoral were no less an ordeal for the Prime Minister than anyone else, save the Queen. On one occasion, when Disraeli wrote to his wife, 'I was glad there were no [Highland] Games', one can sense the depth of his relief.[92]

Disraeli's honeyed words to Victoria were not enough to save his government; in December 1868 he was ousted. When Victoria received the seals from the outgoing Ministers, she noted that, 'they had never been in better hands'.[93] This was an alarming breach of protocol. Albert would have expressed personal sympathy, carefully untainted by political bias. But, however much Victoria might revere his memory, she would always do what was best for Victoria.

In truth, some of the outgoing Ministers were almost as relieved to exit government as had been Disraeli, their master, to escape the Highland Games. Victoria was still 'indifferent to business, except where pressed on by relations.'[94] Yet she was paradoxically 'jealous lest anything be kept back from her.'[95] In 1869, to the new arrival, Gladstone, she made the same lame excuses for not opening Parliament that she had been repeating for most of the decade. Sympathy had long since expired. The Queen was viewed widely as, in effect, hiding behind a doctor's sick note. Writing to Gladstone, a concerned General Grey made it clear that he regarded Victoria as derelict in her duty:

> ...nothing will have any effect but a strong – even a peremptory – tone. In spite of Sir William Jenner, I believe that neither health and strength are wanting, were [her] inclination what it should be. It is simply the long, unchecked habit of self-indulgence that now makes it impossible for her, without some degree of nervous agitation, to give up, even for ten minutes, the gratification of a single inclination, or even whim.[96]

Lest Gladstone have any doubt as to the gravity of the situation, Grey wrote a second letter, urging him to rouse the monarch from her self-imposed seclusion. Any postponement would ensure that 'the fight, which must come' would be even 'more painful and difficult.'[97]

Gladstone was in full agreement with Grey's prognosis. He blamed Victoria's 'fanciful ideas... about her own health' on her 'feeble-minded doctor' who was 'producing in a considerable degree the incapacity which but for him would not exist.'[98] Easier to blame the doctor than the royal patient; but it was the royal patient who was dictating many of the doctor's utterances.

Disraeli had wooed the Queen with honeyed words; Gladstone, like most of Victoria's Prime Ministers, had no such skill. For him, the Queen's wilful 'retirement' was causing damage that might be climactic and irreversible. Privately, even Disraeli agreed. When Stanley, one of the ousted ministers, spoke with Disraeli at dinner in March 1869, he found him:

> ...out of spirits, says he thinks the monarchy in danger, which he never did before: not from immediate causes, nor from any feeling against it of a strongly hostile character, but from gradual loss of prestige; the Queen has thrown away her chances, people find out that they can do without a court, etc.[99]

Even Victoria's half-sister, Feodora, was critical of the determined 'want of being able to enjoy anything, at times.'[100] Although Feo cited 'growing older' as an excuse (Victoria had just turned fifty and had reigned for thirty-two years), she was adamant that, 'Occupation, and having the satisfaction to feel that one is of use to others, is the only help...'[101]

Yet Victoria remained unswerving in her views on 'occupation.' She had been given 'a very difficult task, one for which I feel myself in many ways unfit, from inclination and want of power [physical and psychological strength].'[102] God, who had given her his task, also:

> gave me happiness and He took it away, no doubt for a wise purpose and for the happiness of my beloved one, leaving me alone to bear the heavy burden in trying and troubled times.[103]

To General Grey, Victoria was 'the royal malingerer.'[104] To Gladstone, the danger of Republicanism was growing ever more acute. Victoria exuded regal disdain. Gladstone struggled in vain to persuade her to 'maintain the full influence of the Monarchy.'[105] When she agreed, most reluctantly, to remain at Windsor for an extra week in summer to facilitate government business, she made much of the inconvenience. She emphasised that '…so serious a trial of her strength' might only be justified by a 'very uncommon crisis in public affairs.'[(106)] Such a concession 'must be regarded as an entirely isolated case, and that it must NEVER be made a precedent for any similar representation on the part of her Ministers to her in succeeding years.'[(107)]

Despite her warm relationship with Disraeli, Victoria exhibited the same unpleasant racism as many of her subjects. When the subject of a suitable honour was raised for the eminently deserving Sir Lionel Rothschild, she was adamant in her opposition. The Queen 'cannot consent to a Jew being made a Peer – tho' she will not object to a Jew baronet – and she is quite certain that it wd do the Govt harm instead of good.'[(108)] Given her lack of sympathy with Gladstone's government, her sentiments amounted to little more than personal bias. In any case, her continued seclusion was doing the government immeasurably more 'harm instead of good.'[(109)]

Another entreaty to open Parliament in 1870 was dismissed curtly with 'out of the question' and the threat of 'madness'.[(110)] Later that year, Bismarck lured France into a futile war with Prussia. The result of the war changed the political landscape of Europe. Germany was united in a manner which Albert would have deplored. France was declared a republic. Emperor Napoleon III and Empress Eugénie became political refugees in England. The two themes of Republicanism and anti-Prussian feeling in England deepened. Did the electorate still want a pro-Prussian monarch who refused continually to do her duty?

What Does She Do With It? was the title of a timely pamphlet which emerged to popular acclaim. The Queen received the then enormous sum of £385,000 each year. She did not seem to earn it; she did not seem to spend it. As a monarch, she appeared singularly poor value for money.

On December 3rd 1870, Gladstone wrote to Lord Granville about the 'Royalty question'.[(111)] 'To speak in rude and general terms, the Queen is invisible and the Prince of Wales is not respected.'[(112)] Nor were many of Victoria's other children much liked. Half a dozen British cities, including London, boasted Republican clubs. The movement was gathering momentum.

In 1871, it had been five years since the Queen opened Parliament. The previous year it had been 'out of the question' due to the threat of 'madness'. This year was very different. Victoria had need of another annuity for a son and another dowry for a daughter. To many of her subjects, her attendance, for the same mercenary reasons as previously, was pure hypocrisy. Victoria's timing could not have been more ill-conceived. Attitudes hardened still further.

In March 1871, Victoria made a public appearance in London, before an audience, many of whom had not seen her for ten years. Typically it was for a subject close to her heart – the opening of the Royal Albert Hall. In front of some 8,000 people she felt 'quite giddy.'[(113)] At the crucial moment, when she had to declare the hall open, she called Bertie to her and whispered that she simply could not do it. In inimitable fashion, her despised Bertie rose to the occasion by striding to the front of the stage and stating simply, 'Her Majesty declares this Hall now open.'[(114)]

In April 1871, a third son was born to Bertie and Alix. *Reynolds's Weekly Newspaper* announced the birth as 'Another Inauspicious Event.'[(115)] The following day, the poor child died. In an attack of sickening viciousness, the death was announced as 'A Happy Release.'[(116)]

> We have much satisfaction in announcing that the newly-born child of the Prince and Princess of Wales died shortly after its birth, thus relieving the working classes of England from having to support hereafter another addition to the long roll of State beggars they at present maintain.[(117)]

Still the Queen seemed intent upon ignoring the ever-increasing vitriol of the national mood. In the summer, Gladstone asked her once again to postpone her holidays for a few days to facilitate the business of government. She responded bitterly that she, 'a woman no longer young' refused 'to be driven and abused till her nerves and health will give way with the worry and agitation and interference in her private life.'[(118)] '...overwork and worry' had 'killed her Beloved Husband...'[(119)] Rather than share a similar fate, she would abdicate and the 'heavy burden' would be entrusted 'to other hands.'[(120)] The Queen was playing at brinkmanship. Whose 'other hands' were there to take over but those of Bertie, the son she had failed conspicuously to groom as King? Faced with this unpalatable ultimatum, Gladstone had little choice but to back down.

To Victoria, her escapes to Osborne and Balmoral were blessed relief. The dates of departure had come to assume almost mythical significance. Changing them meant breaching her psychological refuges. For her, it was agonising. To the Prime Minster however, it was perverse that the Queen should create such a fuss about a few days missed holidays when the very future of the monarchy was at stake. After Victoria had ignored two letters from Gladstone, he noted bitterly, 'Smaller and meaner cause for the decay of thrones cannot be conceived. It is like the worm which bores the bark of a noble oak tree and so breaks the channel of its life.'[(121)]

Even Victoria's children were becoming alarmed. Vicky drafted a petition to 'our adored Mama and our Sovereign', alerting her to the threats to the monarchy 'which are daily spreading.'[(122)] She never received it. By the time it was ready, her health had failed to such an extent that it could not be given to her.

* * *

On August 1st, the Commons voted in favour of an annuity for Prince Arthur. Nevertheless there were fifty-four votes against the motion, together with a considerable degree of acrimony. Three days later, Victoria awoke with a sharp pain and a swelling under her right arm. She thought that these symptoms were due to an insect bite. The swelling subsided, although she continued to feel out of sorts, with a marked loss of her renowned appetite. Two weeks later, she went to Scotland. A Court Circular noted that she 'bore her journey to the north well, but continues indisposed.'[123]

The August 19th edition of *The Lancet* contained a curious anonymous article tendering a medical justification of the Queen's withdrawal from public life:

> We have seen with regret the attacks on the Queen, based on Her Majesty's absence from evening entertainments and on her brief residence in London… Her Majesty is not physically capable of bearing the effects of crowded or overheated rooms [a symptom of porphyria], or of prolonged residence in London…[124]

The article gave a list of porphyria symptoms, including appetite loss, debilitating headaches and inability to sleep. It ended with a plea:

> The profession will readily, without our entering more fully into so delicate a subject, understand the necessity for Her Majesty's medical advisers exercising the greatest diligence…[125]

Sir Henry Ponsonby, Victoria's private secretary, tackled Dr Jenner, her physician, as to the authorship of the article. 'I suppose it was written at the Queen's desire,' he accused.[126] An embarrassed Jenner could not look him in the eye. 'If not,' Ponsonby pointed out, 'I may say I think it most unfortunate, as it will enable the abdicationists to say at once, 'Why should we wait any longer – she promises not to do more, but positively to do less.'[127] Jenner, perhaps blinded by loyalty, protested feebly that, 'There is no feeling against the Queen.'[128] Ponsonby scoffed and told him bluntly that even Gladstone, the Prime Minister, was making public utterances about an 'alteration of our form of government.'[129] To many, it seemed that the monarchy was hanging by a thread and the 'royal malingerer' had, with typical selfishness, taken herself off on her customary holiday to Scotland.

The reality was that the Queen was desperately ill. This was not malingering. Victoria lost two stone. A report which appeared subsequently in *The Lancet* (and was almost certainly written by Jenner) stated:

> ...the Queen began to suffer pain a little below the right arm, at which part a swelling, that subsequently suppurated, made its appearance. Her Majesty's health was again gravely disturbed at the time, in connexion with the formation of the abscess, and for days Her Majesty was unable to take any food.[130]

For the following few weeks there was what we would now term a 'royal cover-up' as to the true nature of the Queen's condition. It is deeply ironic that, while continued justifications of royal ill health had appeared to chase the 'sympathy vote', when the Queen was in genuine danger, the knowledge was withheld from her subjects.

The initial diagnosis had been an insect bite; perhaps Victoria had developed a severe anaphylactic reaction to it. However the Queen's illness lasted for nearly three months. The abscess under her arm was followed by a severe abscess in her throat. The Victorian term for peritonsillar abscess was quinsy; before the discovery of antibiotics, it was often fatal.

The abscess in Victoria's throat burst and fluid drained into her oesophagus. She recalled, '...something seemed to give way in the throat & the choking sensation with violent spasms ceased.'[131] To her alarmed doctors, there were two new dangers. The infection could move into the brain; or blood poisoning could develop. Either of these conditions would, almost certainly, be fatal. Jenner thought it likely that the Queen would be dead within the day.

Given the gravity of Queen Victoria's condition, Lady Churchill asked Sir Thomas Biddulph why on earth her children had not been summoned to her bedside. 'Good heavens!' Biddulph expostulated, 'That would have killed her at once.'[132] Ponsonby was in complete agreement. 'Other people have relations, but these relations seem to be the very people the Queen is least inclined to send for.'[133] No more damning indication of Victoria's feelings towards her children may be imagined.

On August 22nd Victoria confided to her journal, 'Never, since a girl, when I had typhoid fever at Ramsgate in '35, have I felt so ill.'[134] Two months later, she would write to Vicky of the tribulations of being 'fed like a baby which lasted three days and a half – the food being put into your mouth, your nose blown and everything done for you.'[135]

At Balmoral, the desperately ill Victoria received one of 'the very people the Queen is least inclined to send for' – her daughter Alice. The 1860s had not been kind to Alice, the young princess who had gone to 'a dull family in a dull country'. She had struggled hard for the betterment of her small portion of that country. She had seen her husband go to war. She had endured military invasion and had been forced to flee with her children. In 1866 she had written to the Queen: 'Life is meant for work, and not for pleasure.'[136] Now she nursed her mother, with the same relentless dedication as she had nursed her father. Yet, for all her loving care, Albert had died.

On September 4th, Doctor Joseph Lister, the leading authority on antisepsis, was brought in to strengthen the medical team. He froze a terrible abscess on the Queen's arm and lanced it. 'In an instant, there was relief. I was then tightly bandaged and rested on my bed… Felt very shaken and exhausted.'[137] Her relief was temporary for, in the words of Alice:

> Mama was weak and unwell when I arrived, as she was getting over two serious illnesses – a very bad throat infection, and then the abscess… on her arm which had to be operated on. Four days after our arrival a third illness appeared, by far the most painful – rheumatoid arthritis… she was confined to the sofa and could not move at all without help.[138]

The Queen's debilitating state continued. More than a week later, when Ponsonby saw her, she was 'thinner and paler.'[139] She had no energy. She was under heavy medication to combat her sleeplessness. Her feet became painfully swollen. All of these symptoms are consistent with porphyria.

Jenner held Gladstone and the other politicians accountable for the Queen's illness; their efforts to make her postpone her visit to Balmoral had brought on the condition. 'By heavens!' he exploded to Ponsonby, 'if she had died I would have borne testimony that they had killed her!'(140) As a woman, she had been bullied; if she had been a man, the Government would never have dared subject her to such 'outrageous' coercion.(141) Ponsonby replied coolly, 'No, they would simply have turned her off the throne.'(142) He cited the ever-increasing dissatisfaction with her seclusion. Jenner would have none of it. 'Nonsense!' he snapped back.(143) For him, the issue was not the Queen's behaviour. It was 'the advancing democracy of the age.'(144)

Only in mid-September, with the Queen finally recovering, albeit slowly, was it considered appropriate to break the news of her serious illness to the public. Despite 'the advancing democracy of the age,' sympathy was widespread. The British electorate, which had hitherto regarded their Queen as under-worked, suddenly began to see her as over-burdened. On September 15th *The Daily News* declared that the entire country was 'ashamed' of its previous criticisms and 'rebukes itself for uttering them.'(145) Three days later, *The Times* also apologised for its assertions of royal malingering.

Sensing the rapidly changing political mood, Disraeli eulogised the Queen. Her health was in jeopardy; for a long time she had been 'morally and physically incapacitated' from fulfilling her ceremonial duties.(146) However she had continued the underlying business of government 'with a punctuality and a precision which have certainly never been surpassed, and rarely equalled, by any monarch of these realms.'(147) The Queen's signature:

> has never been put to any public document of which she did not know the purpose... There is probably no person living in this country who has such complete control over the political tradition of England as the Sovereign herself... May she still continue a reign which has been distinguished by public duty and private virtue.(148)

Unfortunately Disraeli's honeyed encomium was open to misinterpretation. *The Daily Telegraph* pounced upon the phrase 'morally and physically incapacitated.' Disregarding the context, with rare malice, it contended that Disraeli's words constituted an admission that the Queen was unfit to reign as the head of government. A horrified Disraeli hastened to tender his apologies to Victoria. But it was too late. Yet another royal public relations débâcle had ensued. Gladstone summed up the affair, writing thus to Granville, 'Disraeli has done her & the country a left-handed service… The right aim is to keep her up to work…'[149]

On September 11th, when Victoria's bandages were removed, it was 'almost a third illness.'[150] Her ordeal continued, with fever, exhaustion, swelling in both legs, 'violent' pain in her right shoulder and her right hand 'quite unable' to be moved.[151] A month later, she observed:

> A most dreadful night of agonising pain. No sedative did any good. I only got some sleep between five and eight this morning. Felt much exhausted in awaking… Had my feet and hands bandaged. My utter helplessness is a bitter trial, not even being able to feed myself… Was unable all day hardly to eat anything.[152]

Yet again, these symptoms are consistent with a prolonged attack of porphyria. For the Queen, the only consolation, was that her right hand had recovered enough to do justice to the interminable stream of official documents. 'Was able to sign, which is a great thing.'[153] While Disraeli's 'punctuality and precision' were more relevant to Albert, Victoria was far from being the idle parasite of fevered Republican opinion.

Victoria's ordeal continued into November. Traditional British decency and 'support for the underdog' continued to mute public criticism of the monarchy. Many of the Queen's most severe Republican critics remained silent, either from personal sympathy or from a consideration that politically the time was not right. One Republican critic who took a very different view was the Liberal M.P.

for Chelsea, Sir Charles Dilke. On November 6th, while his Queen was still suffering, Dilke made a keynote speech at Newcastle-upon-Tyne. The speech was entitled 'Representation and Royalty.' For Dilke, the cost of the 'waste, corruption and inefficiency' of the monarch amounted to nearly a million pounds a year.[154] From her sickbed, Victoria dashed off a reply to Gladstone, protesting about these 'gross misstatements and fabrications, injurious to the credit of the Queen, and injurious to the Monarchy…'[155] However, only three days after Dilke's speech, at the Lord Mayor's banquet in London, Gladstone declared that every Englishman possessed the right to speak out 'without any limit at all' about 'the institutions under which we live.'[156] It may be that Gladstone hoped Dilke's criticisms would goad the Queen into performing her duty. If she could not be persuaded, then perhaps she might be shamed.

There was a media uproar. Having apologised for its assertions of royal malingering two months previously, *The Times* castigated Dilke's accusations as 'recklessness bordering on criminality.'[157] A variety of views were voiced. The public mood towards the monarchy had swung one way, then another. Now it hung in the balance.

Meanwhile Bertie had been taking the waters at the spa town of Scarborough. Calamity struck when he and his entourage contracted diarrhoea. Subsequently the *British Medical Journal* contended that Scarborough, despite its vaunted spa label, was 'the worst drained town in England.'[158]

The foul drains of Windsor may have contributed to the death of Albert. When Bertie returned to Sandringham for his thirtieth birthday celebrations, diarrhoea was progressing to typhoid fever – the same illness that allegedly had killed his father. On November 24th the parallels became more ominous when Sir William Jenner and three other physicians issued a bland medical bulletin declaring that 'There are no unfavourable symptoms.'[159] Hardly anybody believed it. The bulletin was horribly reminiscent of the pious waffle uttered by Albert's doctors while he died.

Having nursed the Queen through the worst of her illness at Balmoral, Alice discovered that her continued presence was unwanted. With her husband Louis, she had gone to Sandringham as guests of Bertie and Alix. Instead of returning to Germany with Louis, she stayed on and 'became the moral hope and stay of the house, taking charge of her sister-in-law, quiet and confident and responsible, and serving in the sick-room as a trained nurse.'[160] For the next few weeks, the Prince of Wales fought for his life. In that time, Alice wrote seventeen letters to Louis. They chronicle a nightmarish struggle. The first one states bluntly, 'It was a hard blow that it turned out to be typhoid fever after all – Papa's dreadful illness, which I know so well.'[161] Albert's doctors had not served him well. Alice was determined that the mistake would not be repeated. 'I get very worried sometimes – and Dr. Clayton is by no means the right doctor to have, and is not at all decisive or careful.'[162] A concerned Alix replaced Clayton with Dr Gull; in so doing, she may have saved her husband's life.

As Bertie's fever worsened, Alix 'who knows nothing of such illnesses' became increasingly alarmed.[163] Alice nursed her brother with the same selfless intensity that she had devoted to her parents. Her father had died; her mother's sanity and, a decade later, her life had been saved. Could her favourite brother also be saved? Alice moved through an endless haze of exhaustion. Commending her absent husband Louis not to worry about her, she noted that 'one has twice as much strength in difficult times and mine seldom deserts me.'[164]

It has been claimed that Bertie's fevered ravings were dreadful. With discretion cast aside by the severity of his illness, from his louche lifestyle there were 'all sorts of revelations and names of people mentioned'.[165] At times, for her own good, Alix had to be kept out of his sick-room. Alice soldiered on. Yet the fever worsened. The dread date of December 14th approached.

One editorial summed up the national mood thus:

> It is now ten years tomorrow since the Prince Consort died of a similar affliction. As long as the world lasts there will be superstition in it, and however foolish the feeling, there is real anxiety about tomorrow.[166]

The entire nation seemed gripped by superstition. In a grisly repeat of the death of Albert, Bertie lay surrounded by his family. Victoria, who had never respected her son in life, now steeled herself for his death.

> Alice and I said to one another in tears, 'There can be no hope.' I went up to the bed and took hold of his poor hand, kissing it and stroking his arm. He turned around and looked wildly at me saying, 'Who are you?' and then 'It's Mama.' 'Dear child' I replied. Later he said, 'It is so kind of you to come,' which shows he knew me, which was most comforting to me.(167)

On December 14th, the fever broke. Throughout the country, there were explosions of relief. Although *Reynolds's Weekly Newspaper* claimed that the illness had been 'purposely' exaggerated as 'a sham panic got up for the occasion to serve a political end,' few people believed this.(168) The Duke of Cambridge chortled gleefully, 'The Republicans say their chances are up. Heaven has sent this dispensation to save us.'(169) He was correct. It was as though a swollen balloon of Republicanism had been pricked. A commentator noted to Disraeli, 'What a sell for Dilke this illness has been!'(170)

In September, *The Daily Telegraph* had twisted Disraeli's words into an indictment of the Queen as unfit to reign. In December, following Bertie's miraculous recovery, it made the sanctimonious statement:

> When we put the Throne of England away in the British Museum, we will, please God, have a nobler reason than that it costs us a million sterling; that is to say, sevenpence three farthings apiece.(171)

Alice remained with her brother for the first part of his recovery. Then she went to Windsor for a few days in the New Year, before returning to Germany. She had played a key role in the drama during which both his fate and that of the British monarchy had hung in the balance. 'I still do not like leaving England before Bertie's convalescence is more firmly established,' she wrote to her husband. 'But his condition improves so slowly that I shall just have to go. And of course Mama would be pleased to be rid of me…'[172] The last utterance is redolent with regret for a mother who had taken so much from Alice yet would always resent her for it.

At the end of February 1872, the Queen and the Prince of Wales, still pale and wan from his ordeal, attended a Thanksgiving Service at St Paul's Cathedral. As they drove through London, Victoria was touched by 'the wonderful enthusiasm and astounding loyalty shown' by the populace.[173] When they returned to Buckingham Palace, she made several appearances on the balcony to wave to the crowds below. Writing to Gladstone, she confessed that she had been moved greatly by 'the immense enthusiasm and affection exhibited towards her dear son and herself from the highest down to the lowest.'[174] For the occasion, Lord Tennyson, the Poet Laureate, composed an epilogue to his work, *Idylls of the King*. In it, he spoke of a 'Crowned Republic'. It was an inspired riposte to British Republicanism.

Two days after this public display of warmth by her subjects, Victoria encountered the sixth of nine attempts upon her life. After a visit to Hyde Park, as her carriage came back to Buckingham Palace, an assailant attacked at Garden Gate. The attacker was the seventeen-year-old Arthur O'Connor, a great nephew of Fergus O'Connor, the Chartist leader. Brandishing a pistol, O'Connor got within a foot of the Queen before John Brown 'with wonderful presence of mind', jumped down and apprehended him.[175] Upon examination, it was discovered that the pistol was not loaded. The attack was a ludicrous ruse to force Victoria to sign an order for the release of Fenian prisoners. Evidently O'Connor failed to realise that the Queen was made of much sterner stuff and would never have signed such a missive. For his pains, he received a twelve month gaol sentence. His intended victim protested that he deserved worse punishment.

The Queen's undoubtedly genuine illness, the near death and miraculous recovery of the Prince of Wales, the glorious Thanksgiving

Service at St Paul's, Tennyson's 'Crowned Republic', O'Connor's foul attack on a defenceless woman... all of these combined to sway the electorate away from Republicanism. Shortly afterwards, when Dilke attempted to speak at a meeting in Bolton, he was shouted down by impromptu outbursts of *God Save the Queen!* and *Rule Britannia!*[(176)] On March 19th 1872 he addressed the House of Commons with a proposal for the formation of a Select Committee to scrutinise the Civil List. Out of 280 members present, only two supported his motion. Politically Dilke was a spent force. Some years later, he publicly disowned 'the opinions of political infancy'.[(177)] They had been expressed at the tender age of twenty-three, when he was still 'rather scatter brained.'[(178)]

The abrupt collapse of the Republican movement in 1872 is a fascinating political phenomenon. It may be argued that an essentially conservative British electorate had never really embraced the continental enthusiasm for republics and therefore needed little more than convenient excuses to repudiate them. If so, the most amazingly convenient excuses were provided entirely by circumstance. Sometimes even the most determined conspiracy theorist must bow his head before fate.

The Duke of Cambridge's comment that, 'heaven has sent this dispensation to save us' caught the amazing timeliness of Bertie's recovery on December 14th 1871, the tenth anniversary of Albert's death. This was the pivotal event. If the Prince of Wales had died, it is likely that Republicanism would have continued unchecked and the monarchy would have been destroyed. It is equally likely that, if Alice had not nursed Bertie at Sandringham, he would have died. In 1861, in saving Victoria's sanity, Alice probably also saved the monarchy; in 1871, in saving the lives of both Victoria and Bertie, she probably also saved the monarchy for a second time.

Throughout history, in times of crisis, there have been unsung, forgotten heroes, who acted decisively, gave unstintingly and asked for no reward of fame or honour. Alice is one such. Victoria's monarchy would endure for another thirty years, to preside over the greatest empire in history. Throughout the following century, the

British monarchy has endured, for the greater good of all, through two World Wars and much painful turmoil. None of this would have happened without the sacrifice of Alice – for which she was to pay dearly. Even today we are in her debt.

Chapter Seven
The Royal Sufferers

Throughout the 1860s, to many of her subjects, Queen Victoria had been, in the memorable words of General Grey, 'the royal malingerer.' Her obviously entirely genuine illness of 1871 had aroused enormous public sympathy. Less well known to her subjects was her terrible childhood illness in 1835. On both occasions, she had been near to death. The conventional view of Victoria is that she was a woman of robust constitution who was almost never truly ill. Her maladies have been dismissed as convenient excuses for shirking her job – or as equally convenient neuroses.

But what if the conventional view is wrong? What if the truth is that Victoria was a woman who was never truly well? As we have seen, the eminent Cecil Woodham-Smith categorically states 'there is no evidence to suggest that Queen Victoria suffered from porphyria or passed it on to any of her children.' As we have also seen, the intrepid team of Röhl, Warren and Hunt has uncovered abundant evidence that Victoria suffered from porphyria and passed it on to certain of her children. Viewed from this perspective, Victoria is no 'royal malingerer'. Instead she is a 'royal sufferer' who bore a horrible affliction for decade after weary decade, when life lacked purpose and seemed devoid of joy. That the most powerful person in the world might be an object of pity might have occurred to few of her subjects, apart from Disraeli. But, more than a hundred years after her death, it is still not too late to revise our opinion of one of the most written-about people in history. For this, we must thank Röhl, Warren and Hunt for their diligence. We must also thank the almost forgotten team of Macalpine and Hunter both for their spirit of scientific enquiry and their willingness to tackle the scientific establishment.

By 1871 the most dominant themes in Victoria's life were apparent. Although she reigned for another thirty years, there were few new themes that would emerge in her life, rather than the expected gradual decline into old age. It is therefore better for this present narrative to focus on dominant themes rather than attempt to emulate so many distinguished predecessors with a full account of her life from cradle to grave. Although we have considered the theme of Victoria's medical condition as it has appeared periodically throughout the preceding narrative, it is illustrative to consider it once more, in total, from the Queen's earliest years to her latest ones. Yet again we are indebted to the researches of Röhl, Warren and Hunt into Victoria's medical history. Hopefully this present account may help to bring their work to the wider audience which it undoubtedly deserves.

Although Victoria's father, the Duke of Kent, regarded himself as being possessed of an iron constitution, his premature death, as a result of contracting the common cold, must lend some doubt as to the validity of his self-diagnosis. Certainly the plump partridge of the young princess seemed of hardy disposition. Nevertheless, by the age of fourteen, Victoria was complaining of backache, severe headaches which left her 'prostrated' with feelings of sickness and biliousness, sore eyes and depressingly frequent colds. Almost certainly, relevant factors would have been the onset of puberty, together with an immune system weakened by the constant stress of Conroy's invidious Kensington System. Nevertheless, by the following year, her indisposition required a month's confinement to her room. 1835 brought a further array of complaints, with nausea, headaches, 'pain in my back', exhaustion, and a loss of her prodigious appetite.(1) At Ramsgate, she collapsed with fever, delirium and a raging pulse of 130. Dr Clark's diagnosis was 'bilious fever', whereas Victoria thought that her affliction was typhoid. As we have seen, at the time of Prince Albert's death, Lord Clarendon opined memorably of doctors Holland and Clark that they were 'not fit to attend a sick cat'.[2] Victoria, who regarded 'Ramsgate in 1835' as the worst illness she ever endured, noted later that Prince Albert's deathbed symptoms (of typhoid?) were 'much what I had at Ramsgate, only that I was much worse and was not well attended to'.[3] Of course medicine was then still in its infancy, with medical diagnosis a risky business. The early 19th century axiom held that French doctors left patients to die, whereas English doctors killed them.

When Victoria was eighteen and newly arrived on the throne, she noted that she was, once again, suffering from 'nausea', which left her 'sick', 'miserable', 'faint' and, generally 'poorly'.[4] After her coronation, she contracted a rash on her hands, which spread to her neck. Lord Melbourne, her first Prime Minister, advised her 'on no account to scratch it.'[5] Melbourne recalled similar rashes on Victoria's aunts and uncles, which may well have been evidence of porphyria. Certainly Melbourne was alarmed. In his view, the young Queen was following a Hanoverian family tradition of over-eating. He advised exercise, in particular, regular walks. Victoria responded by pointing out that she disliked walking; besides making her feet swell, it left her feeling sick and tired. Melbourne worried that lack of exercise would result in losing the use of her legs, as had happened with many other members of her family. It was sound advice, which the Queen disregarded. Eventually she too would lose mobility.

Before Victoria's marriage to Albert, she was 'very nervous and feverish, so much so that they fancied she was going to have the measles.'[6] As we have seen, the joys of marriage were swiftly tempered by her first pregnancy, then successive ones. After the birth of Vicky, the Princess Royal, Victoria succumbed to what we would now term post-natal depression. For the 'first 2 years of my marriage', she noted, she suffered 'aches – and sufferings and miseries and plagues'.[7] In 1853 the birth of her eighth child, the haemophiliac Prince Leopold, was followed by a series of hysterical outbursts. 'I have been lately suffering a great deal from nervousness and am therefore not capable of writing so connectedly as usual', she noted, the next year.[8] Unfortunately, during the following years, such outbursts became the norm, rather than the exception. In 1856 Prince Albert told her, 'I am trying to keep out of your way until your better feelings have returned and you have regained control of yourself.'[9] As we have seen, Albert had admitted to Baron Stockmar feelings of being 'completely cowed'; there was a 'perpetual terror of bringing on the hereditary malady' of George III and his offspring.[10] He watched his wife's mental health as 'a cat watches at a mouse hole'.[11] In order not to exacerbate Victoria's condition, Albert was reduced to commenting upon contentious issues by sending letters (in effect, memos) to his wife, even if she was in the very next room. At times their relationship seemed as therapeutic as it was marital. Concern for his wife's mental health proved ultimately highly detrimental to Albert's physical health.

Nor was Albert the only person gravely concerned with Victoria's well-being. As with Melbourne, Stockmar had severe misgivings. In 1856 Clark wrote that he had never seen Victoria in such a state of nervous exhaustion. Her mental health hung in the balance. 'Regarding the Queen's mind, unless she is kept quiet and still amused, the time will come when she will be in danger… Much depends on the Prince's management… If I could impress him with what I consider necessary I should almost consider the Queen safe.'[12] Thus Albert's role as Victoria's protector developed. 'He [Albert] saw, through the eyes of Stockmar, not a perfectly sane though angry Victoria, but the mad ghost of George III.'[13]

In 1858 Victoria had 'a sharp attack of neuralgia'.[14] Writing to Vicky, she confessed that 'horrid neuralgic pains' 'flowed' across her face.[15] In 1861 the death of her mother caused her first nervous breakdown. Again confiding to Vicky, she noted that 'My head is so very bad – so fearfully sensitive; I can't bear the least noise or talking in the next room even… [The Prince of Wales'] voice made me so nervous I could hardly bear it. Altogether I never felt in such a state of nerves for noise or sound.' The condition persisted. Weeks later, she told Vicky, 'My nerves are still very bad, I suffer very much from my head and from that dreadful sensitiveness [to noise]'[16] Her self-confidence was at a low ebb. 'I am dreadfully nervous just now... Every new person I see makes me so fearfully nervous.'[17] As the weeks became months, her condition remained dire. 'My spirits are very bad, my nerves terribly weak – and there is a heavy weight which weighs upon me and makes everything seem weary work! ...I am so dull and listless still...'[18] She was in thrall to a 'great depression'.[19]

When Prince Albert contracted his final illness, Victoria fell prey to 'a violent, sick headache and retching!'[20] The second nervous breakdown, following the death of Albert, was even deeper and far more protracted than had been the first. In 1862 she told Vicky, 'I am so terribly nervously affected now; my pulse gets so high, it is constantly between 90 and 100 instead of being 74! This wears me terribly. It exhausts me so and I am so weak, and then my poor memory fails me terribly.'[21] In 1863 she wrote, 'You never will believe how unwell and how weak and nervous I am, but any talking or excitement is far too much for me. I must constantly dine alone.'[22] Bertie's voice was 'quite too much for my very shattered nerves.'[23] Throughout the following years, nerves and neuralgia were frequent complaints. In 1864 she was 'very poorly; very weak and exhausted...'[24] She noted sadly, 'I never was in greater agonies, continuously.'[25] In 1865 her 'poor nerves' were absolutely 'shattered'.[26] In 1867 the pain felt 'as though my head were of china'.[27] It left her 'broken down in body and spirits'.[28] Her feet were badly swollen; even talking to people proved intolerable. In 1868 she noted that 'the noise of London, and driving in the streets tires my head and nerves very much.'[29]

In 1871 Victoria had the second of her two great illnesses, both of which might easily have killed her. Although she recovered, her health remained poor. In 1873 there was the return of 'a violent neuralgic attack in my face...'[30] The following year saw terrible headaches. In 1879 she suffered from a 'bad, feverish, bilious derangement'.[31] In 1883 a fall on the stairs provoked bouts of rheumatism, leaving her unable to walk or even stand. In 1884, 'I am still very cripply [sic] – I can't stand except for a few minutes'.[32] Her servants had to help her climb stairs and get into carriages. 1885 saw a return of her old enemy, neuralgia. Backache ('sciatica'), rheumatism and lameness meant that, by 1887, 'I can't stand hardly at all any more and hot dinners and standing about after dinner and much talking are impossibilities.'(33) The 1890s saw a considerable loss of both mobility and eyesight as the Queen entered old age.

Although Queen Victoria lived to the then very great age of eighty two, it will be seen that her whole life was a cacophony of ill-health. Mostly she put this down to a combination of 'nerves' and neuralgia. As we have seen, her nervous breakdowns and prolonged grieving, firstly after the death of her mother and then after the death of her husband, proved inexplicable both to her subjects and to her doctors. After a decade of seclusion, the monarchy was saved only by a rare and unforeseen combination of circumstances.

Once Victoria's life is viewed in the context of porphyria however, it is possible to arrive at a very different interpretation. Avoiding vexing noise, keeping temperatures cold and over-eating all resemble instinctive ways of managing the condition. Victoria begins to appear both as a 'great sufferer' and a 'great survivor'. Her lapses of enthusiasm for the business of government become entirely understandable for a person with persistent ill-health and consequent lack of energy. Those of us who have suffered chronic pain will testify readily how body and mind become utterly drained. As noted previously, in their examination of porphyria in the royal house of Hanover, Röhl, Warren and Hunt conducted an investigation of the medical histories of the generation preceding Victoria. They discovered that nearly all of George III's thirteen adult children exhibited symptoms of porphyria, ranging from mental disturbance, acute headaches, pain in the side, chest and back, lack of breath, constipation and vomiting. When the medical histories of the generations following Victoria are examined, a similar tale of woe was uncovered. In particular, the lives of Victoria's daughter Vicky, Vicky's daughter Charlotte, and Charlotte's daughter Fedora were all ruined by chronic ill-health.

* * *

Queen Victoria's first child, Vicky, the Princess Royal, was born in 1840. As a young girl, she had poor digestion and was often ill. The proffered medical remedies were calomel and a restricted diet. To Albert, Vicky's concerned father, these were taken to counterproductive extremes. He charged Vicky's doctor, James Clark, of starving her and 'poisoning her with calomel'.(34) As we have seen, Victoria had an almost naïve belief in her doctors, who, in turn, seemed to have an almost naïve belief in their remedies. Bitterly Albert wrote to his wife, 'Take the child [Vicky] away and do as you like and if she dies you will have it on your conscience.'(35) To Victoria, Vicky was plagued with the same 'nerves' as herself. 'You had not good nerves as a child and young girl, which is natural as I always was very nervous, an *inheritance* of my family...' [Italics added](36)

In 1858 Vicky married and went to live in Germany. Soon after arriving, she contracted toothache, headaches and nausea. In 1859 she became bedridden for a time. 1860 brought colic and a severe headache, which forced her back to her bed. 1861 saw 'violent lumbago' making her bedridden once again.(37) A horrible facial rash developed. Writing to Victoria, she noted, 'My face is quite swollen and red on one side and hurts me so much as if I had had a bad bruise.'(38) Later on in the year, she suffered two weeks of agonising headaches, together with a recurrence of the rash. 1862 brought 'violent pains in the left side & back.'(39)

Vicky had the same detestations of heat and noise as Victoria. Writing in the summer of 1862 she declared 'The heat is something awful today. I am in a state which I can not describe – almost suffocated, and everybody else is enjoying so much, and wonders that I find it warm.'(40) Foreign trips, with climatic variations, proved enervating. Back at home, even the freezing German winters brought little comfort. '...there is something irritating and exciting in the [winter] air without being bracing.'(41) Social occasions proved fraught; of one, she noted that it was 'so stiflingly hot and so late that I had a violent headache all day yesterday in consequence.'(42)

The 'perpetual noise' of workmen in the palace gave her a 'racking headache'.[43] As with Victoria, she was criticised for making insufficient social appearances.

In 1864 Vicky was 'feverish from nervous mood swings', followed by migraine and a 'ghastly headache'.[44] In 1865 she had earache and headaches. In 1866 a fever made her pulse race to 128; it was followed by 'rheumatic headaches', lumbago and migraine.[45] The mid 1860s saw Bismarck's wars of Prussian expansionism. Vicky, an English princess in a hostile Germany, was exposed to constant stress. In 1866, when her husband was at war, she suffered 'tormenting abdominal pains'.[46] Rather than being a source of solace, her mother-in-law, Queen Augusta was yet another stressor. Vicky confessed, 'I have been quite ill after [meeting with Augusta] – my knees shaking and my pulse galloping.'[47] Even relations with her domestic staff proved problematic. After one encounter, she confided, 'I am suffering again from a hysterical nervous pressure in my throat.'[48]

In 1868 Vicky had an attack of 'most severe neuralgic headache!' with 'the most excruciating pain'.[49] Feeling that 'I cannot go on like this any longer', she resorted to quinine.[50] Although it brought a respite from the neuralgia, as Vicky had feared, it also heralded a return of the severe, disfiguring facial rash. 'My face has swelled to a dark red sphere… my skin is taut and itches & burns in a way that is as hard to describe as it is to bear.'[51] Vicky's 'fire-red shapeless mass' of a face was humiliating.[52] 'There is only a hint of eyes, nose & mouth, & I look such a fright that I ask forgiveness of everyone for having to lay eyes on such a sight! It's a pitiful condition to be in…'[53] Although Vicky hoped that her disfiguration would be brief, she was disappointed. Nearly two weeks later, 'My eyelids, ears & hands are swollen… the itching is practically unbearable.'[54] Although Vicky was assured that facial rashes were relatively normal allergic reactions to quinine, Röhl, Warren and Hunt point out that Vicky's disfigurement could equally have been a symptom of porphyria. Although Vicky believed that quinine was necessary 'for there is no other sure means of curing these raging, gruelling nerve pains', her 1868 experiences convinced her that the cure was nearly as bad as the disease. She never took quinine again.(55)

The attacks continued. In the summer of 1868, Vicky wrote to Victoria: 'The last few days have been quite too much for me… I have had cholics [sic] and Diarrhoea & feel quite wretched; the heat is really intolerable, & the nights are as bad as the days.'(56) The following year, her 'neuralgia' returned. 1870 saw 'such violent pain in my side that 'I… was truly at my wit's end'.(57) It also saw a return of the dreaded facial rash. 'What a state my skin is in I am quite ashamed of – and can hardly show myself I am such a figure. My forehead, nose and chin are covered with large red blotches…'(58) The presence of rash could no longer be attributed to quinine. The rash – and the pain in Vicky's side – are classic symptoms of porphyria.

The 1870s, 1880s and 1890s brought an intensification of Vicky's symptoms: 'neuralgia' in the face, head and ear, 'agonising rheumatic pains', 'severe nervous headaches', pains in the back and legs, sleeplessness, 'sciatica pains', 'colic' and depression.(59) Stoically she suffered a nearly unbearable existence. Two of her children died; her husband, Fritz, lost his battle with cancer. The political liberalisation of Germany remained a pipe-dream. Despite her title as Empress Frederick, a powerless Vicky was forced to watch in dismay as her son, Kaiser Wilhelm II, began a series of political blunders which would culminate in the wholesale carnage of World War I.

* * *

In 1860 Vicky's first daughter, Charlotte, was born. She too was sickly. 'Alas, she is an unsatisfactory child, poor little thing,' Vicky wrote to Victoria.(60) Early on, Charlotte was 'very sensitive and nervous', thin to the point of 'nothing but skin and bones', hyperactive and as poor a student as her uncle Bertie had been.(61) As with Bertie, there were childish 'Hanoverian' tantrums, 'such outbursts of rage and stubbornness that she screams blue murder'.[62] At fourteen, her lack of physical development was remarkable. Vicky reported to Victoria:

> She grows so little that you would think she was nine or ten, has not an atom of figure, or waist, and shows no sign of her health beginning to change... Charlotte is in everything – health, looks and understanding like a child of ten![63]

Puberty brought two changes in Charlotte. Physically she grew a large upper body, which looked ungainly when contrasted with her extremely short legs. Psychologically a childhood trait towards malice reappeared in 'Charlotte the Brat', as she termed herself.[64] At sixteen, Charlotte married her cousin. Just before the wedding, Vicky made the following remarks to her husband Fritz about her daughter's character:

> I cannot tell you how it saddens and troubles me to think of Charlotte! - That pretty exterior - & the empty inside, those dangerous character traits. Everyone is initially enthralled, & yet those who know her better know how she really is – and can have neither love nor trust nor respect! It is too sad.[65]

Charlotte's twenties brought the all too familiar symptoms of porphyria – neuralgia, fainting, fever and loss of mobility in the legs. When she was twenty-eight, her brother Wilhelm became the new Kaiser. Bitter at his elevation, Charlotte became a princess of malice. She is considered to have been the power behind an outbreak of poison pen letters circulating at her brother's Court. In short, she became a troublemaker, par excellence. Vicky regarded her as 'dangerous in the extreme' and confided to Victoria, 'I am really quite afraid!'[66]

Charlotte's thirties brought a collapse of her health, involving an array of symptoms including rheumatism, pains in her legs, headaches and sleeplessness, 'anemie' [anaemia] & broken down nerves'.[67] To this litany of pain was later added 'dentical torments'

– inflamed roots and abscesses of the gums and teeth.[68] In 1902, shortly after the deaths of her mother, Vicky, and grandmother, Victoria, medical opinion held that Charlotte was suffering from 'a form of scurvy'[69] If so, it was a form of scurvy that was not susceptible to cure, either by diet or medicine. Charlotte described her gums as being 'disgusting… lumps of crimson, or strings of white flesh' that had to be hidden to avoid embarrassment.[70] Charlotte insisted that her 'dentical torments' were not a problem of dentistry, per se, but part of a much broader malaise. In her words, the 'excruciating pains that nearly drove me mad… do not come from my teeth, which are perfectly in order, but abscesses, also on my body, all over the gums: else I should have mine out.'[71] To these abscesses were added abdominal pains, back pains, swollen legs, boils, swellings of the cheek, glands and side of the head, constipation, lameness, giddiness and fainting fits. Charlotte's maladies were textbook symptoms of porphyria.

A 1905 visit to Cannes held the promise that the 'blue sea & sky' would 'soon pick me up again'.[72] When Charlotte arrived, it was 'quite a dream to be here…'[73] The awful reality was that, for a porphyria sufferer, the warm air and bright sunlight of Cannes were guaranteed disaster. And so it proved. Charlotte suffered an agonising attack. She took aspirin 'because I truly could no longer bear the excruciating pains in my eye sockets, nose & forehead… For I cannot see a thing for the pain.'[74] In a letter to her doctor, she noted the last ghastly symptom of porphyria, 'Urine dark red.'[75]

Subsequent visits to Cannes brought a recurrence of the attacks, accompanied by 'an insufferably itchy skin rash'[76] In continuing to visit the Mediterranean, Charlotte failed to realise the dreadful connection. In 1908 she wrote, 'The weather is ideally beautiful: brilliant warm sunshine', not realizing that it was causing her 'atrocious & so dismaying' 'disorders & pains' which were 'almost unbearable'.[77] Pathetically she wrote, 'My pains are not to be endured! And are now accompanied by new symptoms…'[78]

The remainder of Charlotte's life was a miserable porphyria-ridden existence. She died, eighteen years after Vicky and Victoria, in 1919, when the policies of her brother, Wilhelm, had turned northern France into a charnel house. Ever-assiduous in their research, Röhl, Warren and Hunt carried on to investigate the medical situation of Charlotte's long-forgotten daughter, Feodora of whom they noted that, previously, 'Not a line has been written about her in any history book.'(79)

* * *

Vicky's grand-daughter, Feodora, was born in 1879. As with her mother, Charlotte, she was a tiny, anaemic child, although with a disproportionately large head and 'such old sharp [facial] features, much too big for her diminutive body'.(80) Her nickname 'Babes' seems truly ironic for, even at twelve, Vicky thought her 'sharp pinched features are more old looking than ever… I do wish she could grow – she is the shortest child I ever saw.'(81) Vicky also had reservations about Feodora's character. She was 'very fond of telling stories – and hardly ever says exactly the truth! I am afraid she will be her Mama over again.'(82)

At the age of ten, Feodora was prostrated by mysterious attacks involving pain in the head, back and limbs, together with diarrhoea and shivering. As Vicky reported to Victoria, '… she [Feodora] has had an attack similar to mine!'(83) Although Feodora's health seemed to improve, her relationship with her mother, Charlotte 'the Brat' became fraught. As had Vicky and Charlotte, Feodora married young. Shortly after her marriage in 1898, she began to look 'tired… pale & thin.'(84) Charlotte became increasingly disapproving both of Feodora and her husband Heinrich. The rift between mother and daughter widened. Charlotte stormed 'Babes is incomprehensible to me!'(85) Revealingly she continued, 'I never was blind about her faults & character, but never thought she would turn round against me.'(86) Feodora riposted, 'The lies she [Charlotte] has told Papa… about me… are really disgusting…'(87) For her part, Charlotte asserted of Feodora that 'She is beyond my comprehension…'(88)

In a state of trauma from her bitter battles with her mother, Feodora's earlier illness, 'the old story', returned.[89] She believed that the cause was influenza. 'I had a severe attack of Influenza which kept me in bed over a week, half paralysed. I could not move a limb excepting my arms; neck, whole back & legs were totally stiff; & the frightful pains are not to be described.'[90] A further attack in 1900 was accompanied by a 'bowel disorder'.[91] Feodora was confined to bed for another three weeks; the pain and disorientation made her 'half idiotic'.[92] Later attacks were thought to be malaria. Feodora took quinine, as had her grandmother, Vicky. A temporary cessation of pain was followed by 'raging headaches' which she described memorably as being akin to hammers banging away inside her head.[93]

In 1900 Feodora met Victoria, Vicky and Charlotte respectively. Vicky thought her 'anemic & delicate' and was extremely concerned by her 'superficiality'.[94] As we have seen, Vicky had held such reservations about the character of the young Charlotte. As though history was repeating itself, Charlotte harboured similar reservations about Feodora. She declared herself horrified by the 'hatred, disdain & flippancy which came out of that child'.[95] But then she went further. In words which make one's blood run cold, she thus described her daughter:

> . . . pale, thin, ugly, all freshness gone, funnily dressed, hair parted on the forehead (like a dairy maid), talking of dancing, acting, Lieutenants, not looking at anything, inquiring after nobody!! I could hardly believe this curious, loud personage had been my child!!... I could not cherish motherly feelings any more... I cannot love her! & my heart seemed & felt a stone.[96]

Again and again throughout our narrative, there have been tantalising mentions of an otherwise unnamed 'Hanoverian malady' crossing the generations. In Charlotte's words, Feodora's husband, 'tactless as usual, named the illness straight out'.[97] He asked bluntly, 'why I would not say so, [since] all the world knew it.'[98] This suggests that Feodora's husband was laying her ill-health at the door of the family. Conversely Charlotte wrote in 1901:

> Astonish me, her condition does not in the least: I know full well what it comes from, but cannot entrust to pen & ink. All her & his!! fault, & nothing to be done, except a long treatment both flatly refuse to undergo, as naturally [it would] put him in bad light & fault.[99]

Several months later, her assertions became even more pointed. Rejecting a medical opinion of appendicitis, Charlotte named Feodora's condition as 'an internal inflammation!!! I have been dreading for years!!!'[100] Finally Charlotte came out with it, naming Feodora's malaise as venereal disease contracted via her husband. This diagnosis does not appear to have been accepted either by other family members or by Feodora's doctor.

After a year of continuous illness, there was a brief respite, then a recurrence when Feodora felt 'wretched' and her 'head & limbs ache[d] violently'.[101] Feodora spoke of 'beastly migraine' and 'anaemia'.[102] This latter term, ironically the one used previously by her mother, became the accepted family euphemism. In the next few years, Feodora suffered from the same symptoms as had Charlotte – toothaches, headaches, extreme sensitivity to heat, sleeplessness, tiredness, 'terrible, dreadful colic and fainting fits'.[103] After spending many years trying unsuccessfully to conceive, a criminally botched attempt at artificial insemination by her doctor, left her ovaries and uterus in a dire condition. Charlotte's bitter criticism of the doctor seemed to implicate Feodora also. It seemed as though, for Charlotte, Feodora could do nothing right.

In 1913, Feodora wrote:

> There seems no life in me any more, I am sick of it, & all & everything. I have battled against these feelings with all my might & main, till I crashed down completely, & thought I was going

> mad. I saw & heard all sorts of stupid things, was giddy & sick, & dead tired, only longed for sleep & rest.[104]

Treatment, involving arsenic injections, was deemed to have been of limited success. However in 1914, after the onset of war, Feodora's husband went to fight on the Western Front. Her troubled relationship with her parents deteriorated still further. Stress seems to have engendered first depression then a return of the dreaded physical attacks. Again Feodora wrote:

> I have been very ill… First I had a severe bronchitis with fever, up again for a few days, then that terrible abdominal inflammation with a high temperature that came & went, & incredible pains…[105]

Early in 1915 she wrote:

> The three feverish illnesses I had some months ago have brought me to the point of collapse. My stupid nerves don't want to go on any more, I can't do what I want or should. My energy is gone, & there's no point in fighting it…[106]

In late 1916 the twenty-year-old correspondence between Feodora and her lifeline, Baroness Heldburg, ceased. The reason remains unknown. Röhl, Warren and Hunt offer the most likely suggestion: that Feodora, in some unknown manner, caused grave offence to the hitherto tolerant Baroness and, stubbornly, refused to apologise. As we have seen, Charlotte died in 1919. The deeply troubled relationship between mother and daughter seems to have brought out the worst in both of them. With the death of Charlotte, one might have expected Feodora to relent and make some kind of accommodation with her family. There is no evidence that she did so. Did the deadly enmity between the two women extend beyond the grave?

The remainder of Feodora's life is a mystery. All we know is that, on August 26th 1945, as Germany once again collapsed into the chaos of defeat, Feodora and her companion, Meta Schenck, put their heads in an oven and gassed themselves. It was a sad, dreadful ending for Queen Victoria's great-granddaughter.

* * *

In our examination of King George III and his thirteen children, there is case after case of lives blighted by the symptoms of porphyria. In our examination of Queen Victoria's daughter, grand-daughter and great-grand-daughter, we have three lives blighted by exactly the same symptoms. For all the face-saving talk of 'nerves', 'neuralgia', 'influenza' and 'malaria', it seems likely that Victoria, Vicky, Charlotte and Feodora knew very well that a nameless and horribly life-disfiguring disease was being passed across the generations. These royal sufferers had no name for their malaise; there was no cure for it. The best doctors in Europe proved ultimately powerless. Finally the royal sufferers had no other option but to endure it.

Confronted with such a cornucopia of evidence, it is almost certain that Vicky, Charlotte and Feodora all suffered from porphyria. It seems very likely that Victoria had porphyria in intermittent remission and suffered sporadically from it. As noblewomen, Vicky, Charlotte and Feodora struggled, largely unsuccessfully, to manage lives befitting their eminent social positions. When we view Queen Victoria in the context of these royal sufferers, it is almost inconceivable how she ever managed to be more than a semi-invalid recluse. Yet, again and again, when danger threatened her country, she roused herself to equal, if not better, the efforts of the finest of politicians and career diplomats. Truly history has judged her harshly.

Chapter Eight
The Tragedy of Princess Alice

From the previous chapter, it may be seen that porphyria can justifiably lay claim to being 'the royal disease', at least in terms of the English and European royal families of the 19th century. Surprisingly however, the title of 'the royal disease' belongs to another medical condition; even more surprisingly, it is one that is also associated with Queen Victoria. Open any biology textbook and look up 'haemophilia'. Invariably Victoria will be cited as perhaps the most famous carrier of this formerly dread disease.

Both porphyria and haemophilia are extremely unusual. Different types of porphyria have different incidence rates, varying from one person per 5,000, to one person per 50,000. Haemophilia is similarly rare, with typically one person per 10,000 suffering from haemophilia A and one person per 50,000 suffering from haemophilia B.

The word 'haemophilia' comes from two Greek words 'haima' (blood) and 'philia' (love). Normally when we cut ourselves, or suffer internal bleeding, our blood clots within a short time. (If it did not clot, we would simply carry on bleeding until we died through blood loss.) The clotting is caused by so-called 'clotting factors'. Genes contain the genetic information for clotting factors to be produced in the body. The relevant genes are contained in the X chromosome. A male has an X chromosome and a Y chromosome, whereas a female has two X chromosomes. If an X chromosome has an altered (mutated) form of the relevant gene, a clotting factor may not be formed. A female with one affected X chromosome will still have another normal X chromosome and thus another method of producing the clotting factor. She will be a carrier, although not a sufferer of haemophilia, and can pass this disease on to her descendants. However a male with a dysfunctional gene on his X chromosome has no 'biological backup'. He is condemned to be a sufferer. Formerly this was tantamount to receiving a death sentence from either internal or external bleeding. In addition, pressure of internal bleeding into joints and muscles made haemophilia one of the most painful conditions known to medicine. Even if one survived bouts of internal bleeding, haemorrhages into the joints often meant that the sufferer would be crippled.

Although no name for this distressing condition then existed, haemophilia was known in the ancient world. The Talmud stated that male circumcision might be waived if two brothers had died previously during the operation. In the middle ages, Albucasis, an Arab physician, wrote an account of a family where the males bled to death, following minor injuries. An American, Dr John Conrad Otto, studied three generations of descendants of a woman who settled in New Hampshire in 1720. In 1803 Otto wrote of 'a haemorrhagic disposition existing in certain families'.(1) As with Albucasis and the writers of the Talmud, Otto recognised the familial, male-oriented nature of the disease. Moreover his studies convinced him that it was hereditary. The term 'haemophilia' first appeared in 1828, in an academic paper written by Hopff and published in Zurich.(2)

As we have seen, Queen Victoria was the issue of an arranged marriage between two royal families – those of Hanover and those of Saxe-Coburg-Gotha. Unlike porphyria, there is no evidence of haemophilia having existed previously in the House of Hanover; neither has it been detected in the House of Saxe-Coburg-Gotha. Therefore it appears that Victoria – or her mother – was the first person in her bloodline to develop the X chromosome with the faulty blood-clotting gene. It may be that the Queen was quite simply unlucky.

Recently a book was published which advanced a different, rather startling explanation. In 'Queen Victoria's Gene', two brothers,

Malcolm and William Potts, both respected professors, advanced a theory that Queen Victoria was illegitimate and that her (unknown) father was a haemophilia sufferer.[3] On the face of it, this theory, while intriguing, is unlikely. Certainly Victoria's father, the impoverished, debt-ridden Duke of Kent, was a desperate man, possibly willing to take desperate chances. But it is difficult to imagine the priggish former martinet, stiff with pride, being a willing cuckold. And while Victoire, his wife, may have been under his influence (as she was, later, with Captain Conroy), she seems too honest and ingenuous a person to be party to such a stratagem or, indeed, indulge in an extra-marital affair. Additionally, nothing in her life-long devotion to Victoria suggests any mixed motives or dark family secrets.

Could an illegitimate child have been smuggled into Victoire's bedroom in the advanced stages of pregnancy? The body of clergymen waiting in the immediate vicinity included one man decidedly not of the cloth. The doughty Duke of Wellington, survivor of so many bloody European battlefields, would have been alert to any such ruse. Could Wellington have been fooled by the Duke of Kent? It is most unlikely. Could he have been compromised? It is well-nigh unimaginable. As with Victoire, nowhere in Wellington's decades of loyal service to Victoria is there any suggestion of a dark secret.

Conversely the imperious, demanding and temperamental Victoria seems Hanoverian to the core. And there is another reason why it is almost impossible that she was the issue of an unknown haemophilic father. As we have shown repeatedly, both Victoria's ancestors and her descendants were rife with symptoms of porphyria – which appears nowhere in her mother's family. To support the facts, an unknown, haemophilic father would also have had to be suffering from porphyria – and this is stretching credulity to its limits. Regretfully our body of evidence must compel us to reject the novel theory of 'Queen Victoria's Gene'. More happily, the Queen's bloodline – and those of her many illustrious descendants – remains unblemished.

First porphyria; then haemophilia. The popular assertion that 'it was all due to inbreeding' falls rather short of the truth. Both the

Houses of Hanover and those of Saxe-Coburg-Gotha suffered from inbreeding; thus do royal families concentrate power. Although inbreeding may have had little or nothing to do with Victoria contracting haemophilia, the reduced gene pool due to inbreeding meant a higher rate of incidence among her descendants than, say, from a typical commoner with a genetically wider mixture of ancestors. Similarly porphyria may have been acquired randomly, perhaps by Mary Queen of Scots, and passed on to her descendants (for instance, George III and his children) with a much higher incidence rate than would have happened with commoners. Although inbreeding, per se, may not have been responsible for the introduction either of porphyria or haemophilia, it probably increased greatly the chances of them being passed on to descendants.

With odds of, say, 30,000 to 1 in the general population against having either porphyria or haemophilia, the odds against a member of the general population having both diseases are massive. Of course, it may be argued that, as a member of an inbred, and therefore genetically restricted family, Victoria stood an excellent chance of having the pre-existing porphyria. From whatever viewpoint we adopt, our sympathies go to Victoria as being extremely unfortunate to have contracted both diseases. And yet, ironically, her personal sufferings were relatively minor. Her female status meant that, with haemophilia, she was a carrier and not a sufferer. With porphyria, perhaps in intermittent remission, she escaped lightly, compared to her ancestors, such as King George II and his children, and her direct descendents, such as the wretched Vicky, Charlotte and Feodora. Although haemophilia made no difference to her personal health, it would prove calamitous to one son and to the families of two of her daughters. In addition, haemophilia and medical malpractice suffered by the royal family would become catalysts in triggering not only the onset of the First World War (which laid the foundation for the Second World War) but also the Russian Revolution, whose legacy of injustice and misery remains with us almost one hundred years later. In the twentieth century, the Kennedy family, of American presidential fame, were perceived to be suffering from a curse. Much the same might be said of Victoria and her progeny.

* * *

In 1853 Prince Leopold, Duke of Albany, Victoria's fourth son and eighth child was born; he was named after Victoria's mentor, her uncle Leopold. At first, all seemed well and Victoria was able to report to Leopold that his young namesake was 'a jolly fat little fellow'[(4)] Sadly, and to the bewilderment of his parents, the symptoms of haemophilia soon began to appear. Initially the condition was described as 'rheumatism'. When it became clear that Leopold's condition had nothing to do with rheumatism, a stunned Victoria could only murmur that the then recently named haemophilia was 'not in our family', i.e. the House of Hanover.[(5)] The inference was, of course, that Leopold's haemophilia had come from Albert's family. The rumour machine of the time was swift to ascribe it to old and increasingly tired canards of 'the bad blood' and 'the curse of the Coburgs'.

Leopold was the youngest of Victoria's four sons; he is also regarded as having been the most intelligent and, in many ways, the most interesting. At Oxford he developed friendships with such luminaries as Oscar Wilde, John Ruskin and Charles Dodgson, of 'Lewis Carroll' fame. However his life was blighted by his health, which was diplomatically referred to as being 'very delicate'. In addition to haemophilia, he appears to have been mildly epileptic. A conventional career, such as the military, was out of the question. Instead, by his mid-twenties, Leopold had become an unofficial private secretary to his mother, ironically being entrusted with the red boxes of official correspondence which were so carefully withheld from his elder brother, Bertie, Prince of Wales. This role necessitated Leopold exchanging the spirited intellectual life of Oxford for the stifling social routines of Balmoral and Osborne. An attempt at rebellion failed. The

Queen exhorted her other children to put pressure on Leopold to perform his duty by a process of social ostracism. He was, in effect, to be sent to Coventry socially by not being invited to events such as dinners, parties, balls and the racecourse. In the words of his stern, unrelenting parent, 'He must be made to feel that such conduct to a mother and Sovereign cannot be tolerated.'[6] The phrase 'tough love' became prevalent almost a century and a half later. It scarcely does justice to Victoria's inimitable brand of caring and selfishness.

For Leopold, marriage represented virtually his only hope of escaping his mother's hearth and home. However haemophilia made his quest for a bride a difficult one. Various possibilities came to nothing. It has been suggested that he considered Alice Liddell, daughter of the Vice-Chancellor of Oxford University, for whom Charles Dodgson wrote *Alice in Wonderland*. The Queen took a hard-line position, stipulating that her children, as royals, should only marry into other currently reigning royal families. (She allowed a single exception – the marriage of her daughter Louise to a commoner.) Little did she know of the world-shattering events which would result from her policy.

In 1882, at Windsor Castle, Leopold married Princess Helene Friederike, daughter of the Prince of Waldeck-Pyrmont. The following year, Helene gave birth to a daughter, named in memory of Leopold's beloved sister Alice, who had so often pleaded his case with their mother. In early 1884, with Helene pregnant once again, Leopold went to Cannes to escape the British winter. (In common with many haemophilia sufferers, he suffered from severe joint pains made worse by the cold.) At the Yacht Club in Cannes he slipped and fell, injuring his knee. He died shortly afterwards at the age of only thirty-one. His posthumous son, Charles, succeeded him at birth; one of his descendants became King Carl XVI of Sweden.

While Leopold was a sufferer of haemophilia, both Princess Alice and Princess Beatrice, Victoria's youngest child, were known carriers of it. Thus at least three of Victoria's nine children were affected. (Princess Louise, Queen Victoria's fourth daughter and sixth child, had no children; therefore her status as a carrier cannot be assessed.)

In 1870, during the Franco-Prussian War, Alice's fifth child, Frederick William, was born. His birth gave his mother 'a difficult time, but it went quickly.'[7] 'Frittie' was regarded by his parents as a 'new proof of our love'.[8] Seventeen years previously, Leopold had been 'a jolly fat little fellow'; Frittie too was initially 'fat and healthy', unlike his mother, whose health, by then, was declining.[9] As with Leopold, at first all seemed well. In 1871, the same year that Alice nursed Queen Victoria through her near-fatal illness, she gave birth to another daughter, whom she meant to name 'Victoria' which 'they pronounce too dreadfully in German'.[10] Victoria Alix Helena Louise Beatrice was 'a sweet, merry little person always laughing, with a deep dimple in one cheek just like [her older brother] Ernie'.[11] Alix was known as 'Alicky', 'Sunny' or 'Princess Sunshine'.[12] Unbeknown to Alice, she too was a haemophiliac, whose condition would have a profound effect upon the history of the twentieth century.

For nearly the first two years of his life, all seemed well with Frittie, 'a very pretty winsome child'.[13] Then, as with Leopold, his health started to fail. Alice, who was highly competent at nursing, began to have suspicions of haemophilia; in February 1873 these suspicions were confirmed when Frittie cut his ear and bled for three days. Strangely enough, after this distressing episode, the child's health seemed to improve. However there was now a need for the same ceaseless vigilance that was exercised with Leopold. In March, Alice set off on a tour of Italy, returning on May 2nd. On May 29th, Louis, her husband, was to leave the family home at Darmstadt to review the troops in Upper Hesse. The day before, a family reunion was held. Young Alix was barely old enough to join in the festivities. In Ernie's words:

> We gathered lilies-of-the-valley and Fritz [Frittie], who had a special love for me had some in his little hand which he wanted to give me. I ran further and further away and he with his short little legs trotted behind me and I can still hear how he called out: 'Ernie I wants ou, Ernie I wants ou so much!'; he wanted to give the lilies-of-the-valley to me. This cry was with me for many

> months, yes, even years. I could not get it out of my head and at first I felt quite desperate...[14]

The following day, Louis left early. Alice's bedroom had a window through which she could look through the window of the sitting-room, at right angles to her. In Ernie's words:

> My mother was still in bed in the morning and my brother and I were playing near her. I ran into the sitting room in order to look across at my brother. My mother jumped out of bed to pull me back from the window. During this time my little brother got up on a chair to enable him to look out and before my mother could return the chair tipped forward and he fell down on the steps.[15]

Queen Victoria received a telegram and subsequently a letter from one of Alice's ladies, Fräulein Bauer. The Queen appended a translation of this letter to her Journal, since it gave (and gives) the most detailed account of what had happened. Reporting as of 'Thursday forenoon' from Darmstadt on 29th May, Fräulein Bauer wrote:

> Through the telegram which I despatched to Your Majesty by the Princess's own desire, you have already received the terrible news, which since this morning, agitates the town. Prince Frederick fell out of the window from his Mama's bedroom upon a balcony below. He, as well as Prince Ernest, was with his Mama, no nurse being present at the time; and whilst the Princess went for a moment towards the door to call for the nurse to take the two Princes away, the melancholy event happened. The poor boy was lying on his arm, when they came to pick him up, and was senseless, though no external injury was visible. Doctors were speedily at hand and found that the skull was not fractured nor any limb broken; but they fear that an extraversion of blood on the brain may take place. It is now some time since we have observed a considerable swelling on the side of the forehead; but the

> breathing is pretty quiet, the feet are warm and at one time the Prince moved his little arm! Sensation is complete but otherwise he rests without uttering a sound. The doctors are not without hope but at the same time do not conceal from the Princess the extent of the danger… the Princess is dreadfully alarmed but now calm and composed after having been almost stupefied by the terror at first. She does not for a moment leave the bedside, but watches constantly by the darling child whose life, short as it has been, was already such a source of anxiety to her…[16]

Word was sent to Prince Louis to return as soon as possible. Fräulein Bauer continued her account with a section headed 'Thursday afternoon':

> Thus far I had written when things got worse, and after an hour of dreadful suspense all hope was gone. The doctors were right when they feared that there might be an effusion of blood on the brain, and we had hardly realised the idea of the case being hopeless when the terrible news was announced that all was over! Breathing had gradually become more irregular and heavy; all the feeling of the nerves had ceased and without pain and struggle the young soul had departed… [The Princess] was able to give vent to her grief by tears, and God may give her strength in this hard trial of a mother… I have just seen the Princess at the bedside of the poor little Prince, who represents death in its loveliest form. [The Princess] wishes me to tell Your Majesty that she trusts this trial will not be more than she will be able to bear![17]

Alice never recovered from her loss. She knew that Frittie might not have died but for the internal bleeding brought on by the fall. It is true, as his sister Victoria later put it, that Frittie's 'early death might have saved him from a semi-invalid life'.[18] But this is a grim sort of consolation, voiced at its most hollow by Frittie's fellow haemophiliac, his godfather and uncle. Leopold was very close to Alice, to whom he confided his frustrations at the restrictions the Queen imposed upon him and his desire to escape his mother's hearth. Although Leopold's letters were often bitter, on May 11th 1873, he had written to Alice from Oxford: 'I hope my godson is keeping quite well, and not having any more bruises and in every way unlike his godfather except in being very fond of you and Louis…'[19] But all the horror of May 29th returned when he wrote to Alice from Osborne just after Christmas to thank her for a bust of Frittie which she had sent him:

> It is such a dear, sweet and innocent little countenance, that I cannot help saying to myself that it is perhaps well that the dear child has been spared all the trials and possibly miseries of a life of ill-health like mine for instance. Oh dear Alice, I know too well what it is to suffer as he would have suffered, and the great trial of not being able to enjoy life or to know what happiness is, like others. That old saying (I don't know whether I quoted all right); 'Everything works for good', seems always to me such a truly comforting and good one. When first darling Frittie was taken away from among us, I remember so well people saying: 'It is all for the best, he would never have been well etc.' And I said to myself: 'If anything happens to me, that is what everybody will say', and it made me feel so bitter for a time, but I think that I have now come round to see the justness of the saying which I quoted above…[20]

The effect was hugely disturbing to Ernie, who suffered intensely and in secret, as very sensitive children can sometimes suffer. The fact that, on the previous day, he had run away from his little brother and upset him by not accepting the flowers preyed on his mind. He wrote:

> I cried through many nights and everyone thought I was grieving at his loss; it was only partly that, but it was also my conscience. I had told nobody about it and as he was laid amongst all the spring flowers my mother held me up and I placed the lilies-of-the-valley

> into his cold small hands. Can grown-ups ever realise what a child can suffer?[21]

The various members of the family reacted in their different ways to this pathetic event. Prince Louis made no written entry in his diary; but, on June 2nd, he inserted a photograph of the little boy's dead body surrounded by flowers and a press account of the funeral.

* * *

Flowers and music were the two things that most quickly made memories flood back to Alice of a life that she could scarcely believe had vanished. She could not see a flower along the roadside without having an urge to pick it for her dead son. For many days, her beloved piano remained silent. She dared not face the keyboard from which Frittie's tiny hands had so often pulled away her own when he wanted her to come and play with him. The last piece she had played before his death was Chopin's 'funeral March'. 'The wish that all have who love their own' – as Alice put it – was expressed by Ernie to his mother a whole year later: 'When I die, you must die too, and all the others; why can't we all die together? I don't want to die alone like Frittie.'[22] Ernie, who sometimes dreamed of his dead brother, often returned to his theme of wishing that they should 'die all together'.[23]

Throughout the second half of 1873 and the years that followed, outwardly life returned to its normal routine. Inwardly however, Alice was preoccupied by Frittie's death. At the time of the accident, she had been involved in yet another mediation between her siblings and her mother. On this occasion, it was her brother, Prince Alfred, Duke of Edinburgh, who was engaged to the Czar of Russia's only daughter, Marie. Queen Victoria 'displayed unusual tetchiness', much of which was directed at Alice.[24] In April 1873 Victoria had written to Lord Granville laying it down that 'the Queen wished Princess Alice (who is at home) to be in no way consulted or taken into confidence about this affair of Prince Alfred'.[25] (Princess Alice was in fact in Italy at the time). The Czar refused to present his daughter for pre-marriage inspection at Balmoral; instead the Queen was invited to meet the Russian royal family in Germany. When Alice supported this suggestion, 'Queen Victoria's indignation with her second daughter knew no bounds'. 'You have entirely taken the Russian side,' she wrote indignantly to Alice, 'and I do not think, dear child that you should tell me... what I ought to do.'[26]

This remonstrance was directed at Alice only two months after the death of Frittie. On the day it was despatched, Alice wrote to her mother in a very different vein:

> I am glad that you have a little coloured picture of my darling. I feel lower and sadder than ever and miss him so much, so continually. There is such a gap between Ernie and Sunny, and the two boys were such a pretty pair, and were to become such companions. Having so many girls, I was so proud of our two boys! The pleasure did not last long, but he is mine more than ever now. He seems near me always, and I carry his precious image in my heart everywhere. That can never fade or die![27]

Indeed the shadow thus cast remained for the rest of her brief life. If its enveloping quality rekindled the strong basic faith of a soul paralysed by intellectual doubt, it was something akin to restoring life to a frozen limb by casting it into a flame. But a much more philosophical and more tender strain was introduced into Alice's letters to her mother; her thoughts kept drifting back to the past and to the memory of her father; increasingly her attentions and affections were wrapped up in her children, especially Ernie; and her overall outlook was summed up in 'the feeling that all is in God's hands, not in ours'.[28]

Alice's seventh and last child was born almost exactly a year after the death of Frittie, on 24th May 1874. On July 11th she was christened Marie Victoria Feodora Leopoldine. Her existence matched Alice's last years, when her maternal instincts, in reaction to Frittie's death, were directed with increased intensity toward her three youngest children. Well aware of the Queen's detestation of breast-feeding, Alice nevertheless wrote of thus feeding baby May, as Louis and she called their last child. May was adored by little Alix and was especially close to Ernie, who wrote, 'Now I was the only son and my mother and I clung to each other.'(29) Sadly the long-standing emotional gap between Alice and her husband, Louis, widened. At the end of 1874 she wrote to him:

> The wound that his [Frittie's] death inflicted on me is not yet healed – and so painful – I sometimes need to talk about it, when my feelings become too much for me to bear – then I feel stronger, again. But I don't do it with you – I know it hurts you – and men react differently to sorrow from women.(30)

In her marriage, Alice yearned for a union of like-minded souls; although Louis cared greatly for her, he was unable to provide the kind of relationship she craved. Three years later, she expressed weary sentiments:

> Do not write any more about what I have said – I am really looking forward to your arrival so much, and I have overcome the old feeling of disappointment which has often made me unhappy in the last few years – and I shall not torment you any more. It takes a few years for a nature which thirsts for strong mutual love and intellectual communion to reach the point of cheerfully and contentedly renouncing what it seeks. I must reach that point, and if God wills, I shall reach it. The more one's own self dies, the more one can be to others, and, renouncing one's own personal desires, live in search of something higher and better. Goodbye, and come soon...(31)

In 1876 Alice underwent painful treatment for a long-standing internal complaint due to backward curvature of the womb. She refused to allow either declining health or chronic fatigue to dent her efforts to help those less fortunate than herself. Whereas the young Queen Victoria had been horrified by poverty but did little to ameliorate it systematically, her daughter Alice worked hard to combat it. In 1877, with the respective deaths of Louis' father and uncle, Louis and Alice succeeded to the titles of Grand Duke and Grand Duchess of Hesse. Alice became a new kind of mother, the Landesmutter, or 'mother of her country'. This put even more social pressures on her from a foreign people who often seemed determined to repay her goodwill with ill will. In this, they resembled her mother, Victoria, to whom she had rendered such exemplary service only to be rewarded with persistent ingratitude and downright truculence. Alice's letters to Victoria display apparent harmony; in truth, she was deeply hurt that the Queen so obviously did not want her in England. Alice would have welcomed a chance to go 'home' at this particular time, as the prospects of returning to the 'narrow-minded, malicious criticism of intolerant interfering people' in Darmstadt positively appalled her.(32)

On December 13th 1877, Alice wrote to Victoria:

> For tomorrow, as ever, my tenderest sympathy! Time shows but more and more what we all lost in beloved Papa; and the older I grow, the more people I know, the more the remembrance of him shines bright as a star of pure lustre than any I have ever known.(33)

The events happening on and immediately after 'the dreadful 14th, of December had long been 'defaced' from Queen Victoria's memory.(34) By contrast, they had burned themselves deeply into the conscious and subconscious life of Princess Alice. Victoria had paid little more than lip-service to Albert's meritocratic visions of England and Europe, whereas, in Germany, Alice had furthered her father's aims by promoting education, medicine and commerce for the under-privileged. When Albert was organising the Great Exhibition, Alice, with her friend and collaborator, the celebrated social reformer, Octavia Hill, had ventured into the worst Cockney slums. In early 1877, she made a similar visit incognito to the poorest parts of Metz. As the year progressed, more and more demands were made upon the new Grand Duchess. The scale of her pioneering efforts conspired against her. Now it was she, above all others, who was constantly being sought out. The effect upon her was uncannily similar to what had happened to her father, all those years before. Her spirit withered. 'Too much is demanded of one,' she wrote to Queen Victoria, 'and I have to do with so many things. It is more than my strength can stand in the long run.'[35] To add to her troubles, she seemed to sense no spirit of gratitude among the so-called 'right people' in Darmstadt.[36] Little did they know what her efforts were costing her; it was akin to a lingering death. During one of her husband's absences from Darmstadt, Alice wrote to Louis:

> I feel only moderately well and certainly not cheerful – I am 'sore' about all the many unkindnesses which the endless gossip and stories about me cause. [There had been malicious stories about her supposed lack of kindness toward the former Grand Duke's wife at the time of his death.] Lies, envy – I am no match for such baseness, and it leaves a sting – because it is the 'foreigner' that they are always carping at. I am so tired of it, so sick of it – why can they not leave me in peace? [37]

For Alice, the stupidity of ministers in Darmstadt, coupled with the petty-mindedness of the 'right people', was such a contrast to England, where Ruskin admired her painting, Carlyle agreed with her philosophy and Dean Stanley understood her compassion. Yet one person in England had the power to ravage her soul. Alice wrote a bitter, undated, black-bordered missive to Louis:

> I have had a letter from Mama – so unfair that it makes me cry with anger. I am so cross that I shall not write about it until I am back in D. I wish I were dead – and it probably will not be too long before I give Mama that pleasure.[38]

In 1878 Alice's family paid a visit to Osborne. It was her last pilgrimage to the scene of her earliest childhood memories, some thirty-three years previously. She was followed back to Darmstadt by her brother, Leopold. Upon learning that Leopold had gone out shooting during his visit, the over-protective Queen irately telegraphed Alice. Her telegram successfully upset all concerned.

Life grew no easier for Alice. In the autumn of 1878 she expressed her dismay about the reported prohibition against certain ostensibly harmless trade-union associations in Darmstadt: 'We are getting back to a real police state, don't you think?' she pointedly asked Louis.[(39)] Of herself she wrote very pessimistically, despite feeling able to say: 'I am perfectly healthy.'[(40)] She was being defeated by her lack of strength, and perhaps, by then, her lack of hope. As with her father, seventeen years previously, something vital seemed to have died within her. On 6th November 1878, she wrote to Queen Victoria:

> I am but very middling and leading a very quiet life, which is an absolute necessity. It is so depressing to be like this. But our home life is always pleasant – never dull however quiet. Only a feeling of weariness and incapacity is itself a trial.[(41)]

Superficially, life was 'ordinary' in the sense of being relaxed and unworthy of any special note. But there is a record, a very full one, of what was really happening at this time. Katherine Macbean, who lived in Darmstadt and was a great friend of Alice's, was standing in for one of the ladies-in-waiting. On 5th November Miss Macbean was having tea with Alice in the New Palace; subsequently she compiled a detailed account of the proceedings of that day and the following days. Alice's daughter, Princess Victoria, complained of a stiff neck; Alice thought it might be mumps. She remarked how comical it would be if the condition was infectious and the entire household caught it. Little more was said about the matter. Miss Macbean played the piano, while everybody danced and made merry. But, the following morning, Victoria was pronounced to have contracted diphtheria, which was not only very infectious but also highly dangerous. Due to her extensive nursing experience, Alice had a particular horror and dread of this disease. With the help of the Lady Superintendent and staff of her hospital, she took personal charge of the nursing arrangements. No sooner was her eldest daughter out of danger than she was summoned to examine six-year-old Alix. On Alix's throat were the dreaded patches of white membrane, indicating diphtheria in its worst form. Alix's condition looked as if it could easily bring on a lethal obstruction of the respiratory tract through membrane formation.

As she redoubled her nursing efforts, Alice was plagued by forebodings, especially for her little daughter May. On the same morning as Alix had shown the disease, May had clambered up on to her mother's bed to kiss her, before playing happily on the floor. By midday, the sinister spots had appeared on her throat too. The thought of losing 'my little pet, my little darling' May drove Alice to the edge of despair.[(42)] Although her daughter Ella escaped, both Irene and Ernie also caught the infection, which finally overcame Louis, reducing that proud military man to half-delirious bravado. 'Well, Katie,' said Alice to Miss Macbean, 'you and I are the only ones who are not ill, and we must not be ill, but there is so much to be done and seen after.'[(43)]

Despite their troubled relationship, Alice continued to find time to send reports to her mother, sometimes, in her pathetic anguish, mentioning that such letters were only for the eyes of the Queen and Princess Beatrice. On 15th November she wrote:

> With a heart rung with pain and fear I write a few lines… And my sweet little May so bad – so bad; will she get through it! My little one – my last! Oh it is agony! …Husband and four children between life and death… [May God] protect them and teach us to say 'Thy Will be Done'. This letter is only for you and Beatrice! Please don't have it copied.[(44)]

That night she went to bed exhausted, only to be disturbed soon afterwards: the doctor came to report that a piece of membrane was blocking May's windpipe. She rushed to the nursery, but it was too late. May had choked to death; she was the second of Alice's precious 'innocents' to be snatched brutally away.[(45)] For agonising hours, Alice sat by the bed, distractedly kissing the face and hands of her lifeless child. The following day, at Balmoral, Victoria received a telegram from Darmstadt. It was brought to her by her faithful servant, John Brown. The granite-like former gillie was weeping like a child. The significance of the telegram was horribly evident. 'We guessed at the truth!' Victoria wrote starkly in her Journal. 'Precious little May was gone!! I know how my darling child adored that little angel.'(46) In her telegram, Alice wrote: 'The pain is beyond words but God's will be done. Our precious Ernie still a source of such terrible fear; the others though not safe, better.'(47)

For the following two weeks Alice had to keep the news of May's death from her other children, who were constantly asking after her and attempting to send her their toys and books. Unsupported by any of her family, in a palace that had become more like a nursing home, Alice was forced to endure the ordeal of a near-secret funeral. Wearing the type of long crêpe veil adopted in Germany for such sad occasions, she walked slowly between the rows of court gentlemen and servants at the bottom of the staircase. She entered the room where the coffin was lying. It was covered with white flowers; two large candles burned on either side and a great palm stood at its head. As Alice prayed near the coffin, her hand went out towards it; she clutched a corner of the white satin pall and pressed it to her lips.

> She paused in going back to her room and told her friend to watch and let her know when the coffin was brought out. Kneeling and looking through the banisters, the Duchess [sic] saw it put into the carriage. Then from the Duke's [sic] sitting room she watched it go out of the gates...(48) (The words, of course, should respectively read 'Grand Duchess' and 'Grand Duke's').

Three days later, Ernie was out of danger; he handed his mother a book, asking her to give it to May. The effort of smiling as if nothing were untoward made Alice reel with nausea. Nevertheless she resolved that 'he must be spared yet awhile what to him will be much sorrow'.(49) Only at the beginning of December was she able to tell him that his sister was dead. The pain and shock to the unusually sensitive little boy was even greater than she had feared; at first, he refused to believe it. As little Ernie sat up in bed, talking disconsolately about May, the tears streaming down his face, Alice's heart broke. Despite her constant involvement in nursing her diphtheria-suffering husband and children, she had remained free of the disease. Highly medically competent, she knew that the golden rule was to avoid, as far as humanly possible, physical contact with the patients. In her agony, she broke that rule by clasping little Ernie to her. It was enough to seal her fate. The moment was immortalised in an address of condolence made to the House of Lords a fortnight later by Disraeli, by then Lord Beaconsfield:

> The Princess Alice – for I will venture to call her by that name, though she wore a Crown – afforded one of the most striking instances that I can remember of richness of culture and rare intelligence combined with the most pure and refined domestic sentiments... My Lords, there is something wonderfully piteous in the immediate cause of her death. The physicians who permitted her to watch over her family enjoined her under no circumstances whatever to be tempted into an embrace. Her admirable self-restraint guarded her through the crises of this terrible complaint in safety. She remembered and observed the injunctions of her physicians. But it became her lot to break to her son, quite a youth, the death of his youngest sister, to whom he was devotedly attached. The boy was so overcome with misery that the agitated mother to console him clasped him in her arms – and thus received a kiss of death. My Lords, I hardly know an incident more pathetic. It is one by which poets might be inspired and in which the artist in every class, whether in picture, in statue or in gem, might find a fitting subject of commemoration.(50)

The 'kiss of death' did not have an immediate effect. Alice started to make plans to take the family away. She got through her days in a sort of unreal calm, thankful that the rest of the family had been spared 'the dreadful reality I went through – and alone…'[51] She went to see her elder sister Vicky at the railway station as she passed through Darmstadt on her way to England. On the same day, she wrote to her mother. It was a letter that, for the first time since the diphtheria had struck, contained a hint of resumed cheerfulness. Yet it was the last letter she ever wrote to the Queen. Alice referred to the nurseries being repapered and to them going away 'from Wednesday to Saturday week' to Heidelberg.[52] It could scarcely have been a more ironically worded forecast. Saturday would have been 21st December; the intervening Saturday was the ever-dreaded anniversary – and even the same day of the week – on which the Prince Consort had died. On that Saturday, 14th December, at 8.30 in the morning, Alice murmured like a sleepy child: 'From Friday to Saturday – four weeks – May…' [It was exactly four weeks since her daughter had died.] And then she said, 'Dear Papa…'[53] These were the last words she ever spoke. Seventeen years afterwards to the day, Alice joined her beloved father in death.

As one account has it:

> It is needless to dwell on the grief caused by this event in the British Isles and throughout the Empire and in Germany, especially in Darmstadt and the district, where the deceased lady was universally beloved. It was severely felt by the Prince and Princess [of Wales] to whom the Princess Alice had been most dear, not only from natural ties, but from the beauty of her character, and above all, from memory of her devoted attendance on her brother when, seven years previously, he lay so near to death at Sandringham.[54]

The Prince and Princess of Wales were at Windsor to attend the annual memorial service for the Prince Consort. When the news from Darmstadt arrived, a grief-stricken Queen Victoria came in to see the Princess of Wales and clasped her in her arms. 'I wish I had died instead of her,' Alix murmured sadly.[55] And yet, in a strange way, Alice's rare, elusive gifts as a peacemaker persisted after her death.

For during the sad days which followed, Queen Victoria learned to love her daughter-in-law as never before and to turn to her more and more for support and comfort... 'Dear Alix has been a real devoted sympathising daughter to me,' the Queen noted; from then onwards, her daughter-in-law's place in her heart was unshakably secure.[56] The Prince and Princess of Wales were shattered by the death of Alice. Bertie wrote to Lord Granville: 'She was my favourite sister. So good, so kind, so clever! We had gone through so much together...'[57] The letter was read out in the House of Lords.

The British public was shocked. 'The first break in my circle of children,' as the Queen described it to Disraeli, produced many columns of eloquent comment – surrounded by heavy black borders – in the *Morning Post* and *The Times*.[58] The latter reminded its readers:

> The humblest of people felt that they had the kinship of nature with a Princess who was the model of family virtue as a daughter, a sister, a wife and a mother... Her abundant sympathies sought for objects of help in the great unknown waste of human distress. She had that rich store of pity which, even more than duty, is the route of philanthropic zeal.[59]

The Illustrated London News felt that 'the lesson of the late Princess's life is as noble as it is obvious. Moral worth is far more of a distinction than high position.'[60]

For Queen Victoria, every quarrel with Alice was as though it had never existed. The monarch was devastated by the first death among her children. She owed so very much to the young girl who had, so abruptly, become a woman in 1861. Although Alice failed to save her father, her life exemplified all that he held dear. No more worthy daughter could have been envisaged. Whereas Albert had guarded Victoria's sanity, Alice had saved the Queen's sanity, her life and her throne. So utterly different in character to the roué Prince of Wales, in also saving her dear brother Bertie's life, she had saved a future King of England.

The grief in Britain was echoed in Darmstadt, where multitudes silently lined the route of Alice's funeral procession. The Prince of Wales was chief mourner. Wrapped in the Union Jack, her coffin was placed in the mausoleum at Rosenhöhe. There is no more touching and evocative monument than that which stands over the spot where Princess Alice rests eternally. The work of the sculptor Boehm, it is a statue of the recumbent Princess with her little daughter May lying in her arms. It is difficult, even now, to enter the Rosenhöhe Mausoleum and gaze upon this statue without a lump forming in one's throat. Such was the tragedy of Alice.

Chapter Nine
Shadows Falling Across History

As a baby, Alix had been known as 'Alicky', 'Sunny' or 'Princess Sunshine'. When Alice died, her personality underwent a radical change:

> The death of her mother, at 35, had a shattering effect on six year old Alix. She sat quiet and withdrawn in her playroom while her nurse stood in the corner, weeping. Even the toys she handled were new; the old familiar toys had been burnt as a precaution against the disease [of diphtheria]. Alix had been a merry, generous, warm little girl, obstinate but sensitive with a hot temper. After this tragedy she began to seal herself off from other people. A hard shell of aloofness formed over her emotions, and her radiant smile appeared infrequently. Craving intimacy and affection, she held herself back. She grew to dislike unfamiliar places and to avoid unfamiliar people. Only in cosy family gatherings where she could count on warmth and understanding did Alix unwind. There, the shy, serious, cool Princess Alix became once again the merry, dimpled, loving 'sunny' of her early childhood.(1)

For Victoria, the first death of one of her nine children erased all bad memories of her often fraught relationship with Alice. As the years went by and Alix became her favourite granddaughter, it was as though a form of healing was taking place. When Alix grew into womanhood, the Queen dreamed of a royal marriage between her and Bertie's son, Prince Albert Victor ('Eddy'). After Bertie, Eddy was next in line to the throne. A wedding between royal cousins would have echoed Victoria's own wedding with her beloved Albert. It would have bound Alix even more closely to her. And, to Victoria's shrewd eye, marriage to a strong woman might just been the making of the listless, ineffectual Eddy. However Alix was unenthusiastic. Nevertheless, cognizant of the call of duty, she braced herself. Victoria confided to Vicky, 'if she is forced she will do it'.(2) Otherwise Alix wanted nothing to do with Eddy. To a resigned Victoria, her cherished granddaughter's decision to turn down 'the greatest position there is' showed 'great strength of character'.(3)

Alix's decision was pivotal to the future of the British royal family for a reason which neither Victoria nor she had any way of knowing. As with her mother Alice, and her sister, Irene, she too was a carrier of haemophilia. Had she married Eddy – or his brother, Georgie, the future King George V, haemophilia would have been re-introduced into the British royal family. Instead she married Nicky, cousin to Eddy and Georgie. Nicky became the ill-fated Czar Nicholas II of Russia. Although it was to be a happy marriage, Victoria was fearful for Alix. 'My blood runs cold when I think of her so young most likely placed on that very unsafe throne...'(4)

Alix's sister, Irene, married her first cousin, Prince Henry of Prussia. Their union resulted in two haemophiliac sons. In an incident which is horribly reminiscent of the demise of Frittie, his cousin Waldemar, the younger son, bled to death at four. Although his brother, Prince Henry, survived into his fifties, it was no longer possible to conceal that the 'bleeding disease' had entered the German imperial family.

In 1901, Queen Victoria died in the arms of Willy, her first grandchild. After so many weary decades of waiting, Bertie finally came to power, as King Edward VII. Today, looking backwards through a hundred years of history and more, the Edwardian age seems a coda to the Victorian one, an hiatus between the fin de siècle and the Great War.

Increasingly power became concentrated in the hands of three cousins. Close friends from childhood, Nicky and Georgie had the most uncanny physical resemblance; they might have been brothers, even twins. Sometimes people had difficulty telling them apart. The third member of the triumvirate – Nicky and Georgie's mutual cousin – was Willy, Kaiser Wilhelm II of Germany. In 1859 when Vicky, the Princess Royal, was pregnant with her first child, she had caught her foot in a chair leg and fallen badly. Vicky believed that, due to the fall, her baby had shifted position in the womb. The birth was difficult and protracted; it ended with forceps. Willy was born with a withered left arm which the royal doctor attributed to nerve damage caused by the foetus having moved position. Other proffered opinions suggest that the use of forceps was crude and clumsy. As we have seen, Vicky's father Albert was ill served by his doctors; it may be that she was equally ill served.

Despite (or because of) her nine children, Victoria had never been enthusiastic about child-rearing. Vicky seems to have inherited this lack of enthusiasm. As a child, Willy adored his mother. Conversely she had little time for him, clearly favouring her second child, Charlotte. 'I am so proud of her [Charlotte] and like to show her off, which I never did with him [Willy] as he was so thin and pale and fretful at her age.'[5] Of course, as we have seen, Charlotte, the self-confessed 'brat', grew into an emotional monster. Charlotte's ability to provoke Vicky would become replicated by her own daughter, Feodora, who would use similar bitter methods against her.

Estranged by his mother, despised by his sister, Willy learned to reject both of them. Whatever the cause of his deformity, it left him with a lifelong tendency to overcompensate, with tendencies which we would now regard as 'macho'. When Willy succeeded his father as Kaiser, he proved to be both bellicose and headstrong – a dangerous combination. Elevated to the title of Empress, a powerless Vicky could only look on with dismay as Germany grew ever more domineering on the European political stage.

As Kaiser, Willy believed in his quasi-divine right to do as he saw fit. As a constitutional monarch, his English cousin Georgie, shared no such delusions. By contrast, Nicky had a fatal lack of self-belief. When his father, Alexander III, died prematurely, Nicky confided miserably in his brother-in-law. 'Sandro, what am I going to do? I am not prepared to be a Czar. I never wanted to become one. I know nothing of the business of ruling.'[6]

From the onset, it was as though the reign of Nicholas II was cursed. During his coronation, more than 3,000 injuries were incurred by the hordes of onlookers. A ship, decorated in honour of the new Czar, sank at Kiev, with 300 lost.

These ominous happenings at the time of his accession and coronation were the beginnings of an almost unbroken series of disasters; fresh misfortunes dogged his steps in a hundred different forms and variations. As if subject to an inevitable curse, all Nicholas's enactments, however well meant they might be, turned out badly.[7]

In 1913 Willy, Georgie and Nicky met for the last time at a wedding celebration. Between them, they held the balance of power from the English Channel to the Bering Straits. The following year, a single Balkan assassination was all it took to unleash a tsunami of political instability. Prince Albert had dreamed of a Europe united by peaceful alliances; in 1914 that dream became nightmare when Europe was riven by chain reactions of opposing alliances. Albert and Victoria's grandson Willy was instrumental in plunging Europe into World War I. In four years of horror, millions died senselessly. Afterwards, Willy was forced to abdicate. A defeated Germany could no longer afford the luxury of a Kaiser.

* * *

Unwittingly Alix had carried haemophilia into the Russian royal family. She had four daughters, Olga, Tatiana, Marie and Anastasia, before providing a long-awaited son and heir. A few months after his birth, little Alexis began bleeding from the navel. When the bleeding persisted for several days, it was obvious to Nicky and Alix that she had passed the dread disease on to her son. The condition worsened. Casual bumps of arms and legs resulted in ominously dark swellings. Bleeding into the joints caused agonising pain. By degrees, Alix became a semi-invalid, spending weeks in bed. Out of bed, he was a near-cripple, forced to wear a cumbersome iron brace to support his legs.

Russia, one of the great powers of the world, was a deeply troubled country, accustomed to being held together by despotic government. The weak and wavering Nicholas lacked many qualities, not least of them single-mindedness of vision. The heir to the Russian throne was a sickly child, seemingly immune to medical help. In despair, his distraught parents turned to the only person who seemed to possess the power to help Alexis. Unfortunately for them, this was the demented spiritualist monk, Rasputin. History has had more than its fair share of crazed mystical figures, such as Joan of Arc in the time of Henry II and Savonarola in the age of the Borgias. Few have done greater and more lasting damage than Rasputin, who enjoyed almost unlimited trust from Alix, the doomed last Czarina.

In the face of medical impotence, how could Rasputin have helped Alexis? In the early years of the 20th century, aspirin was regularly administered as a remedy for haemophilia. In reality, it worsened the condition. By advising against Alexis being given aspirin, Rasputin was giving good advice, however unwitting. It is also probable that the charismatic monk's deep gaze induced a calm, hypnotic state in Alexis, slowing his blood flow, ameliorating his symptoms, and giving him the blessed refuge of sleep. To distraught and impressionable parents, desperate to save their child, these improvements may have seemed evidence of superior powers. However Rasputin's help came at a terrible price.

We have seen how Queen Victoria bequeathed her disdain for child-rearing to Vicky with the result that Willy loathed his mother, disregarded her advice and was only too willing to plunge Germany into a war which it lost catastrophically. From the aged Queen Victoria, secure after more than a half-century of power, her favourite grand-daughter Alexis inherited a similar regal disdain for heeding the views of her subjects. The spectacular events of 1871 had rendered Victoria relatively immune to public censure thereafter. She could show herself to the public or hide herself away, communicate with her subjects or not, as she saw fit. Such laissez-faire was accepted by tolerant, law-abiding British subjects of the 1870s, 1880s and 1890s. In Russia, in the second decade of the twentieth century, it was a recipe for disaster. Consorting with the hated Rasputin heightened the growing peril.

A weak Czar, a distraught Czarina who cared little about public opinion, a crippled heir, tortured by haemophilia, and a crazed holy man, enjoying almost unlimited royal patronage... The scene was set for the Russian Revolution of 1917. When an attempt at poisoning had no visible effect on Rasputin, he was shot repeatedly.

In his time of greatest need, Nicky turned to his English cousin Georgie. But King George V had his own problems. The bitter fighting of the First World War had created an anti-German backlash in Britain. Hastily the British royal family moved to dissociate itself from its German antecedents. In what we would now term a process of re-invention, Battenburg became Mountbatten.

As if the anti-German backlash was not enough, George V had a second, related problem. His grandmother Victoria had ruled for over sixty years. Although outstanding courage had been displayed in the Crimea, in India and in South Africa, overall there had been relatively low levels of military casualties. The reign of George's father, King Edward VII, had been a time of peace. But the wholesale carnage of conflicts such as the Somme had shown a military high command callously unperturbed by the mass slaughter of its subordinates. To shell-shocked survivors, staggering home after four years of hell, rule from above must have seemed dreadfully hollow. Unsurprisingly, anti-monarchism was back in vogue. To George V, fearful of his own throne, providing refuge to a deposed Nicholas II might have been an act of deliberate provocation to the anti-monarchist lobby. Perhaps Nicky could find sanctuary in France, which was already republican, and where little further damage would be done by his presence.

In the event, Nicholas II found refuge neither in England nor in France. He was shot to death, along with his wife Alix, their four daughters, Olga, Tatiana, Marie and Anastasia, and their haemophiliac son, Alexis. The Russian royal family was not even awarded the fundamental human decency of proper burial; their bodies were flung down a mine-shaft. With the fall of the Romanovs, communism engulfed Russia; for the following seventy years, it would threaten the entire world. At the time of Alix's marriage to Nicky, Victoria had worried that her favourite granddaughter was going to an unsafe country, that she was courting danger. The Queen's premonition proved horribly true to an extent that neither she nor anybody else could have conceived. Alice had died tragically. Alix, the 'Sunny' of carefree nursery days, the beloved 'Sunny' of the last Czar, also died tragically. In invidious ways, the scourge of haemophilia had contributed to both deaths.

* * *

Victoria's principle of dynastic marriages for her children had resulted in haemophilia being transmitted from the British royal family to the royal families of Germany and Russia. It was also transmitted into the Spanish royal family. Alice's sister, Princess Beatrice, was yet another carrier. Beatrice, Victoria's youngest child, functioned as her constant companion in old age. Even her marriage to Prince Henry of Battenberg ('Liko') failed to remove her from her mother's side. In 1896 Liko, in a belated attempt to assert his independence, made an ill-advised expedition to South Africa. There he was stabbed to death by Zulu spears. With his demise, a devastated Beatrice clung still closer to Victoria. After Victoria's death in 1901, Beatrice devoted herself to her three sons and her daughter. Two of the sons were haemophilia sufferers. Maurice, Prince of Battenburg, was killed in World War I. His brother, Leopold Mountbatten died in 1922 at the age of thirty two. Inevitably his fate arouses memories of his namesake, who died at almost the same age.

Victoria Eugenie ('Ena'), the youngest daughter of Beatrice, was a transmitter of haemophilia. In 1906 she married King Alfonso XIII of Spain. A year later, they had a son and heir, Prince Asturias, who was a haemophilia sufferer. Although subsequent children were born healthy, Ena's last son, Infante Gonzalo of Spain, was also haemophiliac. Both the affected children were dressed in padded suits to guard against life-threatening bumps and knocks.

As with Kaiser Wilhelm II, King Alfonso attempted to be an absolute, rather than a constitutional, monarch. Although he had inherited a strong throne, by the time of Ena's marriage, it was under severe threat from those who wanted democratic political representation. In addition, there were revolutionary elements at work, to the extent that the royal wedding procession was disrupted by an anarchist's bomb. The haemophilia which had blighted Prince Leopold's career, similarly affected his two Spanish nephews. That one of those sufferers was the heir to the throne, weakened the chances of survival of the royal family in exactly the same way as with Alexis in Russia.

After an abortive war with Morocco in 1921, Alfonso dissolved the Spanish parliament. In 1923, he entered into a military dictatorship with General Primo de Rivera. Unfortunately for the dictators however, elections could not be staved off indefinitely. In 1931 the Republican vote prevailed at the ballot box. Alfonso was defiant. 'I renounce nothing of my rights,' he wrote with not a shred of repentance, 'because, rather than my own, they are a deposit accumulated by history.'(8) Immediately afterwards, he fled to Paris, leaving his family to face the Republican wrath. A distraught Ena remained with her children in the huge, abandoned Palacio Real, while angry mobs gathered outside, shouting 'Viva la Republica!' The palace doors were rammed by a lorry. Rebels scaled the walls and draped a Republican flag from the balcony. In a desperate situation, the Queen and her children made a mad dash for the railway line. A company of Hussars, loyal to the end, helped them. Prince Austrias was the heir to a throne on which he would never sit. Too weak to run, he was carried on board a train for Paris. It was a remarkable escape. Queen Ena and her children joined King Alfonso in exile. Spain was set for a fearful, bloody civil war and forty years of fascist rule thereafter.

Once again, haemophilia had played its part in the collapse of a monarchy. Queen Victoria's seemingly far-sighted policy of dynastic marriages was betrayed by her own biology. Many years before, she had exclaimed in despair, 'Our poor family seems persecuted by this awful disease, the worst I know.'[(9)] Haemophilia, the dreaded 'bleeding disease' has been called at different times the 'Curse of the Romanovs' and the 'Curse of the Bourbons'. It is ironical to reflect that in origin it was the 'Curse of England', perpetrated by Victoria, 'the grandmother of Europe'.[(10)]

Chapter Ten
In Conclusion

Queen Victoria was born in 1819, just four years after the defeat of Napoleon at the Battle of Waterloo; after a reign of almost sixty four years, she died in 1901, at the age of eighty one. Her life spans the greater part of the nineteenth century, which was so pivotal in shaping the course of the twentieth century. When we think of long-reigning English monarchs, it is temptingly easy to forget Victoria's grandfather, George III. Instead we tend to cite the reigns of three women: Queen Elizabeth I, Queen Victoria, and our own Queen Elizabeth II. Intriguingly Queen Victoria's uncle, King William IV, wanted her to be called Elizabeth. For him Victoria, the Anglicisation of her mother's name Victoire, was 'never known here before as a Christian name in this country'. So we very nearly had three long-reigning Queen Elizabeths.

George III brought the status of the British monarchy to a very low ebb indeed. As we have seen, it is likely that his 'madness' was porphyria and, for enduring this most unpleasant malady, he deserves our utmost sympathy. Yet, upon his son's accession, the status of the monarchy sank even lower. When George IV died, in 1830, *The Times* commented that 'there never was an individual less regretted by his fellow creatures than this deceased King'.

Queen Victoria was conceived, literally, as an aspirant to the throne. Her function was to provide material security for her father, the financially distressed former martinet, the Duke of Kent, in his old age. The child of two royal families, she inherited unwelcome antecedents. On the English side, there was a 'mad' grandfather and a bevy of 'disreputable uncles'. On the German side, there was the 'bad blood of the Coburgs'. Both families were rife with dissipation. It was an unpromising position for a future monarch. Being female was another considerable disadvantage.

As we have seen, the young Victoria was subjected to the odious 'Kensington Method' of attempted mind control, in a blatant attempt to break her spirit and reduce her to the status of a puppet on the throne. Her overseas uncle Leopold and her obsessive governess, Louise Lehzen, proved almost her only supporters; a more unlikely pair of allies can scarcely be imagined. Victoria's refusal to cede her powers to Captain Conroy – even on her sickbed – shows her steely mettle. Yet one suspects that, by the time of her uncle King William IV's death and her accession to the throne, her spirit was perilously close to breaking. Her near-fatal physical collapse at Ramsgate in 1835 almost certainly marked an outbreak of porphyria, triggered by prolonged stress.

In her teens, Victoria cheated both nervous breakdown and death. Always she was 'the great survivor'. Gaining the throne proved her salvation, exchanging the odious Conroy for the sympathetic Lord Melbourne, the first of her many prime ministers. With grace and patience, Melbourne mentored her; he was also the first of several politicians who devoted themselves to her. Throughout her life, so many people, from all corners of society, devoted themselves to her.

Victoria's defeat of the Kensington Method came at the price of her psychological balance. Ever afterwards, she was torn between obsessive trust and obsessive distrust. Even as a child, she had evinced the 'Hanoverian temperament' of moodiness. Inflamed by post-natal depression and, most probably, intermittent bouts of porphyria, her mood swings became more extreme, reducing the ever-attentive and solicitous Prince Albert to distraction. Losing Albert in 1861 almost cost Victoria her sanity. Almost certainly it was only the unlikely intervention of the eighteen-year-old Princess Alice that prevented the Queen from becoming as witless as her grandfather, King George III. Following on from George III, the even more detested King George IV and the disrespected King

William IV, another failed monarch would very likely have meant the dissolution of the monarchy – especially after the wave of revolution that had swept Europe in 1848. Victoria's near-seclusion in the 1860s, broken only by her occasional self-serving appearances, gave the anti-monarchist lobby a golden opportunity to denounce her. Without the timely re-appearance of Princess Alice in 1871 to nurse first the Queen, then the Prince of Wales, it is likely that one – or both – would have died. Had the Queen died, it would have left a then weak heir to the throne. Had Bertie died, it would have left a then unpopular queen, with no viable heir. Had both died, which was entirely possible, it would have left too great a power vacuum. Amazingly, for a second time, the monarchy was saved by Alice. It is difficult for us to conceive how much this shy, self-effacing creature rose to the occasion, what tremendous reservoirs of inner strength she deployed. Sadly, those reservoirs were never replenished. Alice showed the same extreme courage, the same utter selflessness as men who have won the Victoria Cross on far-off, bloody battlefields.

In the autumn of Queen Victoria's life, from the 1870s to the turn of the century, most of her subjects had known no other monarch. Her longevity became symbolic of the monarchy as a British institution that had always prevailed and would always prevail. Over a century later, this symbolism has grown. The 'widow of Windsor', the dumpy, severe lady dressed in black, has assumed mythical and affectionate status in our national psyche. There are museums, many statues and many more public houses. For a child, the name Victoria, 'never known here before', has become enduringly popular. The Victoria Cross, originally made from iron taken from captured guns, remains our premier award for valour.

Victoria's longevity has served to obscure the historical status of Albert, arguably the greatest uncrowned King of England. Albert's stiff Teutonic manner hid the soul of a true visionary. It took two World Wars for his dream of a united Europe to come about, although, one imagines, he might retain caustic views over diktat by Brussels. On the domestic front, his Great Exhibition of 1851, that triumphant celebration of the meritocracy of free trade, stands as an exemplar of how such public events may be run. In our own time, the organisers of Olympic Games and Cities of Culture might learn much from him.

Under Victoria's aegis, the British Empire doubled in size, with expansion in India, South Africa, Burma and Egypt, together with the acquisition of New Zealand. Truly it was a golden age. There were relatively few wars, yet, intriguingly, all of them prefigured later themes. The Crimea resonates with subsequent European-Russian conflict, with Balkan instability, and with military adventuring where politicians hector, while brave and hopelessly under-equipped men go out to die for no good purpose. The Indian Mutiny resonates with home rule, not only for India but for so many countries which saw living standards plummet with the departure of their British masters. The end of Victoria's reign was overshadowed by the Boer War, which was confidently expected to 'be over by Christmas' and was not. In the film 'Breaker Morant', the eponymous Morant, who is fighting the Boer commandos at their own merciless game, reflects bitterly that 'it's a new kind of warfare for a new kind of century'. He was right. The brutality of small-scale warfare was there to stay. Only a few weeks after the near-miraculous evacuation at Dunkirk in 1940, British commandos would go back across the Channel in dead of night on what were, effectively, suicide missions. Thus would a combative spirit be kept alive as mainland Europe collapsed into Nazism and the future of civilisation hung in the balance. Commandos begat Special Forces units; warfare had moved away from scarlet uniforms and battleground set-pieces. Increasingly, the enemy became terrorist cells.

Victoria came to the throne, viewed as a lightweight and as being tainted with the bad blood of both English and German royal families. The conduct of her life shows that the 'bad blood' argument was patent nonsense. In place of the sexual, financial and personal scandals of her predecessors, she substituted morality and family values. These were not the virtues of the aristocracy (nor even of certain of her descendants) so much as the values of the emerging affluent middle-class. On an interpersonal level, the Queen always seemed most at ease with the supposedly 'common' people, and then the vigorous, hard-working professionals. Often she seemed to look somewhat askance at members of her own class.

Queen Victoria's instinctive appreciation of what the majority of her subjects wanted was undoubtedly one of her greatest strengths. She didn't need to consult focus groups; she possessed an empathy which went straight to the heart of human affairs. When visiting maimed soldiers from the Crimea and the Boer War, she did not shrink from the most gory of sights. With the Crimean War, the Boer War and the Indian Mutiny, she possessed an abundance of percipience, commonsense, tolerance, humanity and determination. Again and again, when it really mattered, she rose to the occasion triumphantly, seeing the bigger political picture very clearly indeed. In strengthening the role of the British monarch as constitutional and not absolute, she followed instinctively Walter Bagehot's dictum that such a monarch has 'the right to be consulted, the right to advise and the right to warn.'(1) Queen Victoria did her fair share of consultation, of giving advice and of warning. Would that she had been heeded more.

Victoria achieves permanent greatness not because she was Queen but because of her beneficial, lasting influence over the lives of her subjects, and because of the importance of her enduring iconic status. Interestingly, whereas Albert was innovative and Alice was progressive, in many ways Victoria was conservative, even reactionary. For instance, she viewed women as second-class citizens who had no need of the vote. She seems to have been entirely devoid of the irony that the most powerful person in the world was the very woman whom she saw each day in the mirror.

Prince Albert had insisted that the monarchy be above party politics. Often Victoria failed to follow his admonition. Her politics – and her prejudices – were clear to all. Nevertheless the Victorian age saw a slew of legislation protecting British citizens. People had far more rights in 1901 than they had in 1837. Queen Victoria might have been distrustful of change but, when her instincts told her, she could move with the times. Certainly the essential – and very British – moderation of both the Queen and her subjects enabled the country to avoid the political extremism which has plagued so many other nations. France went through two dynasties, then republicanism; Spain went through three monarchs, whose absolutism paved the way for fascism; Italy and Germany saw national unity tainted by militarism. Russia, a country long inured to suffering, moved ever closer to regicide. By contrast, Britain was a haven of peace.

The Elizabethan and Victorian eras will probably always be regarded as golden ages in British history. Upon closer scrutiny however, the England of Elizabeth I resembles nothing so much as a police state, seething with unresolved dissent. The Victorian era compares very favourably indeed. Certainly life on the lower rungs of the social ladder was, by contemporary standards, shocking. As we have seen, when the teenage Victoria visited the Black Country, she was appalled by the 'wretched huts and carts and little ragged children'.[(2)] Throughout her long life, she would be active in many philanthropic organisations; it cannot be said fairly of her that she lacked humanity. Nevertheless her innate political conservatism precluded a more equal distribution of wealth. Albert's innovations, such as the Great Exhibition, and Alice's progressiveness, such as the hospitals and trade organisations she inspired in Germany, suggest directions in which the Queen could have gone but did not. 'Trickle-down' economics can take a long time indeed to reach those most in need; and there is abundant evidence that the Victorian entrepreneurial spirit had its uncaring, even dark side.

Undoubtedly the great virtues of the Victorians were their energy and industry. Today we are awash in Self-Help books. The relatively little known Samuel Smiles (1812-1904) had a life which roughly paralleled that of his illustrious Queen. In 1859, eight years after Albert's Great Exhibition, Smiles published Self-Help.[(3)] It began with the axiom that 'Heaven helps those who help themselves'. With characteristic modesty, Smiles declares that he is a second-rater. He advises us to do like him and profit by learning from the lives of the successful, the illustrious, the great. We may not have their genius, but we can emulate their energy, industry and resolution. Self-Help is characterised by 'Victorian' virtues which are as relevant today as on the day it was written. Currently the Self-Help industry is estimated to have an overall value of $12 billion. It is tragic and ironic that Smiles' invention is all but forgotten. No-one, however sophisticated, could fail to profit from reading it.

Prince Albert's Great Exhibition gave a huge boost to the creation of wealth from technology and commerce. The invention of the telephone and the humble Penny Black stamp (with Victoria's ever-youthful image) would revolutionise communication, while the invention of the car and the train would have a similar effect upon mass movement. In particular, the train would allow the vastness of America to be tamed; it made possible the industrial supremacy which ensured that the US became the predominant superpower of the twentieth century. Meanwhile the electric bulb revolutionised interior lighting. Self-flushing lavatories aided sanitation, as did vacuum cleaners. The camera captured all these historical innovations for posterity. The stiff, wooden demeanour of Queen Victoria and her subjects in photographs was largely a consequence of protracted sittings.

Often it is the foibles of great people which make them fascinating; certainly Victoria had no lack of foibles. The odious Captain Conroy failed to break her spirit, but he stole away her childhood. The impoverished Princess knew that always there would be those who would attempt to make her to a pawn in their games. She would be even more determined to resist.

And yet, above all else, she yearned to love and be loved. When Prince Albert re-entered her life, she practically swooned with delight. That this Adonis could love her for herself and not merely for her position as Queen seemed astounding. From his earliest days, her cousin Albert had been viewed as her partner in an arranged marriage of convenience. Yet he transcended any such mercenary arrangement. Again and again, his many detractors in England were proved wrong. This unknown, penniless foreign princeling was truly made of the stuff of kings. He literally gave his life for his wife and his adopted country.

The love story between Prince Albert and Queen Victoria is one of history's great love stories. It did not take many years for the looks of both partners to fade. This was irrelevant. They had eyes only for each other and, to each other, each remained beautiful. That Albert had to watch constantly over his wife's sanity gives their relationship an added poignancy. No man could have loved his wife more.

The tragedy of Albert's death was the tragedy of Victoria's life. For the next forty years she wore black. As a woman who could never re-marry (and certainly never enjoy illicit relationships) her passion was doomed to be unrequited. Scandalous voices were raised about her relationship with her gillie and personal servant, John Brown. But an abundance of gossip fails to distil into an iota of evidence. If Prince Albert was the love of Victoria's life, it is equally certain that the Queen loved Brown and was loved in return. Both the humble born gillie and the penniless princeling loved the Queen for her own sake and not for her position. Unlike Albert, Brown was wont to abuse his position of royal patronage and employ 'the prerogative of the harlot'. Yet his transgressions were dwarfed by his unwavering loyalty. As with Albert, he gave his life – literally – to the Queen.

Famously Isaac Newton remarked that he stood on other men's shoulders that he might see further through the mists of science. Victoria, 'the great survivor', outlasted so many who devoted themselves to her. These included family members, such as Victoire, Albert and Alice; politicians such as Melbourne and Disraeli; men of action such as Wellington and Peel and members of her household such as Lehzen and Brown.

The popular image of Queen Victoria is that of a black-garbed frump. The public image belies her passionate interior. This is the woman who proposed to her future husband. This is the woman who married a man younger than her (if only by a few months). This is the woman who was unafraid to have her future husband under the same roof as her (however innocently) on the night before their wedding. This is the woman who, after forty years of black-garbed mourning, stipulated that she should have a white funeral. Again and again, Victoria proves to be a creature of paradox. Often she defies popular image; invariably the reality is far more interesting. We imagine the Queen as a prude, perhaps not being aware of the erotica with which Prince Albert and she enlivened their monogamous marriage.

Queen Victoria is possibly the public figure with the greatest number of biographies. We have attempted here to capture her essentially passionate and paradoxical nature. The House of Hanover hid not madness or 'bad blood' per se, but rather the distressing condition of porphyria, possibly an unwonted legacy from Mary, Queen of Scots. Porphyria devastated the lives of Victoria's ancestors and descendants; through diet, cold rooms and seclusion, the Queen seems to have managed the condition instinctively. Her status as a porphyria sufferer makes a mockery of the 'royal malingerer' jibe. Had they known the truth, her many detractors would have tendered sympathy, even pity. If this present volume helps to put the record straight, it will have fulfilled a worthy purpose.

We have seen how haemophilia, the dreaded 'bleeding disease' cursed the lives of so many of Queen Victoria's descendants and ruined her otherwise sagacious policy of dynastic marriages. For all her percipience, not even Victoria could have had an inkling of the scale of the disasters, especially in Russia. Death spared her the pain of knowing the dreadful end of Alix, her favourite granddaughter.

When we consider the death of Albert, with royal doctors 'not fit to attend a sick cat', when we think of the cruel forceps delivery of Wilhelm, when we remember the helplessness of the doctors struggling to save young Frittie and May, we must be grateful that medical science has progressed so much. It is heartbreaking to reflect that so many of those who appear in this book, wealthy, privileged people at the apex of world society, led lives of misery due to ill-health. The sad triumvirate of Vicky, Charlotte and Feodora were victims of another 'royal disease', all the more pernicious for lacking any name or identity. Vicky outlived her mother by a few months only. In truth, the Empress Frederick had little enough to live for; perhaps her early death was merciful. As with Victoria and Alix, she was spared the pain of knowing the terrible evil of the Great War, which her son helped to bring into being.

In the nineteenth century, the age of Victoria, we have an almost complete blueprint for the twentieth century: the end of absolute monarchy, the death of colonialism, the rise of the middle-class, the emergence of mass communications and mass travel, the relentless onset of technology and the creation of popular culture. Royal watching and the cult of celebrity were, perhaps, less wholesome innovations. Terrorism, which was destined to be the plague of the twentieth century, was in evidence; Victoria was fortunate indeed to survive the many attempts at assassination. It is horrible to think that such an essentially benevolent monarch – and a woman – should have been plagued by such threats to her life. Always her 'pluck' prevailed and her spirit remained undiminished. When we consider that the remote fastness of Balmoral sometimes housed the most powerful people in the world, guarded by a single policeman, one yearns for innocence lost, now never to be regained.

Finally, what remains with us most strongly is Queen Victoria's indomitable spirit.

Tired and old as she was at the end, enduring a disastrous week in the Boer War in 1899, she displayed the same 'pluck' with which, as a young girl, she had faced down the odious Conroy over sixty years previously. '. . . we are not interested in the possibilities of defeat. . .'[(4)] she commented, rallying lesser souls around her. Thirteen years later, in 1912, facing defeat and a bitterly lonely death in the icy Antarctic wastes, Captain Scott would write similarly, '. . . we have no cause for complaint'.[(5)] Queen and explorer were united in a vision of self-reliance from which people of all places and times might benefit.

On January 22nd 1901, Queen Victoria died at Osborne in the arms of her grandson, Kaiser Wilhelm. She was buried with Prince Albert in the mausoleum at Frogmore. By her side was one of Albert's dressing gowns. In her hand was a piece of John Brown's hair and a picture of him.

Family Tree

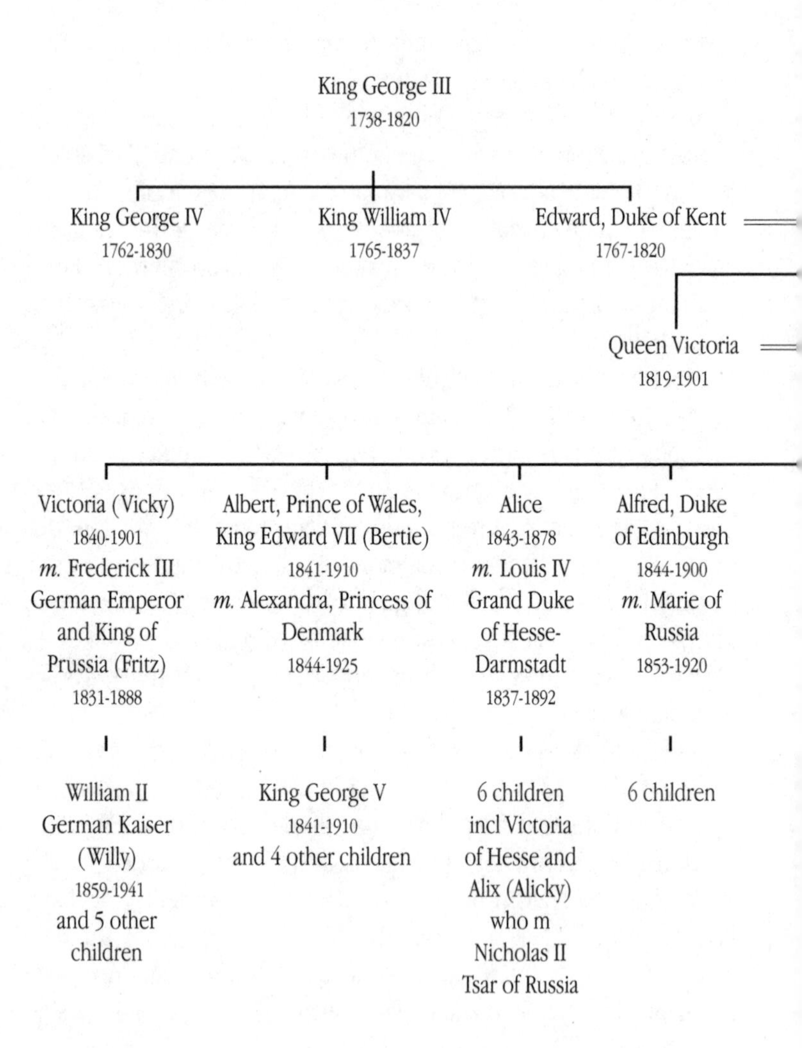
King George III
1738-1820
King George IV
1762-1830
King William IV
1765-1837
Edward, Duke of Kent
1767-1820
Queen Victoria
1819-1901
Victoria (Vicky)
1840-1901
m. Frederick III
German Emperor
and King of
Prussia (Fritz)
1831-1888
Albert, Prince of Wales,
King Edward VII (Bertie)
1841-1910
m. Alexandra, Princess of
Denmark
1844-1925
Alice
1843-1878
m. Louis IV
Grand Duke
of Hesse-
Darmstadt
1837-1892
Alfred, Duke
of Edinburgh
1844-1900
m. Marie of
Russia
1853-1920
William II
German Kaiser
(Willy)
1859-1941
and 5 other
children
King George V
1841-1910
and 4 other children
6 children
incl Victoria
of Hesse and
Alix (Alicky)
who m
Nicholas II
Tsar of Russia
6 children

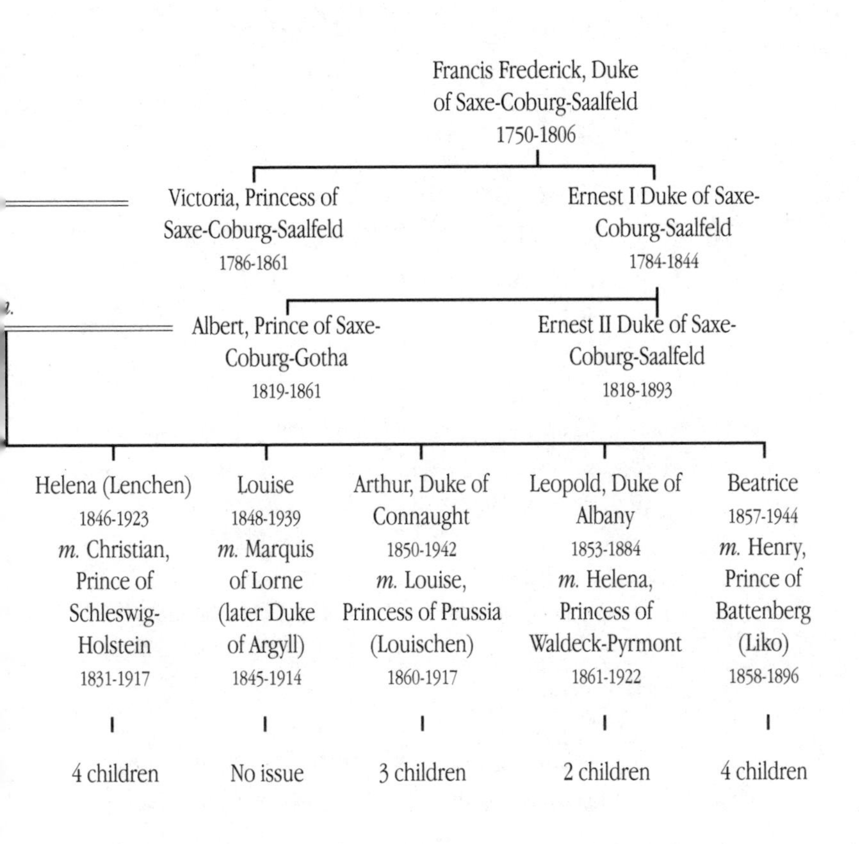

a simplified family tree
showing ancestors and descendants
of

Queen Victoria

Bibliographical Notes

Introduction

1. G. Noel, Princess Alice, Queen Victoria's Forgotten Daughter, 1974
2. C. Woodham-Smith, Queen Victoria, He Life and Times, Vol I, pp. 71
3. J.C.G. Röhl, M. Warren and D. Hunt. Purple Secret: Genes, 'Madness' and the Royal Houses of Europe, (London, 1998) p. 106

Chapter One – The Questionable Madness of George III

1. I. Macalpine and R. Hunter, 'The Insanity of King George III: A Classic Case of Porphyria', British Medical Journal (1966), pp. 65-71.
2. I. Macalpine, R. Hunter and C. Rimington, 'Porphyria in the Royal Houses of Stuart, Hanover and Prussia: A Follow-up Study of George III's Illness', BMJ (1968), pp. 7-18.
3. C. E. Dent to I. Macalpine, 10 January 1966, Macalpine-Hunter Papers (MHP)/Cambridge University Library (CUL)
4. L. Eales and E. B. Dowdle, BMJ, 30 March 1968, pp. 841-2.
5. G. Dean, BMJ, 17 February 1968, p. 443.
6. G. Dean, BMJ, 27 April 1968, p. 224.
7. H. Trevor-Roper, BMJ, 13 April 1968, p. 1105.
8. J. Brooke., King George III, (London, 1972), p. vii-ix.
9. T. B. Macaulay, The History of England From the Accession of James II, (1858) vol. 7, p. 76
10. Purple Secret, p 193.
11. A. Fraser, Mary Queen of Scots, (London, 1969), p. 445.
12. A. Vannotti to C. Rimington, 11 May 1967, MHP, CUL.
13. Purple Secret, p 29.
14. P. Fitzgerald., Royal Dukes and Princesses of the Family of

George III: A View of Court Life and Manners for Seventy Years, 1760-1830 (London, 1882), vol.2, p. 46
15. Purple Secret, p. 94.
16. Zimmermann to King George III, August 1786, quoted in Porphyria – A Royal Malady, British Medical Association, (St Albans, 1968)
17. Purple Secret, p. 95.
18. R. Fulford, ed., Dearest Child: Private Correspondence of Queen Victoria and the Princess Royal, 1858-1861 (London, 1964), p. 335
19. Diary of the Crown Prince (DCP), 23 June 1858, Archiv der Hessischen Hausstiftung, Schloss Fasanerie, (AHH) 21 October – 10 November 1861
20. DCP, 11 June 1862, AHH
21. Diary of the Crown Prince (DCP), 7 and 18 October and 25 December 1864, Archiv der Hessischen Hausstiftung, Schloss Fasanerie (AHH)
22. Quoted in Purple Secret, p. 122
23. Vicky to Fritz 24 April 1868, DCP, 21-24 April 1868, AHH
24. Vicky to Fritz, 26 April 1868; DCP, 26 April 1868, AHH
25. Vicky to Fritz, 29 April 1868, AHH
26. Vicky to Fritz, 11 November 1866, AHH, DCP
27. Quoted in Purple Secret, p. 126
28. Quoted in Fulford, Dearest Mama, p. 84.
29. Quoted Ibid.
30. Vicky to Queen Victoria, 24 and 26 March 1891, Royal Archives, Z50/24, 26
31. Vicky to Queen Victoria, 6 August 1891, Royal Archives, Z51/7
32. Charlotte to Ellen Heldburg, 29 October and 18 November 1902, ThStaMgn, HA 343
33. Charlotte to Ellen Heldburg, 16 November 1905, ThStaMgn, HA 207
34. Charlotte to Lena Schweninger, 7 April 1906, Bundesarchiv Berlin, Schweninger Papers (BABSP)
35. Charlotte to Lena Schweninger, 30 October 1909, (BABSP)
36. Quoted in Purple Secret, p. 215
37. Quoted Ibid.
38. H.E. Bellringer to Röhl, Warren and Hunt, 5 February 1996
39. Quoted in Purple Secret, p. 219
40. G. Dean, British Medical Journal, 27 April 1968, p. 224
41. I. Macalpine and R. Hunter, 'The Insanity of King George III: A Classic Case of Porphyria', British Medical Journal (1966), pp. 65-71.
42. I. Macalpine, R. Hunter and C. Rimington, 'Porphyria in the Royal Houses of Stuart, Hanover and Prussia: A Follow-up Study of George III's Illness', BMJ (1968), pp. 7-18.

Chapter Two – The Child Prisoner of Kensington Palace

1. 'The Tight Little Island' (song), written and composed by Thomas John Dibdin, quoted in C. Woodham-Smith, Queen Victoria Her Life and Times, Volume 1 (1819 – 1861) (London 1972), p 1.
2. William Wilberforce, speaking in the House of Commons in April 1818 after the death of Princess Charlotte. Hansard, Parliamentary Debates, Vol. 38, pp.132-3.
3. Quoted in C. Woodham-Smith, Queen Victoria Her Life and Times, Volume 1 (1819 – 1861) (London 1972), p 3.
4. Quoted in S. Weintraub, Victoria: Biography of a Queen, (London 1987), p. 25
5. Quoted in C. Woodham-Smith, Queen Victoria Her Life and Times, Volume 1 (1819 – 1861) (London 1972), p. 4.
6. Quoted in S. Weintraub, Victoria: Biography of a Queen, (London 1987), pp. 24-25
7. Quoted in G. St Aubyn, Queen Victoria: A Portrait, (London, 1991), p.2
8. Quoted in C. Woodham-Smith, Queen Victoria Her Life and Times, Volume 1 (1819 – 1861) (London 1972), p. 9.
9. Rev. E. Neale, Life of H.R.H. Edward Duke of Kent, 1850, preface, p. xii, quoting a letter to the author from 'a man of high rank'.
10. Ibid.
11. Quoted in G. St Aubyn, Queen Victoria: A Portrait, (London, 1991), p.9
12. Ibid.
13. Royal Archives, M2/2, 3, 8, letter of recommendation from Princess Charlotte, 19 August 1816; Duke of Kent's proposal, n.d.; Princess Charlotte to Princess Victoire, 10 October 1816, trans.
14. Quoted in C. Woodham-Smith, Queen Victoria Her Life and Times, Volume 1 (1819 – 1861) (London 1972), p. 44.
15. Ibid.
16. Quoted in S. Weintraub, Victoria: Biography of a Queen, (London 1987), pp. 24-25
17. Quoted in G. St Aubyn, Queen Victoria: A Portrait, (London, 1991), p.11
18. Quoted in Cecil Woodham-Smith, Queen Victoria Her Life and Times, Volume 1 (1819 – 1861) (London 1972), p. 56
19. Duke of Kent to Duke of Wellington, 4 December 1818. Conroy Papers, Balliol College

Library, Oxford
20. Ibid
21. Quoted in Cecil Woodham-Smith, Queen Victoria Her Life and Times, Volume 1 (1819 – 1861) (London 1972), p. 57
22. Ibid.
23. Quoted in Stanley Weintraub, Victoria: Biography of a Queen, (London 1987), p. 52
24. Ibid.
25. Ibid.
26. Quoted in Stanley Weintraub, Victoria: Biography of a Queen, (London 1987), p. 53
27. Ibid
28. Quoted in Cecil Woodham-Smith, Queen Victoria Her Life and Times, Volume 1 (1819 – 1861) (London 1972), p. 51
29. Charles Greville, The Greville Memoirs 1814-1860, ed. Lytton Strachey and Roger Fulford, 8 vols., Macmillan, 1938, Vol IV, p. 218
30. Royal Archives (RA), Windsor Castle, Queen Victoria's Journal, M7/67 and Add.V2, memorandum by Charles, Prince of Leiningen, 1840, trans.
31. Quoted in Cecil Woodham-Smith, Queen Victoria Her Life and Times, Volume 1 (1819 – 1861) (London 1972), p. 64
32. Ibid.
33. Ibid.
34. Ibid, p. 66
35. Greville, Vol. II, p. 194
36. RA Queen Victoria's Journal, M7/67 and Add.V2, memorandum by Charles, Prince of Leiningen, 1840, trans.
37. Ibid.
38. Conroy Papers. Balliol College Library.
39. RA Queen Victoria's Journal, M7/67 and Add.V2, memorandum by Charles, Prince of Leiningen, 1840, trans.
40. Ibid.
41. Quoted in Giles St Aubyn, Queen Victoria: A Portrait, (London, 1991), p.16
42. Ibid., p.17
43. Ibid., p.25
44. Ibid.
45. Ibid.
46. Ibid.
47. Quoted in Stanley Weintraub, Victoria: Biography of a Queen, (London 1987), p. 70
48. Quoted in Queen Victoria Her Life and Times, p. 79
49. Quoted Ibid
50. Quoted in Queen Victoria: A Portrait, (London, 1991), p.32
51. Quoted Ibid, p.31
52. Quoted Ibid, p.34
53. Quoted Ibid, p.37
54. Quoted Ibid, p.38

55. Quoted Ibid, p.50
56. Quoted Ibid.
57. Quoted Ibid, p.52
58. Quoted Ibid, p.53
59. Quoted Ibid, p.54
60. Quoted Ibid.
61. Quoted in Queen Victoria Her Life and Times, p. 135
62. Quoted in Queen Victoria: A Portrait, p.55
63. Quoted in Queen Victoria Her Life and Times, p. 137
64. Quoted Ibid.
65. Quoted Ibid., p. 138

Chapter Three – Queen Albertine

1. Quoted in Queen Victoria Her Life and Times, Volume I, p. 5
2. Quoted in Queen Victoria: A Portrait, p. 42
3. Quoted Ibid, p. 43
4. Quoted Ibid
5. Quoted Ibid
6. Quoted Ibid
7. Quoted Ibid, pp. 44-45
8. Quoted Ibid, p. 45
9. Quoted Ibid
10. Quoted Ibid, p. 46
11. Quoted Ibid
12. Quoted Ibid
13. Quoted Ibid, p. 125
14. Quoted Ibid
15. Quoted Ibid
16. Quoted Ibid, p. 125-126
17. Quoted Ibid, p. 126
18. Quoted Ibid
19. Quoted Ibid, p. 129
20. Quoted Ibid
21. Quoted Ibid
22. RA Melbourne Papers, Melbourne to Russell, 13 October 1839.
23. Quoted in Queen Victoria: A Portrait, p. 127
24. Quoted Ibid, p. 129
25. Quoted Ibid
26. Quoted Ibid
27. Quoted Ibid
28. Quoted in Victoria: Biography of a Queen, p. 130
29. Quoted Ibid.
30. Quoted Ibid, p. 129
31. Quoted Ibid
32. Quoted Ibid, p. 130
33. Quoted Ibid
34. Quoted Ibid
35. Quoted Ibid
36. Quoted Ibid??, p. 135
37. Quoted Ibid??, p. 136
38. Quoted Ibid??, p. 138
39. Quoted Ibid??, p. 139
40. Quoted Ibid
41. Quoted Ibid
42. Quoted Ibid, p. 140
43. Quoted in Queen Victoria: A Portrait, p. 127
44. Quoted Ibid., 143
45. Quoted Ibid.
46. Quoted Ibid., 150
47. Quoted in Victoria: Biography of a Queen, p. 143

48. Quoted Ibid.
49. Quoted Ibid, p.144
50. Quoted Ibid.
51. Quoted in Queen Victoria: A Portrait, p. 159
52. Quoted in Victoria: Biography of a Queen, p. 144
53. Quoted Ibid
54. Quoted in Queen Victoria: A Portrait, p. 168
55. Quoted Ibid
56. Quoted Ibid
57. Quoted Ibid
58. Quoted in Victoria: Biography of a Queen, pp. 144-145
59. Quoted in Queen Victoria: A Portrait, p. 160
60. Ibid., p. 161
61. Ibid., p. 160
62. Quoted in Victoria: Biography of a Queen, p. 146
63. Quoted in Queen Victoria: A Portrait, p. 161
64. Quoted Ibid., p. 180
65. Quoted in Victoria: Biography of a Queen, p. 149
66. Quoted Ibid., p. 150
67. Quoted Ibid.
68. Quoted Ibid., pp. 150-151
69. Quoted Ibid., p. 150
70. Quoted Ibid., p. 153
71. Quoted in Queen Victoria: A Portrait, p. 162
72. Quoted Ibid.
73. Quoted in Victoria: Biography of a Queen, p. 155
74. Quoted in Queen Victoria: A Portrait, pp. 162-163
75. Quoted Ibid, p. 163
76. Quoted Ibid.
77. Quoted Ibid.
78. Quoted Ibid, p. 159.
79. Quoted Ibid.
80. Quoted Ibid.
81. Quoted in Victoria: Biography of a Queen, p. 157
82. Quoted in Queen Victoria: A Portrait, p. 167
83. Quoted Ibid, p. 208.
84. Quoted Ibid, p. 275.
85. Quoted Ibid,
86. Quoted Ibid.
87. Quoted Ibid, p. 276.
88. Quoted Ibid.
89. Quoted Ibid.
90. Quoted Ibid, p. 277.
91. Quoted in Victoria: Biography of a Queen, p. 159
92. Quoted Ibid
93. Quoted Ibid, p. 160
94. Quoted in Queen Victoria: A Portrait, p. 171-172
95. Quoted Ibid., 172
96. Quoted Ibid., 173
97. Quoted Ibid.
98. Quoted Ibid.
99. Quoted Ibid.
100. Quoted Ibid.
101. Quoted Ibid.
102. Quoted Ibid, p. 174.

103. Quoted Ibid.
104. Quoted Ibid, p. 173.
105. Quoted Ibid, p. 174.
106. Quoted Ibid.
107. Quoted Ibid, p. 175.
108. Quoted Ibid.
109. Quoted in Victoria: Biography of a Queen, p. 167
110. Quoted Ibid.
111. RA, Queen Victoria's Journal, 25 April 1843
112. RA, Y55/9, confidential family papers, 25 April 1843
113. Quoted in Princess Alice, Queen Victoria's Forgotten Daughter, p. 21
114. RA, Queen Victoria's Journal, 25 April 1843
115. E. Longford, Victoria R.I.., p. 66
116. D. Cecil, Lord M (London, 1954), p. 314.
117. RA M51/118, 25 April 1843
118. RA Y91/10, 16 May 1843
119. Quoted in Queen Victoria: A Portrait, p. 183
120. Quoted in Victoria: Biography of a Queen, p. 178
121. Quoted in Queen Victoria: A Portrait, p. 183
122. Quoted Ibid.
123. Quoted in Victoria: Biography of a Queen, p. 187
124. Quoted Ibid.
125. Quoted Ibid.
126. Quoted Ibid, p 188.
127. Quoted Ibid.
128. Quoted Ibid, p. 197.
129. Quoted Ibid, p. 198.
130. Quoted Ibid, p. 196.
131. Quoted Ibid, p. 198.
132. Quoted Ibid.
133. Quoted in Queen Victoria: A Portrait, p. 234.
134. Quoted Ibid, p. 235.
135. Quoted in Victoria: Biography of a Queen, p. 208
136. Quoted in Queen Victoria: A Portrait, p. 235.
137. Quoted Ibid, pp. 235-6.
138. Quoted in Victoria: Biography of a Queen, p. 215
139. Quoted Ibid. p. 215
140. Quoted Ibid. pp. 215-7
141. Quoted Ibid. p. 217
142. Quoted Ibid.
143. Quoted in Queen Victoria: A Portrait, p. 228
144. Quoted Ibid. p. 229
145. Quoted in Victoria: Biography of a Queen, p. 218
146. Quoted Ibid.
147. Quoted Ibid.
148. Quoted Ibid, pp. 218-9.
149. Quoted Ibid, p. 219.
150. Quoted Ibid
151. Quoted Ibid, p. 220
152. Quoted Ibid
153. Quoted in Queen Victoria: A Portrait, p. 230
154. Quoted in Victoria: Biography of

a Queen, p. 221
155. Quoted Ibid.

Chapter Four – Another Death in the Blue Room

1. Quoted in Victoria: Biography of a Queen, p. 225
2. Quoted Ibid, p. 224
3. Quoted in Queen Victoria: A Portrait, p. 259
4. Quoted in Victoria: Biography of a Queen, p. 224
5. Quoted Ibid, p. 226
6. Quoted in Queen Victoria: A Portrait, p. 208
7. Quoted Ibid
8. Quoted Ibid, p. 209
9. Quoted Ibid, p. 277
10. Quoted Ibid, p. 220
11. Quoted in Victoria: Biography of a Queen, p. 231
12. Quoted in Queen Victoria: A Portrait, p. 221
13. Quoted in Victoria: Biography of a Queen, p. 231
14. Quoted Ibid
15. Quoted Ibid, p. 233
16. Quoted in Queen Victoria: A Portrait, p. 293
17. Quoted Ibid, p. 294
18. Quoted in Victoria: Biography of a Queen, p. 232
19. Quoted Ibid, p. 234
20. Quoted Ibid, p. 234
21. Quoted Ibid, p. 234
22. Quoted in Queen Victoria: A Portrait, p. 241
23. Quoted Ibid, p. 293
24. Quoted in Victoria: Biography of a Queen, p. 235
25. Quoted in Queen Victoria: A Portrait, p. 297
26. Quoted Ibid, p. 294
27. Quoted Ibid
28. Quoted Ibid
29. Quoted Ibid, p. 295
30. Quoted Ibid, pp. 295-6
31. Quoted in Victoria: Biography of a Queen, p. 243
32. Quoted Ibid, p. 242
33. Quoted Ibid
34. Quoted Ibid
35. Quoted Ibid, p. 244
36. Quoted Ibid, p. 246
37. Quoted Ibid, p. 253
38. Quoted in Queen Victoria: A Portrait, p. 296
39. Quoted Ibid
40. Quoted Ibid, p 303
41. Quoted Ibid
42. Quoted Ibid
43. Quoted Ibid
44. Quoted in Victoria: Biography of a Queen, p. 260
45. Quoted in Queen Victoria: A Portrait, p. 306
46. Quoted Ibid
47. Quoted Ibid
48. Quoted Ibid, pp. 306-7
49. Quoted Ibid, pp. 307

50. Quoted Ibid
51. Quoted Ibid
52. Quoted in Victoria: Biography of a Queen, p. 261
53. Quoted in Queen Victoria: A Portrait, p. 307
54. Quoted Ibid, p. 307-8
55. Quoted Ibid, p. 308
56. Quoted in Victoria: Biography of a Queen, p. 264
57. Quoted Ibid
58. Quoted Ibid
59. Quoted in Victoria: Biography of a Queen, p. 267
60. Quoted Ibid, p. 268
61. Quoted Ibid
62. Quoted Ibid
63. Quoted Ibid
64. Quoted Ibid, p. 274
65. Quoted Ibid
66. Quoted Ibid, p 278
67. Quoted Ibid
68. Quoted Ibid, p 269
69. Quoted Ibid, p 274
70. Quoted Ibid
71. Quoted Ibid, p 275
72. Quoted Ibid, p 280
73. Quoted Ibid, p 282
74. Quoted Ibid
75. Quoted Ibid
76. Quoted Ibid
77. Quoted Ibid, p 283
78. Quoted Ibid
79. Quoted Ibid, p 287
80. Quoted Ibid, p 288
81. Quoted Ibid
82. Quoted Ibid
83. Quoted Ibid, pp 287-8
84. Quoted Ibid, pp 289
85. Quoted in Queen Victoria: A Portrait, p. 318
86. Quoted Ibid
87. Quoted Ibid
88. Quoted Ibid, p 319
89. Quoted in Victoria: Biography of a Queen, p. 290
90. Quoted Ibid
91. Quoted in Queen Victoria: A Portrait, p. 318
92. Quoted in Victoria: Biography of a Queen, pp. 289-90
93. Quoted Ibid, p.290
94. Quoted Ibid
95. Quoted in Queen Victoria: A Portrait, p. 318
96. Quoted Ibid
97. Quoted Ibid
98. Quoted Ibid
99. Quoted Ibid
100. Quoted Ibid
101. Quoted Ibid, pp 318-9
102. Quoted Ibid, p 319
103. Quoted Ibid, p 318
104. Quoted Ibid
105. Quoted in Victoria: Biography of a Queen, p. 274
106. Quoted in Queen Victoria: A Portrait, p. 276
107. Quoted Ibid
108. Quoted in Victoria: Biography of

a Queen, p. 291
109. Quoted in Queen Victoria: A Portrait, p. 278
110. Quoted in Victoria: Biography of a Queen, p. 291
111. Quoted Ibid, p. 292
112. Quoted Ibid
113. Quoted Ibid
114. Quoted Ibid
115. Quoted in Queen Victoria: A Portrait, p. 322
116. Quoted Ibid
117. Quoted Ibid, p. 323
118. Quoted Ibid
119. Quoted in Victoria: Biography of a Queen, p. 292
120. Quoted Ibid, p. 293
121. Quoted Ibid, p. 292
122. Quoted Ibid
123. Quoted Ibid, p. 293
124. Quoted in Queen Victoria: A Portrait, p. 324
125. Quoted in Victoria: Biography of a Queen, p. 294
126. Quoted Ibid
127. Quoted Ibid, p. 295
128. Quoted Ibid
129. Quoted Ibid
130. Quoted Ibid, p. 287
131. Quoted in Queen Victoria, Her Life and Times, Volume 1, p. 423
132. Quoted Ibid, p. 424
133. Quoted in Queen Victoria: A Portrait, p. 325
134. Quoted Ibid
135. Quoted in Victoria: Biography of a Queen, p. 297
136. Quoted Ibid, p. 297
137. Quoted in Queen Victoria: A Portrait, p. 326
138. Quoted in Victoria: Biography of a Queen, p. 296
139. Quoted Ibid
140. Quoted in Queen Victoria: A Portrait, p. 326
141. Quoted in Victoria: Biography of a Queen, p. 297
142. Quoted Ibid
143. Quoted Ibid, p. 298
144. Quoted Ibid, p. 297
145. Quoted Ibid, pp. 297-8
146. Quoted Ibid, p. 298
147. Quoted Ibid
148. Quoted Ibid
149. Quoted Ibid, p. 299
150. Quoted Ibid, p. 298
151. Quoted Ibid, p. 299
152. Quoted Ibid
153. Quoted in Queen Victoria: A Portrait, p. 327
154. Quoted in Victoria: Biography of a Queen, p. 299
155. Quoted Ibid, p. 300
156. Quoted Ibid
157. Quoted Ibid
158. Quoted in Queen Victoria: A Portrait, p. 327
159. Quoted in Victoria: Biography of a Queen, p. 300
160. Quoted Ibid, p. 301

161. Quoted in Queen Victoria: A Portrait, p. 327
162. Quoted Ibid
163. Quoted Ibid
164. Quoted Ibid

Chapter Five – An Unexpected Saviour of Sanity

1. Quoted in Queen Victoria: A Portrait, p. 129
2. Quoted Ibid
3. Quoted Ibid
4. Quoted Ibid, p. 168
5. Quoted Ibid, p. 152
6. Quoted Ibid
7. Quoted Ibid
8. Quoted Ibid, p. 149
9. Quoted Ibid
10. Quoted Ibid
11. Quoted Ibid
12. Quoted Ibid
13. Quoted Ibid, p. 126
14. Quoted Ibid, p. 158
15. Quoted Ibid
16. Quoted Ibid
17. Quoted Ibid
18. Quoted Ibid
19. Quoted Ibid
20. Quoted Ibid, p. 172
21. Quoted Ibid
22. Quoted Ibid, p. 159
23. Quoted Ibid
24. Quoted Ibid
25. Quoted Ibid
26. Quoted Ibid
27. Quoted Ibid
28. Quoted Ibid
29. Quoted Ibid, p. 165
30. Quoted Ibid
31. Quoted Ibid
32. Quoted Ibid, p. 167
33. Quoted Ibid
34. Quoted Ibid
35. Quoted Ibid
36. Quoted Ibid
37. Quoted Ibid, p. 208
38. Quoted Ibid
39. Quoted Ibid, p. 204
40. Quoted Ibid
41. Quoted Ibid, p. 169
42. Quoted Ibid, p. 170
43. Quoted Ibid, p. 169
44. Quoted Ibid
45. Quoted Ibid
46. Quoted Ibid, p. 169
47. Quoted Ibid, p. 170
48. Quoted Ibid
49. Quoted in Victoria: Biography of a Queen, pp. 289-290
50. Quoted in Queen Victoria: A Portrait, p. 333
51. Quoted in Queen Victoria: A Portrait, p. 318
52. Quoted Ibid, p. 328
53. Quoted Ibid
54. Quoted Ibid
55. Quoted in Victoria: Biography of a Queen, p. 297
56. Quoted Ibid, p. 305
57. Quoted in Queen Victoria: A

Portrait, p. 328
58. Quoted in Victoria: Biography of a Queen, p. 316
59. Quoted in Queen Victoria: A Portrait, p. 328
60. Quoted Ibid
61. Quoted Ibid
62. Quoted Ibid
63. Quoted Ibid
64. Quoted Ibid
65. Quoted Ibid, p. 329
66. Quoted Ibid
67. Quoted Ibid, p. 330
68. Quoted in Princess Alice: Queen Victoria's Forgotten Daughter, p.81
69. E. Fitzmaurice, The Life of Granville, (London, 1905), p: 405
70. Quoted in Princess Alice: Queen Victoria's Forgotten Daughter, p.81
71. Alice Grand Duchess of Hesse – Biographical Sketch and Letters (London: John Murray 1884), p. 9
72. Quoted in Princess Alice: Queen Victoria's Forgotten Daughter, p.31
73. Alice Grand Duchess of Hesse – Biographical Sketch and Letters, p. 6
74. K. Jagow (ed.), Letters of the Prince Consort, John Murray, (London 1938) p. 233
75. Quoted in Princess Alice: Queen Victoria's Forgotten Daughter, p.70
76. E.C. Kenyon, Scenes in the Life of Princess Alice, p. 64
77. State (formerly Grandducal) Archives, Darmstadt, Box 26, No. 4 (II), 3 December 1868
78. G. Barnett-Smith, Queen Victoria, (London 1901) p. 351
79. C. Jerrold, The Widowhood of Queen Victoria, (London 1916) p. 20
80. State (formerly Grandducal) Archives, Darmstadt, Box 23, No.1, 1 January 1862
81. Alice Grand Duchess of Hesse – Biographical Sketch and Letters, p. 20
82. G. Villiers, A Vanished Victorian, p. 309 'The Alice Hospital', Prince Louis of Hesse's 1953 lecture
83. H. Bolitho, A Century of British Monarchy, p. 75
84. The Times, 17 December 1861
85. Alice Grand Duchess of Hesse – Biographical Sketch and Letters, p. 398
86. Quoted in Queen Victoria: A Portrait, p. 331
87. Quoted in Victoria: Biography of a Queen, p. 305
88. Quoted Ibid, p. 307
89. Quoted Ibid
90. Quoted Ibid
91. Quoted in Queen Victoria: A

Portrait, p. 330
92. Quoted Ibid
93. Quoted Ibid
94. Quoted Ibid
95. Quoted Ibid
96. Quoted Ibid
97. Quoted Ibid, p. 329
98. Quoted Ibid
99. Quoted Ibid
100. Quoted in Victoria: Biography of a Queen, p. 304
101. Quoted in Queen Victoria: A Portrait, p. 189
102. Quoted Ibid
103. Quoted Ibid
104. Quoted Ibid
105. Quoted Ibid, p. 331
106. Quoted Ibid
107. Quoted in Victoria: Biography of Queen, p. 313
108. Quoted Ibid
109. Quoted Ibid
110. S. Erskine (ed.), Twenty Years at Court, p. 394
111. Quoted in Victoria: Biography of a Queen, p. 314
112. Quoted Ibid
113. Quoted Ibid
114. Quoted Ibid, p. 315
115. Quoted Ibid, p. 314
116. Quoted Ibid
117. Quoted Ibid
118. Quoted Ibid
119. Quoted Ibid
120. Quoted Ibid
121. Quoted Ibid, p. 315
122. Quoted in Queen Victoria: A Portrait, p. 333
123. Quoted Ibid
124. Quoted Ibid
125. Quoted in Victoria: Biography of a Queen, p. 316
126. Quoted Ibid, pp. 316-7
127. Quoted Ibid
128. Quoted Ibid, p. 317
129. Quoted Ibid
130. Quoted Ibid
131. Quoted Ibid
132. Quoted Ibid
133. Quoted in Queen Victoria: A Portrait, p. 330
134. Quoted Ibid, p. 330-1
135. Quoted in Victoria: Biography of a Queen, p. 318
136. Quoted in Queen Victoria: A Portrait, p. 333
137. Quoted Ibid

Chapter Six – The Monarchy in Peril

1. Quoted in Victoria: Biography of a Queen, p. 309
2. Quoted Ibid, p. 310
3. Quoted Ibid
4. Quoted Ibid, p. 312
5. Quoted in Queen Victoria: A Portrait, p. 331
6. Quoted Ibid, p. 331
7. Quoted Ibid
8. Quoted in Victoria: Biography of

a Queen, p. 313
9. Quoted Ibid
10. Quoted Ibid
11. Quoted Ibid
12. H. Dyson and C. Tennyson (eds), Dear and Honoured Lady, p. 51 (New Jersey, 1971)
13. H. Bolitho (ed.), Further Letters of Queen Victoria, 26 May 1862 (London, 1938)
14. E. Longford, Victoria R.I. p. 309 (London, 1964)
15. Quoted in Victoria: Biography of a Queen, p. 318
16. Quoted Ibid
17. A.L. Kennedy (ed.), My Dear Duchess, (London 1956) p. 197
18. Quoted in Victoria: Biography of a Queen, p. 319
19. Quoted Ibid
20. Quoted Ibid
21. Quoted Ibid
22. Quoted Ibid, p. 321
23. Quoted Ibid
24. Quoted Ibid
25. Quoted Ibid, p. 322
26. Quoted Ibid, p. 323
27. Quoted Ibid
28. Quoted in Queen Victoria: A Portrait, p. 330
29. Quoted Ibid
30. Quoted Ibid
31. Quoted in Victoria: Biography of a Queen, p. 335
32. Quoted Ibid
33. Quoted in Queen Victoria: A Portrait, p. 333
34. Quoted Ibid
35. Quoted Ibid
36. Quoted Ibid
37. Quoted Ibid
38. Quoted Ibid, p. 349
39. Quoted Ibid
40. Quoted Ibid
41. Quoted in Queen Victoria: A Portrait, p. 332
42. Quoted Ibid
43. Quoted Ibid, p. 333
44. Quoted Ibid
45. Quoted in Victoria: Biography of a Queen, p. 326
46. Quoted Ibid, p. 327
47. Quoted Ibid, p. 328
48. Quoted Ibid, p. 327
49. Quoted Ibid, p. 329
50. Quoted Ibid
51. Quoted Ibid
52. Quoted Ibid
53. Quoted Ibid
54. Quoted Ibid, p. 330
55. Quoted Ibid, p. 331
56. Quoted Ibid
57. Quoted Ibid
58. Quoted Ibid, p. 332
59. Quoted in Queen Victoria: A Portrait, p. 344
60. Quoted Ibid
61. Quoted Ibid
62. Quoted in Victoria: Biography of a Queen, p. 333

63. Quoted Ibid
64. Quoted Ibid
65. Quoted in Victoria: Biography of a Queen, p. 333
66. Quoted Ibid
67. Quoted Ibid
68. Quoted Ibid, p. 334
69. Quoted Ibid
70. Quoted Ibid
71. Quoted Ibid
72. Quoted Ibid, p. 335
73. Quoted Ibid
74. Quoted Ibid
75. Quoted Ibid
76. Quoted Ibid, p. 343
77. Quoted Ibid
78. Quoted Ibid, pp. 343-4
79. Quoted Ibid, p. 344
80. Quoted Ibid
81. Quoted Ibid, p. 347
82. Quoted Ibid
83. Quoted Ibid, p. 346
84. Quoted Ibid
85. Quoted Ibid
86. Quoted Ibid, pp. 346-7
87. Quoted Ibid, p. 347
88. Quoted Ibid
89. Quoted Ibid, p. 348
90. Quoted Ibid
91. Quoted Ibid, p. 349
92. Quoted Ibid
93. Quoted Ibid, p. 350
94. Quoted Ibid
95. Quoted Ibid
96. Quoted Ibid, pp. 351-2
97. Quoted Ibid, p. 352
98. Quoted Ibid
99. Quoted Ibid
100. Quoted Ibid, p. 353
101. Quoted Ibid
102. Quoted Ibid
103. Quoted Ibid, p. 353-4
104. Quoted Ibid, p. 354
105. Quoted Ibid
106. Quoted Ibid, p. 355
107. Quoted Ibid
108. Quoted Ibid
109. Quoted Ibid
110. Quoted Ibid, p. 357
111. Quoted Ibid, p. 360
112. Quoted Ibid
113. Quoted Ibid, p. 362
114. Quoted Ibid
115. Quoted Ibid, p. 360
116. Quoted Ibid
117. Quoted Ibid, pp. 360-1
118. Quoted Ibid, p. 363
119. Quoted Ibid
120. Quoted Ibid
121. Quoted Ibid
122. Quoted Ibid
123. Quoted Ibid, p. 364
124. Quoted Ibid, p. 365-6
125. Quoted Ibid
126. Quoted Ibid
127. Quoted Ibid
128. Quoted Ibid
129. Quoted Ibid
130. Quoted Ibid, p. 364
131. Quoted Ibid, p. 364

132. Quoted Ibid
133. Quoted Ibid
134. Quoted Ibid
135. Quoted Ibid
136. Alice Grand Duchess of Hesse – Biographical Sketch and Letters, 29 August 1866, p. 147
137. Quoted Ibid, p. 367
138. State (formerly Grandducal) Archives, Darmstadt, Box 23, 25 September 1871
139. Quoted in Victoria: Biography of a Queen, p. 367
140. Quoted Ibid, p. 366
141. Quoted Ibid
142. Quoted Ibid
143. Quoted Ibid
144. Quoted Ibid
145. Quoted Ibid, p. 367
146. Quoted Ibid, p. 368
147. Quoted Ibid
148. Quoted Ibid
149. Quoted Ibid
150. Quoted Ibid
151. Quoted Ibid
152. Quoted Ibid, p. 369
153. Quoted Ibid
154. Quoted Ibid
155. Quoted Ibid, p. 369-70
156. Quoted Ibid, p. 370
157. Quoted Ibid
158. Quoted Ibid
159. Quoted Ibid
160. E. F. Benson, Daughters of Queen Victoria, (New York, 1938) p. 164
161. State (formerly Grandducal) Archives, Darmstadt, Letters from Princess Alice to Prince Louis, 22 November 1871
162. Ibid
163. Ibid, 25 November 1871
164. Ibid, 27 November 1871
165. G. Battiscombe, Queen Alexandra, (London, 1969) p. 115
166. Quoted in Victoria: Biography of a Queen, p. 370
167. Quoted Ibid, p. 371
168. Quoted Ibid
169. Quoted in Queen Victoria: A Portrait, p. 388
170. Quoted in Victoria: Biography of a Queen, p. 371
171. Quoted Ibid
172. State (formerly Grandducal) Archives, Darmstadt, Letters from Princess Alice to Prince Louis, 4 January 1872
173. Quoted in Queen Victoria: A Portrait, p. 388
174. Quoted Ibid
175. Quoted Ibid
176. Quoted Ibid, p. 389
177. Quoted Ibid
178. Quoted Ibid

Chapter Seven – The Royal Sufferers

1. Quoted in Queen Victoria, Her Life and Times, p. 102
2. Quoted in Victoria: Biography of

a Queen, p. 297
3. Quoted in Purple Secret, p. 107
4. (4) Quoted in Queen Victoria, Her Life and Times, p. 151
5. (5) Quoted Ibid, p. 161
6. (6) Wilson, P.W., ed., The Greville Diary (London 1927) vol. 2, p. 130
7. (7) Fulford, R., ed., Dearest Child: Private Correspondence of Queen Victoria and the Princess Royal, 1858-1861, (London, 1964) p. 77
8. Bolitho, H., Further Letters of Queen Victoria (London, 1938) p. 49.
9. Quoted in Queen Victoria, Her Life and Times, p. 330
10. Quoted in Queen Victoria: A Portrait, p. 170
11. Quoted Ibid.
12. Quoted in Purple Secret, p. 108
13. Longford, E., Victoria RI (London 1964), p. 273
14. Quoted Ibid, pp. 278, 292f.
15. Fulford, R., ed., Dearest Child: Private Correspondence of Queen Victoria and the Princess Royal,pp. 48, 54
16. Quoted Ibid, pp. 324f., 327.
17. Quoted Ibid, pp. 330-3.
18. Quoted Ibid, pp.342.
19. Quoted Ibid, pp.362f.
20. Quoted Ibid, pp.364ff.
21. Quoted Ibid, p.74f.
22. Quoted Ibid, pp.164f., 168f.
23. Quoted Ibid.
24. Quoted Ibid, p. 305.
25. Quoted Ibid, p. 319, 322, 326f.
26. Fulford, R., ed., Your Dear Letter: Private Correspondence of Queen Victoria and the German Crown Princess, 1865-1871 (London 1976), p. 236
27. Quoted Ibid, pp.150, 162f.
28. Quoted Ibid
29. Quoted Ibid, p. 181f
30. Longford, E., Victoria RI., pp. 79, 81
31. Fulford, R., ed.,Beloved Mama: Private Correspondence of Queen Victoria and the German Crown Princess, 1878-1885 (London 1981), p. 83
32. Ibid, p. 157
33. Ramm, A., ed., Beloved and Darling Child: Last Letters Between Queen Victoria and Her Eldest Daughter 1886-1901 (Stroud, 1990) pp. 48, 53
34. Quoted in Queen Victoria: A Portrait, p. 171-172
35. Quoted Ibid
36. Fulford, R., ed., Darling Child: Private Correspondence of Queen Victoria and the German Crown Princess, 1878-1885, (London, 1976) p. 160
37. Fulford, R., ed., Dearest Child, p. 335

38. Quoted Ibid, p. 339
39. Diary of the Crown Prince (DCP), 11 June 1862, Archiv der Hessischen Hausstiftung, Schloss Fasanerie (AHH)
40. Fulford, R., ed., Dearest Mama, p. 93.
41. Quoted Ibid, pp. 290, 293, 302
42. Quoted Ibid, p. 232.
43. Fulford, R., ed., Dearest Mama, p. 123.
44. DCP, 7 and 18 October and 25 December 1864, AHH.
45. DCP, 7-9 January, 21 July, 5 and 14 November 1866, AHH ; Vicky to Fritz, 14 November 1866, AHH.
46. Vicky to Fritz, 4 August 1866, AHH.
47. Ibid, 11 November 1866.
48. Ibid
49. Ibid, 24 April 1868
50. Ibid, 27 April 1868
51. Ibid
52. Ibid
53. Ibid
54. Ibid, 7-8 May 1868
55. Ibid, 1 May 1868
56. Vicky to Queen Victoria, 19 August 1868, The Royal Archives, Windsor Castle, Z22/11
57. Vicky to Fritz, 9 May 1870, AHH.
58. Dearest Mama, p. 261.
59. Purple Secret, pp. 126-133.
60. Pakula, H., An Uncommon Woman: The Empress Frederick, Daughter of Queen Victoria, Wife of the Crown Prince of Prussia, Mother of Kaiser Wilhelm, (New York, London, Toronto, Sydney, Tokyo, Singapore, 1995), p. 335
61. Vicky to Fritz, 8 April 1864, AHH. Vicky to Fritz, 9 May 1864, AHH.
62. Vicky to Fritz, 2 May 1862, AHH.
63. Fulford, Darling Child, pp. 138f.
64. Feodora, Princess of Reuss to EH, 28 December 1908, ThStaMgn, HA 382/IV
65. Vicky to Fritz, 28 October 1877, AHH.
66. Vicky to Queen Victoria, 2 November 1888, 20 August 1890 and 31 March 1891, RA, Z43/32, Z49/8 and Z50/30.
67. Charlotte to EH, 13 August 1894, ThStaMgn, KHA 342.
68. Charlotte to EH, 21 September 1901, ThStaMgn, KHA 343.
69. Quoted in Purple Secret, p. 140
70. Charlotte to EH, 29 October and 18 November 1902, ThStaMgn, KHA 343.
71. Charlotte to EH, n.d., ThStaMgn, HA 207
72. Charlotte to EH 16 November 1905, HA 207
73. Ibid.
74. Quoted in Purple Secret, p. 144
75. Charlotte to Shweninger, 7 April 1906, BABSP
76. Quoted in Purple Secret, p. 145

77. Charlotte to Shweninger, 7 January 1908, 21 January 1908, 13 February 1908, BABSP
78. Charlotte to Shweninger, 13 March 1908, BABSP
79. Purple Secret, p. 155.
80. Quoted in Purple Secret, p. 156.
81. Quoted Ibid.
82. Quoted Ibid.
83. Vicky to Queen Victoria, 15 October 1890, RA, Z49/19-20.
84. Quoted in Purple Secret, p. 157.
85. Quoted Ibid, p. 158.
86. Quoted Ibid.
87. Feo to EH, 26 November 1899, ThStaMgn, HA 382/I.
88. Charlotte to EH, 22 April, 10 and 29 May, 4 June, 23 July and 12 September 1900, ThStaMgn, HA 343.
89. Feo to her grandfather, 21 September 1899, ThStaMgn, HA 382/I.
90. Feo to EH, 15 November 1899, ThStaMgn, HA 382/I.
91. Feo to EH, 9 and 25 March 1900, ThStaMgn, HA 382/I.
92. Ibid.
93. Feo to EH, 10 January 1901, ThStaMgn, HA 382/I.
94. Charlotte to EH, 3 October 1900, ThStaMgn, HA 343.
95. Quoted in Purple Secret, p. 159.
96. Quoted Ibid.
97. Charlotte to EH, 5 December 1900 and 28 March 1901, ThStaMgn, HA 343.
98. Ibid.
99. Feo to EH, 30 November 1901, ThStaMgn, HA 382/I.
100. Charlotte to EH, 27 March 1902, ThStaMgn, HA 343.
101. Charlotte to EH, 31 December 1902, ThStaMgn, HA 382/II.
102. Charlotte to EH, 14 May and 23 June 1903, ThStaMgn, HA 382/II.
103. Heinrich Reuss to EH, 12 and 13 February 1910, ThStaMgn, HA 383/IV.
104. Feo to EH, 5 May 1913, ThStaMgn, HA 383/II.
105. Feo to EH, 6 December 1914, ThStaMgn, HA 383/III.
106. Feo to EH, 1 April 1915, ThStaMgn, HA 383/III.

Chapter Eight – The Tragedy of Princess Alice

1. 'An Account of a Haemorrhagic Disposition Existing in Certain Families' Dr J C Otto, (Philadelphia, 1803)
2. 'Über Die Haemophilie Oder Die Erbliche Anlage Zu Todlichen Blutungen', Dr F Hopff, (Zurich, 1928)
3. 'Queen Victoria's Gene' D.M Potts, W.T.W. Potts (Stroud, 1999)
4. Victoria, Biography of A Queen, p. 224

5. Quoted in Queen Victoria, A Portrait, p. 259
6. Ibid.
7. State (formerly Grandducal) Archives, Darmstadt, Letters from Princess Alice to Prince Louis, 9 October 1870
8. Quoted in Princess Alice, Queen Victoria's Forgotten Daughter, G Noel, p. 166
9. Quoted Ibid., p. 208
10. Alice Letters, 17 June 1872, p. 279
11. Ibid, 14 August 1872, p. 281
12. Quoted in Princess Alice, Queen Victoria's Forgotten Daughter, G Noel, p. 209
13. Marchioness of Milford Haven 'Reminiscences'
14. Prince Ernest Louis, 'Private Memories'
15. Ibid.
16. The Royal Archives, Windsor Castle, Z379/163, 29 May 1873
17. Ibid.
18. Marchioness of Milford Haven 'Reminiscences'
19. State (formerly Grandducal) Archives, Darmstadt, Box 27 14c, 11 May 1873
20. Ibid, 30 December 1873.
21. Prince Ernest Louis, 'Private Memories'
22. Alice Grand Duchess of Hesse – Biographical Sketch and Letters (London 1884) 26 April 1874, p. 321
23. Quoted in Princess Alice, Queen Victoria's Forgotten Daughter, G Noel, p. 213
24. E Longford, Victoria R.I. (London 1964), p. 234
25. Granville Papers, 4 April 1873 (Public Record Office)
26. The Royal Archives, Windsor Castle, S27/129-30, 26 July 1873
27. Alice Grand Duchess of Hesse – Biographical Sketch and Letters (London 1884) 26 July 1873, p. 308
28. Ibid., 17 December 1874, p. 331
29. Prince Ernest Louis, 'Private Memories'
30. Quoted in Princess Alice, Queen Victoria's Forgotten Daughter, G Noel, p. 221
31. State (formerly Grandducal) Archives, Darmstadt, Letters from Princess Alice to Prince Louis, 5 August 1877.
32. Ibid., 1 August 1877.
33. Alice Grand Duchess of Hesse – Biographical Sketch and Letters (London 1884) 13 December 1877, p. 359
34. Ibid., 21 December 1877, p. 359
35. Ibid., 30 October 1877, p. 359
36. Quoted in Princess Alice, Queen Victoria's Forgotten Daughter, G Noel, p. 230
37. State (formerly Grandducal)

Archives, Darmstadt, Letters from Princess Alice to Prince Louis, 31 October 1877
38. Ibid., undated except for 'Friday'; probably late November 1877
39. Ibid., 3 November 1878
40. Ibid., 4 November 1878
41. Alice Grand Duchess of Hesse – Biographical Sketch and Letters (London 1884) 6 November 1878, p. 367
42. Quoted in Princess Alice, Queen Victoria's Forgotten Daughter, G Noel, p. 236
43. Quoted Ibid.
44. Broadlands Archives, 15 November 1878
45. Quoted in Princess Alice, Queen Victoria's Forgotten Daughter, G Noel, p. 237
46. The Royal Archives, Windsor Castle, Queen Victoria's Journal, 16 November 1878
47. Broadlands Archives, 16 November 1878
48. S. Tytler, The Queen, (Toronto, c 1885) p. 112
49. Broadlands Archives, 22 November 1878
50. Hansard, 17 December 1878
51. Alice Grand Duchess of Hesse – Biographical Sketch and Letters (London 1884) 6 December 1878, p. 374
52. Quoted in Princess Alice, Queen Victoria's Forgotten Daughter, G Noel, p. 239
53. Quoted Ibid., p. 240
54. E. Sanderson and L. Melville, Edward VII, (London, 1910) p. 164
55. Quoted in Princess Alice, Queen Victoria's Forgotten Daughter, G Noel, p. 240
56. G. Battiscombe, Queen Alexandra, (London, 1969), pp. 148-9.
57. T. Martin, Queen Victoria As I Knew Her, (for private circulation) (Edinburgh, 1901) p. 113
58. W.F. Monypenny and G.E, Buckle, The Life of Benjamin Disraeli, Earl of Beaconsfield (London, 1929) p. 1,341
59. The Times, 16 December 1878
60. Illustrated London News, 21 December 1878

Chapter Nine – Shadows Fallig Across History

1. R.K. Massie, Nicholas and Alexandra (London 1968)
2. Quoted in S. Weintraub, Victoria, Biography of a Queen, p. 520
3. Quoted Ibid.
4. C. Hibbert, Edward VII, the Last Victorian King, (London 1976), p. 329
5. Ibid

6. Ibid
7. R. Fulop-Miller, Rasputin the Holy Devil, (New York, 1928), p. 84
8. Quoted in T. Aronson, Grandmama of Europe: The Crowned Descendants of Queen Victoria, (London, 1974), p. 284
9. Quoted in Princess Alice, Queen Victoria's Forgotten Daughter, G Noel, p. 219
10. Ibid.

Chapter Ten – In Conclusion

1. Walter Bagethot, The English Constitution (London, 1867), p. 81
2. Quoted in Queen Victoria: A Portrait, (London, 1991), p.31
3. S. Smiles, Self-Help, (London, 1859)
4. Quoted in S. Weintraub, Victoria, Biography of a Queen, p . 611
5. Captain R.F. Scott, Message To The Public, 1912

List of Abbreviations

Archive of the Hessische Hausstiftung, Schloss Fasanerie (AHH)

Broadlands Archives (BA)

Letters from Princess Alice to Prince Louis (LAL)

Private Diary of Prince Louis (DPL)

Royal Archives, Windsor Castle (RA)

State (formerly Grandducal) Archives, Darmstadt (DA)

Thuringian State Archive, Meiningen (ThStaMgn)

Victorian Additional Manuscripts, Royal Archives (RA Add)

Index